Decriminalizing Abortion in Northern Ireland

Decriminalizing Abortion in Northern Ireland

Legislation and Protest

Edited by
Fiona Bloomer and Emma Campbell

BLOOMSBURY ACADEMIC
LONDON • NEW YORK • OXFORD • NEW DELHI • SYDNEY

BLOOMSBURY ACADEMIC
Bloomsbury Publishing Plc
50 Bedford Square, London, WC1B 3DP, UK
1385 Broadway, New York, NY 10018, USA
29 Earlsfort Terrace, Dublin 2, Ireland

BLOOMSBURY, BLOOMSBURY ACADEMIC and the Diana logo are trademarks of
Bloomsbury Publishing Plc

First published in Great Britain 2022

Cover design by Paul Smith
Cover image: When They Put Their Hands Out Like Scales, Abortion
Journeys 6, 2012, by Emma Campbell

A catalogue record for this book is available from the British Library.

A catalog record for this book is available from the Library of Congress.

ISBN: HB: 978-0-7556-4257-1
         ePDF: 978-0-7556-4259-5
         eBook: 978-0-7556-4258-8

Typeset by Integra Software Services Pvt. Ltd.

To find out more about our authors and books visit www.bloomsbury.com
and sign up for our newsletters.

Contents

Acknowledgements

We would never be able to include everyone we wanted to in a volume spanning decades, therefore we would like to acknowledge some important contributors to the movement towards change, such as Dawn Purvis, Clare Bailey, Paula Bradshaw and Gerry Carroll, the team at BPAS and MSI and more, their work continues to be key to reproductive rights in NI.

We would take five volumes just to name all the volunteers – those fighting for change for decades up to those more recently involved. We know thousands of people have signed petitions and donated money, people have made cakes, made art, jogged, swam, sang karaoke, held burlesque nights, yoga sessions and marches for choice. We are grateful to people who canvassed for Repeal, who paid for other people's bus seats to rallies, who made banners, who spoke to a mercurial public, who submitted their first-hand experiences as evidence to committees, who spoke to journalists and lit candles in memory of Savita.

We want to give our heartfelt thanks to peer reviewers: Judith Cross, Máiréad Enright, Noirin MacNamara, Maeve O'Brien, Kellie O'Dowd, Catherine O'Rourke, Claire Pierson, Jennifer Thomson, Rosa Thomson, Kellie Turtle, Ann Rossiter, Naomi Connor, Rachel Powell and Danielle Roberts, all of whom brought generosity and expertise to the project. We are grateful to the anonymous reviewers of the book proposal who were so positive about the project and to the anonymous reviewer of the draft manuscript.

We also thank those who supported our late nights and writing focus: partners (Stephen; Mo), children (George, Martha; Luca), colleagues and parents. We also must thank Alliance for Choice (AfC) for supporting the book so wholeheartedly from the beginning. Ulster University has given unwavering support for us both to continue our research by writing on this important topic and recognizing the impact of the work that Ulster University continues to do alongside AfC. We would also like to thank each other, because we have worked so well together and have been able to trust one another's writing and editing, complement each other's organizing, understand our motivations and most of all friendship. Not everyone expects a late-night ping-pong of an idea to become a reality!

Contributors

Les Allamby was the Chief Commissioner at the Northern Ireland Human Rights Commission from 1 September 2014 to 31 August 2021. He was formerly the Director of Law Centre (NI) and Chair of the Commonwealth Forum of National Human Rights Institutions. He has written extensively on human rights, legal and policy issues.

Fiona Bloomer is Senior Lecturer in the School of Applied Social and Policy Sciences, at Ulster University, UK. Her research focuses on abortion policy. She has written extensively on this subject; she is the co-author of the book *Reimagining Global Abortion Politics* (2018). She has been research advisor to AfC since 2008 and is a member of the Northern Ireland Abortion and Contraceptive Taskgroup (NIACT).

Emma Campbell is completing her PhD on photography as an activist tool for the abortion rights movement, at Ulster University. Emma is also a member of the Turner Prize winning Array Collective, exhibiting internationally. An activist with several NI groups and current co-convenor of Alliance for Choice, she comments frequently on abortion in NI, most recently in a joint article on Abortion Doula work in NI for the *BMJ Sexual and Reproductive Health Journal*.

Stella Creasy is a British Labour and Co-operative politician who has been Member of Parliament (MP) for the London constituency of Walthamstow since 2010. Her doctorate in Social Psychology (the London School of Economics) focused on social exclusion. Creasy has been advocating for a change to abortion law in NI since 2017. She succeeded in bringing about decriminalization following an amendment to the Northern Ireland (Executive Formation, etc.) Act 2019.

Judith Cross is a public policy analyst with a focus on equality and human rights. Working in the public policy arena she has worked across several sectors, including the public sector and the NGO sector with a focus on women, disabled people and older people. She has been a key member of AfC for many years campaigning and lobbying for access to abortion for women and young girls in Northern Ireland using the equality and human rights frameworks.

Máiréad Enright is Reader in Feminist Legal Studies at Birmingham Law School. Her research interests focus on reproductive rights, 'historical' injustice and feminist legal theory. She is currently a Leverhulme Research Fellow and co-director of Feminist Constitutional Futures; an emerging network of feminist scholars and activists considering how we can re-imagine constitutional law for the future of Ireland and Northern Ireland.

Emma Gallen is a volunteer coordinator for AfC, she organized the Saturday stall from 2016 and was an organizer of Rally for Choice 2016. She has written about abortion activism in Belfast for the *Telegraph*, *Refinery 29* and the *Independent*.

Anna Manwah Lo MBE settled in Northern Ireland from Hong Kong in 1974. Initially, she worked for the BBC in Belfast as a secretary and a freelance contributor for the Chinese Service. After qualifying in social work in Ulster University, she worked in social services and Barnardos before becoming the director of the Chinese Welfare Association in 1997. She was elected to the Northern Ireland Assembly in 2007 and retired in 2016. Her autobiography *The Place I Call Home* was published in 2016. Anna was awarded an honorary doctorate from the Open University in 2018.

Maria Amélia Ponte Lourenço is a health- and social-care worker.

Susan McKay is an author, journalist and feminist. She is writing a book about borders and received an Arts Council NI major individual award to do so. Her latest book is *Northern Protestants – On Shifting Ground* (2021). She was a founder of the Belfast Rape Crisis Centre in 1981.

Maeve O'Brien is a Postdoctoral Researcher in Healthcare Communication at the Royal College of Surgeons, Dublin. A Tyrone native, her research interests include medical stigma, reproductive justice and twentieth-century women's writing. From 2020–2021, Maeve ran the Archiving the 8th Project at University College Dublin. Recent publications include The Bloomsbury Handbook to Sylvia Plath (2022) and the FSRH briefing paper Abortion Reform in Northern Ireland: What Does It Mean for Healthcare Providers? (2021).

Kellie O'Dowd is a feminist and trade union activist. She was co-chair of AfC Belfast from 2012 to 2019. She was one of the first clinic escorts in Belfast for the Marie Stopes Clinic 2014–17 to stop the harassment by anti-choice protestors of women trying to access healthcare services. Kellie has been facilitating workshops on abortion for ten years in the community, trade union and voluntary sectors. She has published academic research on the issue of abortion and best practice strategies when working in morally conservative settings.

Claire Pierson is Senior Lecturer in Politics at the University of Liverpool. Her research interests are feminist politics, reproductive justice, activism and gender security. She is the co-author of Reimagining Global Abortion Politics (2018) and is currently working on a monograph on feminist politics in Northern Ireland for Manchester University Press. She is currently co-chair of the Feminist Studies Association of the UK and Ireland.

Ruairi Rowan is Director of Advocacy and Policy for Informing Choices NI (ICNI) and formerly Advocacy Manager for the Family Planning Association. ICNI advocate for sexual and reproductive health services to meet the needs of all citizens in Northern Ireland and following the introduction of a new abortion framework in Northern Ireland launched a Central Access Point – enabling women to contact a single telephone number to access non-directive information, pregnancy choices counselling and abortion care up to 10 weeks gestation.

Catherine O'Rourke is Professor of Global Law at Durham University Law School. She previously taught human rights and international law at Ulster University. Her research interests are in gender, human rights, conflict and international law. She co-authored the submission to the CEDAW Committee requesting an inquiry into access to abortion in Northern Ireland.

Cara Sanquest is co-founder of London-Irish Abortion Rights Campaign, a grassroots campaign with the aim of bringing people in London together to campaign for free, safe and legal abortion across the island of Ireland.

Audrey Simpson was the Director of FPA NI from 1988 to 2015. In April 2019, when the London-based Trustees of FPA UK decided to close the organization, she became Chair of Informing Choices NI (ICNI) when it was formally established in May 2019. ICNI was committed to continuing the work of FPA NI in promoting sexual and reproductive healthcare for ALL in Northern Ireland. She has a PhD in Sociology and in 2005 was awarded an OBE for promoting women's healthcare in Northern Ireland.

Grainne Teggart is Campaigns Manager for Amnesty International UK in Northern Ireland where she manages campaigns, strategic litigation, public affairs and is a Spokesperson on a range of human rights issues including sexual and reproductive rights, human rights in the UK and legacy of the Northern Ireland conflict. Grainne led Amnesty's campaign for abortion rights; working closely with those impacted by the former abortion ban including Sarah Ewart, challenging the law through the courts, and advocating for change at Westminster. Grainne serves (in 2021) as a Director of Informing Choices NI and Integrated Education Fund.

Jennifer Thomson is Senior Lecturer in Comparative Politics in the Department of Politics, Languages and International Studies at the University of Bath. She is the author of *Abortion Law and Political Institutions: Explaining Policy Resistance* (Palgrave, 2019), which explores abortion in Northern Ireland in the context of the devolved United Kingdom. Her work on reproductive politics has been published in *British Politics*, the *British Journal of Politics and International Relations* and the *International Political Science Review*.

Ashleigh Topley is an HR Officer in Portadown. In her first pregnancy in 2014, she was denied a termination after learning that her daughter had a fatal foetal abnormality. She has shared her story in order to elicit change and was an intervenor in the recent Supreme Court case. She manages the social media accounts for In Her Shoes, Northern Ireland.

Lynda Walker is a member of Belfast Trades Council, and a civil rights activist, a founder member of the NI Women's Rights Movement and active on abortions rights since the early 70's. She is a founder member of Reclaim the Agenda and member of Alliance for Choice. She was Director of Women's Studies in Belfast Metropolitan College. Lynda is a member of the Communist Party of Ireland since 1969 and has written articles and booklets on women in Ireland.

Introduction

Emma Campbell and Fiona Bloomer

Why did we imagine this book?

In October 2019 abortion was decriminalized in Northern Ireland (NI). As a result, it became one of the few countries in the world to have achieved this; the others include Canada, Cuba, most of Australia and New Zealand (Centre for Reproductive Rights, 2021; Children by Choice, 2021). This book tells NI's story from the perspective of those directly involved in the struggle for legal change. It is unique, in that it represents first-hand accounts of abortion seekers, activists, NGOs, policy and academic perspectives on this change.

We have included those who were involved in the early days of campaigning as well as recently. We have brought together those who were denied abortions; those who risked criminality and those who had to travel outside of NI to access abortions. We have highlighted those that stepped in where the state would not. We have accounts from health professionals and policymakers. We have covered a range of activist organizations who led the charge to dismantle the law and challenge the oppressive norms which allowed stigma and silence to flourish. Our aim was to reach an audience beyond academics: activists, writers, providers, abortion seekers and more from across the globe, where we know similar struggles continue.

The writing of the chapters was conducted during the COVID-19 pandemic, during lockdown, whilst authors were juggling all the responsibilities and anxieties that this brought. We are in awe of their work and thankful for their time and efforts.

We could never capture every story and would encourage those who want to contribute personal reflections to go to the book website DecrimAbortionNI. com where we will have space to share additional historical artefacts and further information for researchers.

Context

As a campaign to decriminalize the abortion law in NI, this volume describes how it was necessary 'to work towards change in three different jurisdictions'. (Campbell, 2019)

Working across NI, Ireland and the UK is important strategically and politically for issues in NI. Given that for three years until early 2020, there was no acting devolved assembly in NI, it made England and Ireland even more crucial in the path to decriminalization. Across the island of Ireland, the grassroots campaigners had built a strong reciprocal solidarity, but whilst there was a clear cultural mutual understanding, dealing with the legal and healthcare differences was often difficult. In the UK environment, the Westminster campaign was not about whether Parliament was pro-choice, it is in fact overwhelmingly pro-choice. Instead, it was about the reach of the state, to figure out who was responsible for human rights in a complex, devolved union and whether there was ample evidence from the people of NI that they needed the change in the law. Many of the chapters in this volume grapple with this complex issue, borne out of NI's conflict.

For further detail on the timeline for abortion law change in NI, the UK, Ireland and globally, refer to Appendix 1.

Structure of the book

The idea for this book emerged in December 2019, with an initial list of fifteen chapters that soon increased to over thirty, leading to two volumes of the book being developed. Volume 1 is organized into two themes: Law; Campaigning and Activism; Volume 2 is organized into two themes: Allied Organizations/Activities; and Abortion Provision. We encourage our reader to embrace the different voices, modes of reflection and analysis as many are from personal experience and others from a strategic political standpoint. As editors we endeavoured to retain the richness and variation of approaches to portray an authentic account of the campaigns and their impact.

Volume 1

In the Law section we begin with a personal perspective from Anna Lo, admirably one of the first politicians in the Northern Ireland Assembly (NIA) to declare she was pro-choice. As Lo notes, the need for abortion is a universal experience and can further impact those already marginalized by poverty and immigration. Claire Pierson offers an analysis of how the NIA responded to the restricted abortion provision in NI. Further she reflects on their contribution to abortion myths on the one hand and how others conversely developed their limited perspective to become advocates for widening legal access to abortion. Insight into the role of the Northern Ireland Human Rights Commission is provided by Les Allamby, who documents the international national and regional tools used to frame legal challenges regarding the restrictive law as well as some of the organizational limitations faced by NIHRC.

The focus moves to Westminster with Jennifer Thomson providing an analysis of the UK government largely ignoring abortion in NI for the best part of fifty years until forced in 2018. The lack of action from both the Assembly and Westminster provided context for the actions of Family Planning Association (FPA), NI Women's European Platform (NIWEP) and AfC, whose request for intervention from Convention on the Elimination of All Forms of Discrimination Against Women (CEDAW) is detailed in the chapter by Judith Cross, Catherine O'Rourke and Audrey Simpson. The authors of this chapter provide a critique not only of government failure to act but also of the human rights organizations who until recently failed to support the campaign for change. The CEDAW report provided the foundation for action within Westminster to bring about historical legal change. In Working within Westminster, Stella Creasy and Cara Sanquest tell the story of how this was achieved, capturing just a fragment of the intensity and tenacity of the lobbying and persuasion in Parliament.

In the next chapter we have a change of pace, with Susan McKay relating the heart-breaking story of how Sarah Ewart became involved in the campaign for abortion law change, having been denied an abortion in NI. Interviews with Sarah, her mother Jane Christie and Grainne Teggart (Amnesty UK) provide insight into the challenges of campaigning and involvement in judicial reviews and Supreme Court cases. In the following chapter, Grainne Teggart and Ruairi Rowan provide their perspective on engaging with Westminster, detailing the relentless efforts to raise awareness and gain support for a change in the law.

Concluding this section Máiréad Enright centres the work of AfC in creating historic legal change and frames their activities as feminist law making, in challenging not only the letter of the law but also the means by which we understand legal work.

Having documented the legal perspective, we move on to theme 2, Campaigning and Activism. We begin this section with a view of activism from 1960s to 2008. Veteran activist Lynda Walker charts the development of key grassroots and NGO groups during that period and discusses how, despite their work feeling at the time as moving with glacial speed, in truth it laid the foundations for the campaigns to come. The development of these activists continued and built the base for a reinvigorated AfC by 2008. Kellie O'Dowd, Judith Cross and Fiona Bloomer document the development of this work from public meetings, lobbying politicians, petitions and marches to a highly developed campaign approach which encompassed training education and research and the development of work with allied organizations, up until 2016. AfC laid the building blocks of a social movement for change: they designed and created new conditions for engagement on abortion. In Reflections of an Activist, Maria Lourenco presents a personal perspective on motivations to become involved in the campaign for legal reform from 2008 onwards. Maria's insight offers a unique perspective as a woman who was new to NI and at times perplexed by the stagnation on abortion and at others, buoyed by the camaraderie in the campaigning groups. The chapter about 'In her shoes NI' is written by Ashleigh Topley, a key figure for her involvement in the NIHRC JR, CEDAW and continuing activism around bringing other women and pregnant people's stories to light, it is a heart-breaking but important reminder for why this work is necessary.

In presenting the continuing story of AfC from 2017 to 2020, Emma Campbell details the rationale of the organization to pivot focus towards Westminster and includes some of the local and internal difficulties inherent in that strategy, which ended in intervention from the UK government to decriminalize abortion in NI. Alongside which we learn how AfC Derry continued its activism focusing on street actions and grassroots work, as told by Maeve O'Brien. FPA/ ICNI highlight their important role in underlining workable, published medical guidelines, as well as the continued harassment of their workers and clients, as told by Ruairi Rowan and Audrey Simpson. Emma Gallen finally details the outreach work of volunteers in AfC Belfast, who used long-tested letter-writing campaigns in parallel to social media engagement and supportive de-escalation training, to guide the person on the street grappling with the poignant issues and put individual direct experience on the desks of influential politicians.

This multitude of voices offers a broad insight into the motivations and modes of campaigning in the North of Ireland. It spans decades and acknowledges hundreds of individuals and dozens of organizations who have brought us to this seismic change for reproductive justice. Yet it is still only a snapshot of the totality of emotional, physical, bureaucratic, caring and imaginative labour that went into decriminalization. The time it spans has witnessed sporadic moves back and forth, towards and away from progress across the globe, it saw the normalization of the use of misoprostol and the fourth wave of a more intersectional feminist movement, we intend that this volume will encourage our readers to delve into the second volume, that will outline the importance of solidarity work both globally and across issues of interest. Mostly we hope this is a source of comfort and inspiration for thousands of our global siblings faced with seemingly insurmountable roadblocks and regression, to know that decriminalization is possible.

Theme 1

Law

2

Reflections from a Northern Ireland politician

Anna Lo MBE

I suspect my mother had one or even two abortions in the 1950s in Hong Kong. My parents had six children with the first five being born in relatively quick succession but there's a gap of five years between me and my younger sister, the last of my siblings, was born. My mother, a trained teacher, adored children and must have agonised over the decision to end her pregnancy or pregnancies but my father's shipping business went bust shortly after my birth and we were in debt and living with my maternal grandparents in very crowded accommodation. Who could blame my parents for not wanting to bring another child into the world under such stressful circumstances? My mother would probably have a backstreet abortion and was lucky not to have been butchered to be able to have my younger sister some years later.

As the director of the Chinese Welfare Association in Northern Ireland, I supported my staff to help several immigrants with no legal status to seek abortions in England. These women, with no legal status, could not register with a General Practitioner (GP) to access any National Health Service (NHS) services, let alone maternity care. The only choice they had was to end their pregnancies.

However, it was not solely because of my speculation of my mother's plight or my empathy for these undocumented workers' helplessness that made me pro-choice. To me, it was also a class issue in that only those who could find a couple of thousand pounds for the costs of the operation and travel could make their way to England for the private medical procedure. Those who were on low incomes or social benefits simply could not come up with that sort of money in a hurry, which could also lead to delays in accessing the termination. More and more people were being forced to take risks by purchasing abortion pills online and administering them without medical supervision. Women would be reluctant to seek after-care from their doctors for fear of prosecution and the potential of a life sentence in prison. It is about fairness and equity of treatment too. We all contribute to the NHS through paying taxes and why should women in Northern Ireland (NI) not be able to avail of the same free medical services as other women in other parts of the UK?

Fundamentally, I believe that it is the woman's right to have autonomy over her body when faced with a crisis pregnancy. It is my strong view that the 1861 Offences Against a Person's Act is totally archaic and out of step not only with the UK's 1967 Abortion Act but also with the opinion of the majority of the local population wanting changes to the law that has been evidenced by repeated surveys and opinion polls (Cross O'Rourke Simpson, Teggart Rowan, this volume; Gray volume 2).

Yet our politicians have vehemently opposed any update of the law to live up to the twenty-first century. As a liberal, I view it as barbaric to force a woman to continue with an unplanned, unwanted pregnancy particularly horrendous when the pregnancy is a result of sexual crime or would end at birth due to foetal, fatal abnormality.

When elected to the Northern Ireland Assembly in 2007, I made no apologies making it known that I advocated for changes to the abortion law. I recall a seasoned politician from the Social Democratic and Labour Party (SDLP) giving me a 'piece of advice' soon after I got elected as we sat beside each other in a coach to a conference. He said, 'Anna, you have a niche in politics and that's a good thing for any politician, but you must stop claiming to be pro-choice. That's going to lose you votes'. Wanting to effect positive change for this society was my motivation to get into politics and if what I believed did not appeal to voters, I could only try to persuade them to see my point of view. However, during my re-election canvassing, I did come across people asking for my stance on abortion, but I encountered more support, particularly amongst younger people, than opposition from the general public.

However, in my two terms of nine years in the Assembly, there were only four publicly declared pro-choice MLAs. There is so much hypocrisy amongst most of our politicians, who are conservative middle-aged males, that they prefer to export pregnant women to England for abortions than to show compassion and common sense to let them have legal abortions in their own country under the NHS with family support close by. This is a health matter, not a criminal-justice issue. Women should not be stigmatized and criminalized for wanting to decide what to do with their bodies, nor for wanting to have children at the appropriate time and under circumstances of their own choosing.

Soon after becoming an Assembly member, I joined the advisory board of the Family Planning Association Northern Ireland (FPA NI) which campaigned to extend the Abortion Act to NI. The Labour MP Diane Abbott agreed to submit an amendment to the Human Fertilisation and Embryology Bill in the autumn of 2008 in Westminster. The Association sent facts and figures about abortions to MLAs to try to debunk myths, many of the carefully drafted leaflets probably went straight into the bin! Dawn Purvis MLA and I wrote to MPs to urge them to support the amendment and received some encouraging replies including from John Bercow, the then Speaker and Nick Clegg, the then leader of the Liberal Democrats. Disappointingly, as a result of political pressure, the Labour government used a timetabling motion in the House of Commons debate, which killed off a series of proposed amendments including Diane Abbott's (Thomson, O'Dowd Cross Bloomer, Creasy Sanquest, this volume). We were obviously crestfallen as we feared that we had lost the last chance of getting the law extended to NI before criminal-justice powers were devolved to the Assembly later that year. We suspected rightly that it would be extremely difficult if not impossible to amend the existing abortion law through the Assembly itself.

Extending the Abortion Act to NI might be a big ask for our MLAs but one would think at least they could issue abortion guidelines for the Health Service staff. Yet there was a fifteen-year battle to seek clarification on the abortion law for health professionals (Rowan Simpson, this volume). In 2001, the Family Planning Association sought a judicial review of the Department of Health's failure to issue guidelines to ascertain when an abortion is legal in NI. In 2004, the Court of Appeal ordered the department to draw up such a policy document, but it was not until 2007 that the department issued draft guidelines. However, the attempt was thwarted by the Assembly's health committee, led by Iris Robinson DUP, which succeeded in having the guidelines rejected on moral grounds. New guidelines were re-issued a year later, but it was legally challenged by the Society for the Protection of the Unborn Child. Further revised rules were again published for consultation in 2010. It was frustrating and bewildering to witness the obstruction of the attempt to clarify medical practices for our doctors and nurses to do their job. The anti-abortion lobby warned that it was a 'back door to bring in abortion on demand', which seemed to chime well with many Assembly members in the DUP.

I had repeatedly asked questions in the Assembly regarding the progress for guidelines and wrote a feature piece published in the *Belfast Telegraph* following a meeting with a hospital consultant who expressed serious concerns of medical staff working without guidelines. The years of long delay had created a vacuum of clarity within the health service, leading to uncertainties and a chill factor for health professionals who tended to err on the side of caution rather than to provide abortions for cases such as fatal foetal abnormality which used to be done routinely without any qualms. Their caution was understandable. If a health worker was judged to have carried out an illegal abortion, he or she could go to jail for life.

The abortion guidelines were eventually published in March 2016, days before the end of the term of the Assembly, twelve years after the court ordered the Department of Health to do so (Rowan Simpson, this volume). Obviously, if there was the political will to set out a clear framework for the health professionals then it could have been completed within months.

The huge publicity in 2013 regarding the heart-breaking experience of Sarah Ewart who had to go to England for an abortion when she discovered that her baby had anencephaly, a malformation of the brain and skull, sparked another momentum for change in the abortion law (McKay, this volume).

Following a public consultation in 2014, the then Justice Minister David Ford failed to get agreement from the Executive to propose legislative change to the law to allow abortion on the grounds of fatal foetal abnormality. Meanwhile, in a judicial review sought by the Northern Ireland Human Rights Commission, the Belfast High Court ruled that prohibition of abortion in cases of fatal foetal abnormality and sexual crime violated human rights. The court placed the onus on the Assembly to make legislative change (Allamby, this volume).

The next option to effect changes in the law was to submit amendments to the Justice (No. 2) Bill during its consideration stage. My former Alliance Party colleagues put in an amendment for foetal fatal abnormality but had reservations if an amendment on sexual crime would succeed in getting enough votes in the chamber. However, I decided to go it alone in forwarding an amendment on sexual crime in my own name, even though it would most likely not succeed into the statute. I thought it was essential to make a point. Likewise, Steven Agnew from the Green Party and Basil McCrea of NI21 jointly put in brief amendments on fatal foetal abnormality and sexual crime.

While Sinn Féin endorsed all the amendments, the DUP, SDLP and most of the UUP members voted against all of them, stymieing the attempt to at least bring a bit more humanity into our strict ban on abortion and to become compatible with the European Convention on Human Rights.

I retired in March 2016 but was hopeful that there was a momentum for change of this Victorian law in NI. Little did I know big changes were afoot! Stormont then collapsed in January 2017 leaving a political and legislative vacuum that inadvertently paved the way for the decriminalization of abortion in NI. It was also timely that UN's Convention on the Elimination of all forms of Discrimination against Women (CEDAW) conducted an inquiry on our most restrictive abortion law following extensive lobbying from FPA NI, AfC and NIWEP (Cross O'Rourke Simpson, this volume). I was delighted to participate in the CEDAW stakeholder consultation held in Belfast. Its 2018 report found that the UK was guilty of grave and systemic human rights abuses by forcing people to have to travel from NI to England for abortions. It further stated that Westminster will always be ultimately responsible for human rights in NI even if the devolved region continued to refuse to comply with the European Convention. It was gratifying to witness Westminster stepping in to legislate after years of prevarication from Stormont (Creasy Sanquest, this volume).

I thought it was pathetic that the DUP attempted to recall the Assembly to return to the mothballed chamber in October 2019 for the first time in almost three years to protest the extension of abortion rights to NI. Mind you, perhaps some politicians were quietly content that controversial and difficult issues such as abortion and equal marriage were sorted out by Westminster so that they could always blame the Tory Government for it and not risk losing votes from the electorate!

At long last after decades of tireless campaign by organizations, community groups and individuals, abortion regulations came into law in March 2019 and ratified in June in the House of Commons and the House of Lords over the heads of our politicians who were absent from the empty Parliament Buildings in Stormont (Enright, Rowan Simpson, this volume; Morgan, McLaughlin, Kavanaugh Kirk, volume 2).

I hope our MLAs would be humble and wise enough now to stop blocking changes in order to let the Department of Health to commission effective services and provide unambiguous guidance for health professionals and abortion seekers. It has been a long time for this catching up with a modern society where women's autonomy in respect of their health and wellbeing is respected.

3

Power-sharing and patriarchy: An analysis of the role of the Northern Ireland Assembly in abortion law reform

Claire Pierson

The role of the devolved Assembly in changes to abortion law in Northern Ireland (NI) can most accurately be described as obstructive. Since the introduction of the 1967 Abortion Act in Britain there has either been little reference to abortion by Northern Irish politicians or overt attempts to ensure that there is no relaxation of the law. After the reinstatement of the Stormont Assembly after the Good Friday Agreement (GFA), debates on abortion became more prevalent yet largely displayed anti-abortion rhetoric and misinformation about abortion. In addition, if moves are made at the national and international level to effect change, the response of political parties has largely been to prevent any reform.

The example of NI does not fit with most accounts of devolved power which largely position devolution as positive for women's representation and rights and gendered institutional change. Power-sharing, in the form of consociationalism, and its prioritization of ethno-national identity has been documented as creating an environment which deprioritizes gender issues (or any issues which do not directly correspond to ethno-nationalism). The reification of a particular form of identity, based on a moral conservatism and religious observance, may hold more resonance for explaining the long-term, cross-party resistance to any change to the law.

Recently, party policies and political positions on abortion have become more diverse, largely in response to changing public opinion, women publicly (and emotively) recounting their experience of accessing abortion (Topley this volume), and legal developments in the Republic of Ireland. The shift in party positions appears to have happened from a bottom-up position, with activism and public opinion polls illustrating how out of step politics is with the electorate. In addition, power-sharing has enabled a proliferation of smaller parties not situated in constitutional issues to become vocal and propose pro-choice arguments from a variety of perspectives. As such, politics has been out of step with the public and is only catching up.

This chapter traces the role of the NI Assembly (NIA) in abortion law reform, focussing predominantly on the post-GFA period to the present, considering the role of structures of governance, changing discursive framings of abortion in political debate and evolving political party policy on abortion. Without the intervention of Westminster, it is likely that legal reform of abortion undertaken with support of the NIA would have been stymied or limited to liberalization of the law in extreme circumstances such as fatal foetal anomaly (FFA) and sexual crime.

'The special social and political situation in Northern Ireland'[1]: Devolution, power-sharing and the NI Assembly

Analysing the role of the NIA regarding the lack of progression on abortion law reform can most usefully be explained through its position as a devolved legislature and its relationship to Westminster, in conjunction with the specific form of governance set up in NI through consociationalism. Layered over both structures of governance are embedded conservative gender roles and their hybrid relationship to militarized forms of masculinity and conservative religious morality.

Devolution is generally presented as positive for women. This is largely in reference to the descriptive and substantive representation of women and the potential for new political arenas to shed the traditional masculinity of older institutions (Mackay and McAllister, 2012). For example, academic work on Scotland and Wales points to a less adversarial form of politics and the pursuance of woman-friendly policies (Mackay and McAllister, 2012). NI has not been presented in this same light. Thomson (2016b) outlines how the Assembly may suffer from 'nested newness', the idea that institutions cannot be blank slates and are informed by their institutional legacy. The Assembly cannot simply go from an institution that had historically low representation of women and a highly masculinized and sectarian form of politics to a woman-friendly arena without significant institutional and cultural transformation – such transformation takes time to embed women as political actors.

The Assembly has been slower than the other devolved Assembly's to increase women's descriptive representation, but representation has vastly increased. In 1998, representation of women stood at 13 per cent, by 2019 this had risen to 32 per cent (Uberoi et al., 2020). Women also lead four of NI's political parties (the DUP, Sinn Féin the Alliance Party and the Green Party). However, with an increase in female leadership a more progressive focus on gender policy issues cannot be assumed. Women may not automatically represent women or more liberal policy positions. Research on devolved Assemblies in the UK has noted the particularly male-dominated and intimidating space of the NIA for women, and the distinct challenge for women to find their voice in such space (Shaw, 2013).

In terms of institutional legacy, Northern Irish politics before the Agreement suffered from very low representation of women coupled with what has been described as a 'martial' form of politics (Wilford, 1996). Between 1921 and 1969 only nine women were elected to the Assembly, and in the interim periods of devolution in the 1970s and 1980s, only four women were elected in each time period (Wilford, 1996). Politics and political parties were based on a militarized notion of protecting and defending the Union (for unionists) and challenging and ending this Union (for nationalists), coupled with the political violence of the Troubles, the political arena was not viewed as suitable for women. This is aptly summed up by Peter Robinson (former leader of the DUP and former First Minister) in a statement about the NI Women's Coalition (a party who formed for the sole purpose of ensuring women were represented during Agreement talks), 'they (the NIWC) haven't been at the forefront of the battle when shots were being fired or when the constitution of Northern Ireland was in peril' (Peter Robinson quoted in Fearon, 1999, p.14). Here, political participation is predicated on having taken part in violent political action and connected with male violence. Accordingly, women were not 'legitimate' actors on this stage. In many ways this assumption still exists, I point to the low representation of women in talks about policing, community relations and legacy issues as continuance of delegitimizing women's voice in politics (Pierson, 2019).

The structures of governance borne out of the Agreement may not facilitate the progression of gender policy issues (Kennedy et al., 2016). The Assembly is formed through a consociational mode of governance which includes a cross-community, power-sharing executive with minority veto rights and cultural respect for both Protestant and Catholic communities. Ethno-national identity is specifically linked to religious affiliation. This has entrenched party political structures and voters as focussed on protecting ethnic interests. The right to veto and the parity of consent model positions all issues along an ethno-national divide, making legislation more difficult to pass and in effect furthering sectarian politics. This model impacts on raising issues which are not ethno-national in nature, deprioritizing and invisibilizing those linked to gender, race, sexuality (dis)ability, for example (Kennedy et al., 2016). Issues become easily sectarianized under this model, for example, equality and human rights have been presented as part of a 'nationalist agenda' by some sections of unionism, despite their benefit to everyone. Regarding abortion, it has allowed the Assembly to block movement on the law, using the issue to display cross-party unity which is rarely seen in the politics of NI.

Layered over these structures of governance are cultural norms embedded within politics in the region. NI is viewed to have a particularly conservative gender order, emerging from ethno-religious framings of women's appropriate roles in both conservative Catholicism and evangelical Protestantism. Religious and national ideologies depend on explicitly conservative notions of women and gender (Pierson, 2018). Common themes, such as the elevation of motherhood (and a subsequent rejection of abortion), the role of women as helpers to political movements rather than actors and a particularly conservative view of women's sexuality and respectability limit women's voices in politics and the ability to challenge gender norms and issues within political arenas. The prominence of religion within NI's ethno-national identities also provides a socially conservative context from within which women's rights are easily marginalized.

Law and policy making under a devolved Stormont operates a 'lowest common denominator' approach resulting in stagnancy and socially conservative policies (McLaughlin, 2007). Gray and Birrell (2012) found evidence of difficulty agreeing in some instances on a lowest common denominator leading to a failure in policy development and falling behind standards in the rest of the UK. Lack of agreement can also be explained through the 'zero sum game' approach which typifies most ethno-national politics in the region, where each gain is seen as a loss for the 'other side', leading to a lack of consensus. Under this regime, changing law and policy on even uncontested issues can be difficult, but on an issue such as abortion may prove impossible. The following section will outline developments and (in)actions taken by the NIA on abortion focussing on the post-devolution period where most debate has taken place.

This we shall maintain: The Northern Ireland Assembly and abortion

As Jennifer Thomson documents in this volume, little discussion took place over NI in the creation of the 1967 Act. British politicians lacked understanding of and an unwillingness to intervene in NI and were happy to accept a portrayal of NI as somewhere 'different'. NI MPs did nothing to disavow them of this notion and relied at times on these stereotypes of a precarious peace process and vastly differing public opinion on abortion to inhibit change (Thomson, 2016b). Both the NIA and Westminster had little discussion of abortion in the run up to the 1967 Act and after, up until the period of devolution. The NIA records no debate between 1922 and 1974 with any substantive reference to abortion, and the only references to abortion and NI in Westminster were in the form of questions by backbenchers which were quickly dismissed.

It is in the period post-Agreement where discussion of abortion became much more prevalent. One of the first debates in the Assembly, in 2000, was specifically to oppose any extension of the 1967 Act to NI despite policing and justice powers not being devolved by that period and no mention of any extension of the Act by Westminster had been announced. It appears that this debate was tabled in order to put forward an anti-abortion stance from the majority of MLAs and this was clear from language used during the debate including mythology around the negative mental and physical effects of abortion, negative portrayals of women seeking abortion and the idea that restricting access to abortion would decrease demand (Pierson and Bloomer, 2018).

In the following years, debates cropped up sporadically largely with the aim of opposing or restricting access to abortion. These include debates on opposition to the introduction on guidelines on abortion for healthcare providers, opposition to the provision of abortion in private clinics (related to the opening of a Marie Stopes International clinic in Belfast in 2012) and two amendments to the Criminal Justice Bill to allow for abortion in cases of FFA and sexual crime (both of which were voted down). The fact these debates were framed mostly in opposition to abortion indicates the nature of the debates, largely focused on negative portrayals of abortion, setting up a dualism of rights between the pregnant woman and the foetus and misinformation on abortion. In more recent years, more pro-choice voices became heard in debates, a more empathic presentation of women seeking abortion and nuanced perspectives is found; however, this was still not enough to pass amendments even on the most limited liberalization. Abortion has also been blocked through guidelines provided for healthcare professionals, as detailed by Rowan and Simpson in this volume. Whilst the most restrictive guidelines were replaced in 2016, their legacy is perceived to have a longer-term chilling effect on health practice in abortion care.

Between 2007 and 2015, the Assembly had an All-Party pro-life group. All-Party groups provide a forum by which MLAs and outside organizations and individuals can meet to discuss shared interests on a particular cause or subject. All-Party groups have no formal role in policy making and do not have the powers of an Assembly Committee (niassembly.gov.uk, 2020); however, they provide a useful forum for external groups to present their views to MLAs and for cross-party discussions to take place. The secretariat to the All-Party pro-life group was initially provided by the DUP, and then by Bernadette Smyth, founding member of Precious Life. Precious Life is an anti-choice group which is well-known in NI for its visible anti-choice campaigning and protests outside sexual health clinics. During the operation of the all-party group, it held private meetings at the Assembly, access to which had to be approved by Smyth.

MLAs repeatedly state that they oppose the intervention of Westminster into abortion law (Thomson, this volume). For example, Jim Wells of the DUP noted that he supported the 2006 St Andrews Agreement (an agreement between the British and Irish governments and NI's political parties to restore the NIA in 2007 and stating Sinn Féin's support of the Police Service of NI as it would enable policing and justice powers to be devolved to the region therefore putting the control of abortion law within the hands of the Assembly (Tonge et al., 2014). The rejection of Westminster intervention was also stated clearly in debates leading up to decriminalization, with leader of the DUP, Arlene Foster, sending an open letter to the Secretary of State stating, 'the DUP along with other parties believe the Assembly chamber is the appropriate place to deal with abortion' (BBC News, 2019a).

Even after changes were established, members of the Assembly attempted to block their enactment. Despite the Assembly not sitting for almost three years, Unionist parties triggered the Assembly's recall through a petition with the intent to pass legislation in the form of a Defence of the Unborn Child Bill 2019. MLAs were told the Assembly could not do any business until a speaker was elected with cross-community backing, which became impossible when the SDLP left the chamber. Since the regulations drafted by the NIO at the end of March 2020 came into force, access has not been guaranteed. The Department of Health delayed granting approval to health trusts to provide services despite trusts statement that they were ready to provide services. Telemedicine which was rolled out in the rest of the UK in response to COVID-19 restrictions in travel was not approved for NI. This resulted in women continuing having to travel to England during a pandemic. At the time of writing, abortion up to ten weeks was available in most health trusts, but after ten weeks access routes are less clearly defined (Bloomer, 2020). In June 2020 the Assembly debated and passed a motion disagreeing with the legalization of abortion on the grounds of (non-fatal) foetal anomaly.

As this section has set out, the role of the Assembly in abortion law reform has been obstructive to any change and has attempted to roll back progress made in other forums. However, there is evidence to suggest that party positions have more plurality regarding abortion and that the power sharing model has allowed a diversity of positions on abortion to come forward. The following section will detail developments on political discourse on abortion.

Talking about abortion: Political discourse in the Assembly

Debates that have taken place in the NIA highlight the shape that political discourse has taken on abortion and its contribution to the intransigency of legal reform. The majority of debate has taken an anti-abortion stance based on abortion myths and misinformation, arguments about religion and morals, the positioning of foetal rights against women's rights, positioning women's rights against disability rights and presenting a perception of women needing to access abortion as being vulnerable and in need of protection. For more detailed discussions on abortion mythology, see Pierson and Bloomer (2018), and on discussions of the discourse of rights see Pierson and Bloomer (2017). This section will outline three key discourses in the NIA which contribute to its contemporary opposition to reform; firstly, the positioning of NI as different from Britain on its views on abortion, second, the emotive use of foetal rights arguments to oppose abortion and thirdly the notion that the NIA is protecting women by limiting abortion. These themes can be internationally contextualized and contribute to continued stigmatization and difficulty of having open and evidence-based discussions in the political realm.

As noted above, a cross-party argument, often repeated, is that any change to NI's abortion laws should come from the NIA. For example, in the most recent 2020 debate on the motion to oppose abortion for non-fatal foetal anomaly the DUP consistently referred to 'constitutional indignities' and 'constitutional abuses' in reference to abortion regulations. This suggests that Westminster has overreached its powers but fails to consider that the NIA had not sat for almost three years prior to decriminalization. In addition, it assumes that no power continues to rest at Westminster for NI. However, the UK is the signatory to CEDAW and as such has a duty to ensure human rights compliance; with no action taken by the Assembly, Westminster had a duty to act (Pierson et al., 2018).

Other means by which MLAs attempt to distance NI is through arguments of difference, with references to the peace process or the special circumstances of NI having halted debate in the past. Distinguishing NI via its ethno-national status is an attempt to use misunderstandings of NI in Westminster to delegitimize any actions taken there. For example, in the 2020 debate, Delores Kelly from the SDLP notes the overreach of the British government and the 'right to life of unborn Irish children' (Hansard, 2020). Weaponizing identity is a strategy that has consistently been used to oppose abortion, the DUP have even called on an all-Ireland identity based on opposition to abortion (prior to Repeal of the Eighth Amendment). These arguments position the Assembly as the only legitimate forum to amend abortion law through their positioning of Westminster as unknowledgeable and acting beyond their powers.

A consistent argument throughout political debate attempts a balancing of rights in abortion. This argument developed globally both from a recognition of the legitimacy of rights-based defences and a need to provide a counterargument, coupled with the development of high-quality ultrasound which has enabled the presentation of the idea of foetal personhood through graphic imagery. This positions pregnant women and the foetus in an adversarial relationship, where women need to be regulated in order to protect the foetus. Women are present and yet not present in foetal rights arguments, whose imagery depends on the erasure of women and the foetus as a free-floating independent being. The moralistic position of the foetal rights argument posits the foetus as morally equivalent to a rights-bearing person, that it is innocent and therefore morally superior, and that choice-based arguments are inferior to the right to life (Bloomer et al., 2018). Within debate in NI the phrase 'unborn child' is used much more frequently than 'foetus'. This also reflects Northern Irish anti-abortion activism which uses slogans such as 'Love Them Both' and 'Both Lives Matter'. Politicians have also framed their foetal rights arguments as a moral right, linked to religion or when lives lost in the conflict of NI are conflated with lives lost through abortion. Such arguments are emotive and designed to position anti-choice politicians as protectors:

> Surely the most vulnerable life in our society is the life of the unborn child. Those boys and girls have nobody to speak for them. They are totally reliant on what we do in this House. They are protected by the cross-community will of Northern Ireland. However, a democratic deceit has been perpetrated against them … Is it not a shame that, in our United Kingdom, the most dangerous place for a child is in its mother's womb?
>
> (Jonathan Bell, DUP, Hansard, 2013, p. 23)

An extension of this argument can be seen in arguments around the right to life of the foetus with regard to disability rights. This was the focus of the most recent debate which attempted to roll back regulations from Westminster. Such arguments are of course complex, and many disability rights advocates are not against abortion per se but oppose abortion in cases of what can be termed 'weak eugenics' that is 'promoting technologies of reproductive selection via non-coercive individual choices' (Shakespeare quoted in Sharp and Earle, 2002). However, in political debate the case of disability has been raised by those who are against abortion under any circumstances, and it appears that disability is simply another means by which to begin to restrict abortion completely.

Alongside foetal rights is a growing propensity to position women seeking abortion as in some way 'vulnerable' or 'at risk'. Global anti-abortion discourse argues that 'restrictions on legal abortion are necessary to stop weak and irrational women from making bad decisions that harm them' (Cannold, 2002, p. 174). This switched tactics from previously positioning those seeking abortion as bad or selfish, to now as weak or vulnerable. Northern Irish political debate reflects these trends as words such as 'vulnerable' and 'protect' are used more often, particularly debates attempting to limit provision of abortion from private providers (a response to the opening of Marie Stopes International in 2012), politicians here positioned themselves protecting women from unscrupulous abortion providers. The change in tactics reflects a public sentiment of sympathy towards those seeking abortion. This argument serves to hide anti-woman sentiment behind a veneer of protection and reduction of harm-based sentiment and positions politicians as protectors of women rather than enablers of rights.

Outlining some prevalent anti-abortion discourses in NIA debate helps contextualize anti-choice sentiment and attempts of politicians to restrict or roll back abortion access. This is not to say that there has not been development and more nuanced perspectives on abortion. The following section will detail political party positions on abortion and their evolution, attempting to explain a growing plurality of opinion and changes in policy.

'The north is next': Changing party positions and dissenting voices, attitudes and opinions

As noted above, early discussions on abortion pre-devolution were rare, and those after heavily permeated with anti-abortion viewpoints. Dissenting voices in the political realm were rarely heard in debate, Anna Lo from the Alliance Party being a notable exception. This served to ensure a largely cross-party consensus on the position of the law remaining as it was and meant that parties could also lobby Westminster as a group to ensure movement did not take place at that level. However, this hegemonic position has recently been challenged, with the number of dissenting voices becoming louder and the legal change in the Republic of Ireland arguably forcing the hand of nationalist parties to maintain all-Ireland coherence in policy.

The DUP have the clearest party policy on abortion, in that they oppose legal reform under any circumstances and have always done so. Despite their core political project being maintenance of NI's position in the United Kingdom and their lobbying of Westminster to ensure NI maintains the same legal position as Britain, for example on issues such as Brexit, they are happy to maintain this legislative difference. Many of their members are vocally anti-abortion, for example the Former Health Minister, MLA Jim Wells, is on record as stating his opposition to abortion even in cases of rape, he has also compared abortion to the Holocaust (Pierson and Bloomer, 2018). The party also has strong links with anti-abortion groups such as 'Precious Life', and religious groups such as the Caleb Foundation and the Evangelical Alliance, religious 'think-tanks' linked to evangelical Protestantism who have moved their political projects from constitutional issues towards moral and social ones such as abortion and same-sex marriage (Ganiel, 2006).

The UUP do not apply a party whip on the issue of abortion and party leadership appears keen to maintain that approach. This allows representatives to vote according to their 'conscience' on abortion. The position of their elected representatives falls across the political spectrum, with some presenting themselves as pro-life, others pro-choice in limited circumstances and some fully and openly in support of women's rights. Survey research of the UUP and its members indicates that their membership is also in support of liberalization of abortion laws with over 50 per cent supporting that 'abortion should be permitted up to 24 weeks of pregnancy, subject to medical approval, in line with the law in England and Wales' (Hennessey et al., 2018).

Sinn Féin's policy on abortion has been ambiguous. At the 2015 Ard Fheis a motion was passed to allow for abortion in cases of 'fatal foetal anomaly'. A NI council member, Anne Brolly, resigned after this decision. Sinn Féin have also stated that they do not wish to extend the 1967 Abortion Act to NI as it is a piece of British legislation (Pierson, 2018). Within political debate, Sinn Féin use a rhetoric of empathy and emphasize the vulnerability of women across Ireland, more recently they have positioned abortion as an issue of 'modern healthcare'. After the Repeal of the Eighth Amendment to the Irish constitution in 2018, the image of Sinn Féin leader in the south, Mary-Lou McDonald, and leader in the north, Michelle O'Neill, holding up the sign 'the north is next' became emblematic of the bid for legislative change on both sides of the border. Party policy was changed after a vote in 2018 to support abortion within 'a limited gestational period', enabling the party to support change in the south and promote change in the north. This spurred the resignation of some members and the creation of a new party, Aontú, which puts protection of the right to life as one of its core political goals. However, party policy across the island does not support abortion in cases of non-fatal foetal anomaly allowing them to put forward a similar motion to the DUP on restriction of abortion on these grounds.

The Social Democratic and Labour Party (SDLP) openly position themselves as a 'pro-life' party and various members have aligned themselves with anti-choice groups such as Precious Life; however, the party does not apply a whip on the issue and similarly to the UUP allows members to vote on conscience. Days before the referendum in the Republic, the SDLP held a special conference on abortion. The party stated that the conference not only reaffirmed their position as a pro-life party but also supported freedom of conscience voting for elected representatives. Politicians from the SDLP have more overtly linked their position on abortion as being part of their Catholic faith, indicating a form of nationalism built upon and intertwined with religious convictions. Representatives of the SDLP also draw on their status as upholders of civil rights and their stance of non-violence to contextualize their views on abortion.

The Alliance Party also has a position on conscience on abortion, Alliance has grown and in fact doubled its vote in 2019 to become the third largest party in NI (Tonge, 2020). The rise of a centrist party which claims no position on constitutional issues illustrates the growing number of people who either do not align with nationalism or unionism or perhaps do not see it as their primary identifying identity, but also an electorate who wish to progress social issues (this is also illustrated in the growth of parties such as The Green Party and People before Profit – both openly pro-choice parties). The Alliance Party are the only one who have attempted to advance legislation on abortion, their leader David Ford as Justice Minister convened a consultation on abortion and put forward amendments to the Criminal Justice Bill in 2016 to allow for abortion in cases of FFA and sexual crime (both were voted down). The current leader Naomi Long has also stated she is in favour of decriminalization of abortion with strict gestational limits.

Party positions on abortion have mostly moved to more liberal positions, this coupled with the changes in the Republic of Ireland has destroyed the view that NI is opposed to abortion and that abortion is anti-Irish. The growth of dissenting and plural voices about abortion highlights one of the benefits of power-sharing, that with wider representation smaller parties that don't conform to the two communities' model have the potential to be heard and grow and to challenge dominant narratives. However, pro-choice voices have not reached a majority level yet and as such this chapter will conclude by considering what, if any, role the NIA could have played in abortion law reform.

The lowest-common denominator approach: What change could have come from Stormont?

The common refrain from NI politicians is that change on abortion law should come from Stormont. But what form would this change take? This chapter has attempted to outline the action taken by NI politicians, their positions when discussing abortion and the evolution of party policy on the issue. Intertwined with this is the role of structures of governance on furthering or limiting progressive positions on gender-related policy.

The outcome of this is relatively bleak. In December 2021 an attempt to restrict abortion in cases on non-fatal foetal anomaly was rejected by a small majority of 45 to 42 votes. The debate exposing that many political representatives continue to oppose abortion on wider grounds than were being debated. As such, it is clear that this is not the end of the abortion debate in NI and perhaps the beginning of a long battle to ensure that the rights gained are not regressed.

Devolution coupled with power-sharing has not been positive for women in NI. Whilst the number of women represented in the Assembly has increased, the experiences and perspectives of women who seek or have sought abortion are not being adequately represented nor their rights fought for. Public opinion polls on abortion are increasingly showing more liberal attitudes towards abortion and a public will for change; political opinion in this case appears to fall behind and out of step with the public. The increasing number of politicians supporting more liberal legislation (in a variety of forms) is growing, but this growth is not enough yet to ensure a majority.

In this environment, it is likely that abortion would continue to be an issue that the Assembly would struggle to even form a lowest common denominator agreement on; if legislation was to be passed, it would affect a minority of women – those experiencing a diagnosis of fatal foetal anomaly or those who have been a victim of sexual crime. As such, legislation passed by the Assembly would ensure that most women seeking abortion would continue to travel to England or seek abortion illegally in NI. In this case, it is likely that women's rights in NI could only have been met by the shift in power and responsibility back to the Westminster legislature and that future action in the Assembly may be to attempt to reverse any progress that has been made.

Note

1   Alex Salmond in a House of Commons debate on devolution and abortion law HC Deb 31 March 1998 vol 309 c1109

4

The role of human rights organizations

Les Allamby

Introduction

In July 2019 for the first time anywhere, the recommendations of an inquiry from a human rights treaty monitoring body were adopted in their entirety by a Parliament and placed in legislation. Article 9 (1) of the Northern Ireland (Executive Formation etc.) Act 2019 provided that 'the Secretary of State must ensure that the recommendations in paragraphs 85 and 86 of the CEDAW report are implemented in respect of Northern Ireland'. How did this happen and what role did human rights and the Northern Ireland Human Rights Commission play in this change in the law?

Of course, like any significant legal and social reform, the outcome was the result of the work of many including clinical organizations, family-planning providers, abortion-support organizations, women groups, trade unions, human rights and other NGOs, politicians and not least, women who bravely raised their voices and told their stories. The work done by organizations was combined with other circumstances including the reform of abortion law elsewhere in Ireland, the suspension of devolved institutions in NI and legal challenges that helped pave the way for the reform through Westminster. This chapter focuses on the role of the Commission while recognizing the role of many others who fought in hostile circumstances who should take the credit for enabling reform.

The role of the Commission and human rights standards

The Northern Ireland Human Rights Commission was created as part of the Belfast (Good Friday) Agreement in 1998. The Commission's statutory duties include keeping under review the adequacy and effectiveness of law and practice to protect human rights. This sits alongside a role to advise the Secretary of State for NI and the NI Executive and Northern Ireland Assembly (NIA) on legislative and other measures, to be taken to enable human rights. The specific powers include taking legal action, undertaking research and educational activities.

The Commission is part of a global network of national human rights institutions, which must conform to the UN General Assembly resolution 48/134 (the Paris Principles) which include being independent, pluralist and having a sufficient mandate and resources to effectively carry out its role. The platform from which the Commission operates is the international and regional human rights standards created through treaties ratified by the UK government.

While the Council of Europe's regional treaty the European Convention on Human Rights has been incorporated into domestic law through the Human Rights Act, other treaties including the UN treaties have not. In practice, while the courts will draw on, for example UN human rights treaties in certain circumstances they are not directly enforceable as a matter of law. Instead, the UN Treaty monitoring bodies periodically examine the UK government's adherence to the standards through reviews as part of a wider cycle of assessment faced by those member states who have ratified the individual treaties. The UN treaty monitoring reporting procedure looks at the record of the UK government in implementing treaties having considered written and oral evidence provided by the UK government, national human rights institutions, human rights NGOs and others. The treaty monitoring body publishes its concluding observations highlighting progress and deficiencies with recommendations on what needs doing to fulfil the obligations contained within the individual treaty. The process is part of the wider work undertaken to monitor the human rights record of individual states. Among the other powers open to UN Treaty monitoring bodies is the ability to launch inquiries, for example under Article 8 of the Optional Protocol of CEDAW; the Committee may conduct an inquiry where it receives reliable information of grave or systematic violations of human rights. This is done in co-operation of the State party. The UK government agreed to the Optional Protocol in December 2004.

The Commission actively engages in the monitoring processes on individual treaties along with a vibrant voluntary and community sector. The conclusions of the treaty bodies is one pillar that drives its work forward.

The recommendations for change varied between UN monitoring committees and evolved over time. By way of illustration, the UN Convention on the Rights of Persons with Disabilities recommendations focussed on the question of equality of treatment within disability in the rest of the UK and was the subject of significant debate as to its meaning and whether it cohered with recommendations of other committees. This alongside concerns in other global contexts led the CEDAW and UNCRPD treaty monitoring bodies to look at the possibility of producing an agreed joint statement on the issue.

The Commission met with the chair and vice chair of the Committee on the Rights of Persons with Disabilities in March 2018 during the drafting process to emphasize the need for clarity around the compatibility of equal rights and non-discrimination in disability and a woman's right to personal and bodily autonomy. The meeting included a discussion on how the Committee's conclusions had been utilized by the (then) Attorney General to argue in court that abortion law in NI was human rights compliant. On 29 August 2018, the UNCRPD and UNCEDAW committees issued a joint statement 'Guaranteeing sexual and reproductive health and rights for all women in particular women with disabilities'. In its conclusion, the joint statement outlined

> In all efforts to implement their obligations regarding sexual and reproductive health and rights including access to safe and legal abortion, the Committee call upon State parties to take a human rights-based approach that safeguards the reproductive choice and autonomy of all women, including women with disabilities.

The statement sought to clarify the two bodies position on abortion law reform as compatible with their specific roles to promote non-discrimination.

The Commission's High Court legal challenge

Shortly after the CEDAW committee's conclusions in July 2013 calling for the decriminalization of abortion, the Commission wrote to the Department of Health to offer its advice on recently issued guidance on abortion for health and social care staff. The guidance had taken almost a decade to produce following several legal challenges. The Commission also wrote to the Departments of Health and Justice to outline its concern that the law on abortion was not human rights compliant by failing to provide access in cases of fatal and severe foetal abnormality and for victims of sexual crimes. In reply, the Department for Justice outlined its intention to introduce shortly a consultation paper to allow for terminations in cases of fatal foetal abnormality and to consider the issue of abortion for victims of sexual crimes. Ultimately, it took almost a year before the Department of Justice issued its consultation paper in October 2014. It was clear from both private discussions and correspondence that the recommendation from CEDAW was not being considered.

As a result, the Commission sought a legal opinion on the question of whether the abortion law in NI was compatible with the European Convention on Human Rights. The Convention had been effectively incorporated in domestic law through the Human Rights Act and was the clear vehicle for a legal challenge in the courts in NI. The Commission also raised the question of compatibility with the CEDAW obligations though this never became a central feature of the legal submissions or subsequent judgements. From the outset, the issue was managed as a human rights issue and that alone. On receipt of the legal opinion outlining there was an arguable basis for a legal challenge the Commission held long and robust discussions as to whether we should embark on a legal case or wait and see how the consultation process unfolded. A significant majority of Commissioners adopted to press ahead with a judicial review. The challenge lodged in December 2014 was based on whether Sections 58 and 59 of the Offences against the Person Act 1861 and Section 25 of the Criminal Justice Act (NI) 1945 which prohibited access to terminations was contrary to the Convention and Human Rights Act in cases of serious malformation of the foetus or pregnancy resulting from rape or incest. The application was made in the Commission's own name without a victim as there was in practical terms little chance of a woman being willing to take legal action. Moreover, one victim, if found would only have addressed her circumstances and not the wider systemic issue, which is why having the power to take a case without a victim is important.

The Attorney General joined the application against the Department of Justice following the issue of a Notice of Devolution. In addition, several others intervened both in support of and against the Commission's challenge (Campbell, this volume; Teggart and Rowan, this volume; see appendix for list of interveners).

While the case was not taken in an individual's name, the legal papers included the personal circumstances of Sarah Ewart and Ashleigh Topley who were supported by Amnesty International and AfC, respectively (McKay, this volume; Topley, this volume). In addition, anonymized personal stories were submitted in an affidavit from Dawn Purvis in her role as head of the Marie Stopes Clinic in Belfast. The case was heard in June 2015 and judgement given on 30 November 2015.

Mr. Justice Horner held that the law on abortion in NI was not compatible with human rights under Article 8 (the right to private and family life) and a woman's right to personal and bodily integrity in cases of fatal foetal abnormality and for victims of sexual crimes. The challenge failed in cases of serious malformation of the foetus and under Article 3 (freedom of inhuman and degrading treatment) and Article 14 (freedom from discrimination). The right of the Commission to take a case without a victim was upheld, this right having been challenged by both the Department of Justice and the Attorney General.

An interesting and often unheralded part of the judgement was the ruling given on the common law position of whether the unborn have freestanding rights. This was considered at paragraphs 96–109 where Mr. Justice Horner held that the common law in NI was no different from England and Wales. In effect, a foetus has no freestanding human rights of existence save for any rights being inextricably linked to the rights of a pregnant woman. As the judge concluded, 'the position in Northern Ireland law can reasonably be summed up by concluding that the unborn child does not enjoy a full "right to life" under Article 2. However, pre-natal life does have some statutory protection in respect of some of its attributes'.

This analysis remained undisturbed in the subsequent Court of Appeal and Supreme Court judgements and remains the settled law on the issue in NI. In contrast, the European Court of Human Rights has never ruled definitively on when life begins, concluding instead that it is a matter which falls within the discretion of individual countries.

At a separate hearing, the judge considered the question of legal relief. The 1861 Act is primary legislation and the 1945 Act is secondary legislation. Under the Human Rights Act the High Court and above can only issue a 'declaration of incompatibility' except where it is possible to interpret the working of the legislation in a way that gives effect to human rights. Articles 58 and 59 were unequivocal in terms of criminalizing and prohibiting abortion and the wording could not be interpreted to mean that terminations were allowed in certain circumstances. As a result, the judge issued a declaration of incompatibility under Section 4 of the Human Rights Act – in effect, he declared the law was not human rights compliant in cases of fatal foetal abnormality and for victims of sexual crimes, and it was a matter for the legislature to resolve. At the time of the High Court's final judgement in December 2015 the issue fell to the NI Executive and Assembly.

Court of Appeal and Supreme Court legal challenges

The Attorney General and Department of Justice appealed the High Court's decision while the Commission cross-appealed the ruling that the current law was human right compliant in cases of serious malformation of the foetus and that the law was not a violation of Articles 3 and 14 of the Convention. In effect, all the legal issues remained in play before the Court of Appeal. The case was heard in June 2016 by three appeal court judges. Judgement was given a year later in June 2017. The three judges unanimously upheld the appeal issuing individual judgements. Each judgement took a differing nuanced view nonetheless, all three appeal court judges agreed that this was a matter for the legislature and not the courts. In essence, this was captured by Lord Justice Weatherup at paragraph 178 of the judgement where he held 'The Court has to consider whether in all the circumstances it is institutionally appropriate to intervene in respect of the legislation. This judgement may inform further consideration of the issues. As the matter will receive further consideration in the Assembly, I would conclude that it is not appropriate to intervene at this stage'. The Court of Appeal upheld the right of the Commission to take the case in its own name without a victim.

The ball now fell back to into the Commission's court and based on the international standards which continued to evolve, the Commisssion decided to appeal the decision to the Supreme Court. The case was heard in October 2017 with the largest number of interveners in any Supreme Court hearing to date.

The Supreme Court delivered its judgement on 7 June 2018 with five of the seven Supreme Court justices giving their own judgement. The Supreme Court justices by a majority of four to three held that the Commission did not have a legal standing to bring a case without a victim, based on the interpretation of the statutory powers given to the Commission under Sections 69–71 of the NI Act 1998. Normally, the Supreme Court would go no further and leave the substantive legal point untouched. However, in a highly unusual move all five judges set out their views on the question of whether the law on abortion in NI was compatible with human rights. On a majority of five to two and four to three, respectively, the Supreme Court held that the law breached the right to family and private life in cases of fatal foetal abnormality and for victims of sexual crimes. Two judges held that the law reached the Article 3 threshold of amounting to inhuman and degrading treatment while several other judges reserved their views in the absence of facts of an individual applicant. The judgement amounted to indicative legal opinions of the Supreme Court rather than binding judgements. Nonetheless, the Supreme Court's concern about the state of the law of abortion in NI could not have been made clearer. It was perhaps best encapsulated by Lord Mance, one of the judges who held the Commission did not have standing to take a case. He concluded at paragraph 135 that

I am in short satisfied that the present legislative position in Northern Ireland is untenable and intrinsically disproportionate in excluding from any possibility of abortion, pregnancies involving fatal foetal abnormality or due to rape or incest, the present law clearly needs radical reconsideration. Those responsible for ensuring the compatibility of Northern Ireland law with Convention rights will no doubt recognise and take account of these conclusions, at as early a time as possible, by considering whether and how to amend the law, in light of the ongoing suffering being caused by it as well as the likelihood that a victim of the existing law would have standing to pursue similar proceedings to reach similar conclusions and to obtain a declaration of incompatibility in relation to the 1861 Act.

The verdict on the Commission's lack of standing meant no 'declaration of incompatibility' could be issued though the judgement provided a strong indicative opinion as to the unsatisfactory state of the current law and its incompatibility with human rights. The judgement was substantially utilized in a subsequent case taken by Sarah Ewart that the law would continue to prejudice her human rights should she suffer a further fatal foetal abnormality in any future pregnancy (McKay, this volume). Mrs. Justice Keegan ruled that the law was not compatible with human rights in those circumstances though by the time of her ruling the Northern Ireland Executive Formations Act 2019 had passed, so there was no necessity to issue a declaration of incompatibility. The decision to prosecute the mother who supplied pills to her pregnant fifteen-year-old daughter was also subsequently dropped as a result of legal reform.

Other developments

The legal challenge provided a sharpened focus on the issue of abortion law reform each time it was heard in court and judgement were delivered. However, it wasn't the only legal and political development.

In NI in October 2014 the Department of Justice issued its consultation on the criminal law on abortion covering fatal foetal abnormality and the victims of sexual crime. The Department recommended a change in the law to allow for terminations in cases of fatal foetal abnormality and sought views on the need for similar reform in cases of sexual crimes. In April 2015, the Department published a summary of the responses and its proposals concluding there had been a case made for limited change to the law in cases of fatal foetal abnormality. On sexual crimes, the Department decided not to propose any changes. Proposals for limited reform were developed by the Department; however, the changes had to be agreed by the NI Executive and they floundered there (Pierson, this volume).

In February 2016 several amendments were tabled to the Justice (No2) Bill before the NIA from the Alliance Party and the Green Party. The amendments addressed substantively many of the issues contained in the Commission's legal challenge. All the amendments were comprehensively defeated. The debate was, however, a catalyst for the then leader of the DUP, Arlene Foster, to ask the minister of health to establish a working group to examine how the issue of fatal foetal abnormality could be addressed. Following the Assembly election in May 2016, the then ministers of Health (Michelle O'Neill) and Justice (Claire Sugden) set up an interdepartmental working group to look at the issue of fatal foetal abnormality. This initiative had gained the approval of the NI Executive. The report was submitted to both ministers on 11 October 2016 though not published until 25 April 2018. Among the findings was

> the overall recognition by those health professionals who spoke to the group that the existing legal framework prevents them from fully meeting their duty of care to all women in this situation and therefore denies those women who wish to terminate their pregnancy access to proper standards of healthcare. In summary, health professionals considered the current situation to be professionally untenable.

The group proposed a change to the law within the parameters of its terms of reference, namely, to examine only the issue of fatal foetal abnormality. The delay in publishing the report has never been explained.

Elsewhere, in Ireland, the pace of change quickened. In September 2017, Taoiseach Leo Varadkar announced a referendum on whether to Repeal the Eighth Amendment to the Irish Constitution giving equal value to the life of the unborn foetus and pregnant woman. The constitutional and legislative provisions were discussed at a Citizens Assembly and an Oireachtas committee both of which recommended substantial reform. On 25 May 2018 the Irish people voted by just over a two-thirds majority to Repeal the Eighth Amendment. Law reform swiftly followed and in December 2018, the Health (Regulation of Termination of Pregnancy) Act was passed allowing abortion during the first twelve weeks of pregnancy and later in circumstances of fatal foetal abnormality or where the life or health of the woman was a risk (Roberts, volume 2; Gillum and Weiderud, volume 2).

Legal and policy developments were not confined to both parts of Ireland. In Britain in June 2017, the Supreme Court rejected an appeal by a majority of three to two against a challenge to the Department for Health for failing to provide NHS funding in England for abortions provided to women travelling from NI. The Minister for Women and Equalities Justine Greening announced that such funding would be provided and in a later statement, that funding would be extended to cover travel and accommodation costs. The first statement was made in the week judgement was given in the Court of Appeal and the second the week of the Supreme Court hearing (Creasy and Sanquest, this volume; Thomson, this volume). The governments in Scotland and Wales also followed suit.

The House of Commons Women and Equalities Select Committee then launched its own enquiry into the law in September 2018, holding oral sessions in NI and London. The Commission met the committee in Belfast and gave evidence in February 2019. Among the conclusions of the committee's report published in April 2019 was that while respecting the principle of devolution and the responsibility of the NIA to legislate on matters of abortion law, the UK government retains responsibility to meet its international human rights obligations and devolution cannot justify a failure to meet those standards (House of Commons Women and Equalities Committee, 2019). The Select Committee also concluded that the UK government needed to address breaches of women's rights identified in the CEDAW inquiry where there is no government in NI to take this action. By the time the UK government responded in August 2019, the House of Commons had passed an amendment from Stella Creasy MP to the Northern Ireland Executive Formation Bill to implement the CEDAW committee's inquiry recommendations in full.

The CEDAW inquiry

In December 2010 FPA, NIWEP and AfC made a submission to the CEDAW committee under the Optional Protocol to the Convention that the restrictions on access to abortion for women and girls and the criminalization of abortion under the law amounted to grave and systematic violation of human rights. In 2015 CEDAW decided to undertake the inquiry and the UK government consented. The Commission facilitated the inquiry's confidential visit and meetings with a range of stakeholders with a plethora of views. During the inquiry visit, Dr Caroline Gannon, one of only two paediatric pathologists in NI resigned after thirty years' service and went public with her concerns including having to advise a couple to use a picnic cooler bag to return their baby's remains to NI following an abortion in England. The Commission was able to arrange for Dr Gannon to meet the inquiry team.

The Committee's inquiry was published on 23 February 2018, concluding that the UK government was responsible for ongoing grave and systematic violations of rights under the CEDAW Convention (UN CEDAW, 2018). The Committee's recommendations went far beyond abortion law reform to recognize wider systemic issues including effective access to reproductive and sexual health services; the need for age-appropriate, comprehensive and scientifically accurate, rights-based sex education for adolescents; and the need for a strategy to combat gender-based stereotypes (Cross O'Rourke Simpson, this volume).

The inquiry's findings were published alongside the observations of the UK government, which did not accept the committee's conclusions. The UK government promised a substantive response once devolution was restored. The report struck a timely chord during legal challenges and public discussion in NI and political debate in Westminster. Its recommendations provided the framework for a human rights compliant change to the law covering abortion and wider changes to accessing reproductive and sexual health services. The recommendations became pivotal to the agreed amendment to the Northern Ireland Executive Formations Act 2019 and the transformation of the legal landscape on abortion law. The amendment required the decriminalization of abortion and the implementation of the CEDAW recommendations by 31 March 2020 unless the NI Executive returned by 21 October 2019. The NI Executive was not restored by that date.

Little did the original organizations know what impact their submission to the CEDAW committee was to have almost a decade later.

Analysis

A human rights commission worth its salt must start from the bedrock of international and domestic human rights standards. The question is how to turn those standards into a meaningful policy input locally that improves people's lives. The Commission's role is also to promote and protect the human rights of everyone in NI. The challenge is thrown into even sharper relief when dealing with an issue as divisive as abortion. The Commission's task was to embed its approach on the work of UN international treaty bodies and treaties ratified by the UK government. The Commission is required by UN Paris Principles to be pluralist and its members will always have a diverse range of views. The Commission had significant and lengthy discussions on the issue, sometimes difficultly so, yet they were always based on the human rights standards. In essence, the human rights standards must be the guiding light. That pluralism also meant engaging with all sides of the debate, despite the clear conflict between the position of the Commission and some organizations. In its media work, the Commission was resolute in emphasizing the human rights issues at play in our legal challenge. The tone was sober and factual as reflected in the press releases and other media contributions.

We sought to engage with those who opposed the intervention and stance. One of the unlikely by-products of the work of the Commission on abortion is that it acted as a catalyst for a respectful engagement with the Evangelical Alliance. This arose from meeting with the Evangelical Alliance following a protest-cum-prayer vigil outside the Commission's premises. Subsequent meetings led to a partnership on an animation and seminar around the issue of freedom of thought, conscience and religion. As a result of the engagement, the Evangelical Alliance did not resile from its position on abortion and neither did the Commission; the Alliance continues to be publicly critical of our role on the issue, nonetheless, we understand better each other's perspective. That is as it should be. A second initiative was the setting up of a faith and church forum in tandem with the Equality Commission who had also been in the eye of a storm by supporting Gareth Lee in the case against Ashers Bakery which also reached the Supreme Court. The Commission engaged with many other organizations including the Royal Colleges of Midwives, Nursing, Obstetricians and Gynaecologists, pro-choice and pro-life organizations including AfC and Both Lives Matter. We also met political parties and politicians of all stripes in London and Belfast. We engaged with the international treaty monitoring bodies in Geneva, recognizing the issue of women's reproductive rights including abortion, is a global one.

The Commission is not naïve: we knew that by making a strategic legal intervention the case was likely to end up in the Supreme Court. Such an approach would inevitably keep the question of abortion law in the public spotlight and engender a debate. What the Commission did not foresee was that individual women would gain their voices and tell their stories. This shone a public light on how difficult a decision to have an abortion can be and the associated barriers, loneliness and pain women face when taking such decisions.

At the outset, we also did not envisage the combination of circumstances that paved the way for substantive reform. These included the evolution of human rights standards, particularly the recommendations of the CEDAW inquiry's report into abortion in NI, the loss of the NI Executive and Assembly (something the Commission decried), a willingness for MPs in Britain to recognize that human rights standards cannot be left in suspended animation in the absence of devolved government and the pace of change elsewhere in Ireland.

We will never know if the NIA had voted for limited reform in February 2016 or if the Supreme Court had held the Commission had the statutory power to take a case in its own name and issued a declaration of incompatibility, whether the reform of the law would have eventually settled on implementing in full the recommendations of the UN CEDAW inquiry instead.

The stage has now moved on to implementing the law in practice. Within the Executive Formations Act, the Commission has a role to monitor compliance with international standards and the advancement of women's rights in terms of access to sexual and reproductive health including access to safe abortions. The Commission's monitoring report, published in April 2021, revealed the unwillingness of the Department of Health and NI Executive to enable a funded service to be delivered leaving an interim early medical abortion service in place far short of the legal requirements. Moreover, the service was being periodically suspended in a few trusts (Morgan McLaughlin Kavanaugh Kirk, volume 2). Even this service has only been possible due to the commitment of clinicians and managers within health and social care trusts alongside others who set up the NI Abortion and Contraception Taskforce to deliver a service in the absence of formal support from within the Department of Health. The Taskforce produced a report of its own highlighting the shortcomings of the current provision (NIACT, 2021).

The Commission launched a further legal challenge against the Secretary of State for failing to implement fully the CEDAW recommendations under the Westminster legislation and the Department of Health (NI) and NI Executive for not enabling a commissioned and funded service to be introduced. The legal challenge concentrated political minds in both London and Belfast leading to the new 2021 regulations from Westminster giving the Secretary of State for NI the power to direct the first and deputy first ministers and health minister, among others, to fully implement the CEDAW recommendations in line with the Westminster legislation. The legal challenge was heard in May 2021 and judgement is awaited. In a separate development, the Society for the Protection of the Unborn Child issued a wide-ranging challenge to the 2021 regulations which is being heard in October 2021. The Commission has intervened to challenge this legal action. Further, a Private Members Bill has been produced by Paul Givan a DUP MLA to stop terminations in cases of foetal abnormalities. This Bill is currently before the NIA's Health committee.

In practice, there is a legal and local political war of attrition to oppose the right of a woman to personal and bodily autonomy in line with human rights standards. In my view, this war will ultimately fail. In the meantime, the Commission will stay the course in ensuring human rights standards are upheld.

5

A 'United' Kingdom?: The 1967 Abortion Act and Northern Ireland

Jennifer Thomson

Abortion has been legal in the UK since 1967. The 1967 Abortion Act, which covers England, Wales and Scotland was, however, never extended to Northern Ireland (NI), and change in the region has come via different legal avenues. This chapter addresses the exclusion of NI from the legislation, by looking at events from the passage of the 1967 Act until the present day. It draws on a combination of in-depth interviews with key figures (politicians and activists) and Westminster parliamentary debates. The chapter begins by examining why and how a discussion of NI was not included in the initial 1967 legislation. It then examines attempts to change the situation in NI at Westminster from 1967, most especially the failed attempt to extend the Act in 2008 via the Human Fertilization and Embryology (HFE) Bill. A consideration of the difficulties of involving the national government after the 2010 Hillsborough Agreement follows, concluding with a discussion of the eventual legal changes of 2020.

'Completely passed to one side': Abortion and Northern Ireland from 1967 to 1998

Change to abortion laws in the UK came via David Steel (later Lord Steel) of the Liberal party at Westminster. He had been successful in the Private Members' Ballot and was keen to use this to support abortion law reform (BPAS, 1997, p. 50). Any consideration of NI was, however, limited. Indeed, the only reference to the province in the entirety of the Abortion Act is in the final sentence, which baldly declares that 'This Act does not extend to Northern Ireland'. Lord Steel recalled scant mention of NI, believing to have simply been informed by the

Home Office that it was the responsibility of Stormont and not Westminster (Personal correspondence, 2013). Given that Parliament at Stormont was sitting until 1972, NI was not considered for the reform. Whilst key reformers all had close ties to medical and political institutions (Vera Houghton, the Chair of the Abortion Law Reform Association (ALRA), was the wife of Labour MP, Douglas Houghton), their ties were firmly to London-based institutions. Furthermore, there were no similar debates in Stormont. The Northern Irish Parliament of 1922–74 does not record one debate with any substantial reference to abortion. With no pressure at Westminster or Stormont, NI was neglected during the legislation.

This absence continued in the wake of the 1967 Act, even after the suspension of Stormont in 1972. Most references in the following decades were written questions from backbenchers to the Secretary of State for NI, with a simple answer in response that there was no current policy to change the situation. At irregular intervals, backbenchers inquired into the statistics regarding the numbers of Northern Irish women coming to Britain to seek terminations. The question to Kenneth Clarke is indicative of this: 'Mr. Taylor: asked the Secretary of State for Social Services what is the estimated number of women from Northern Ireland who have had to go elsewhere in the United Kingdom for abortions in each of the last ten years' (HC Deb 05 March 1984 vol 55 cc446-7). Occasionally other statistics were requested (the number of women who had died as a result of illegal abortions in NI, 1985 (HC Deb 07 March 1985 vol 74 c591), the Regional Health Authorities in which NI women had sought terminations, 1986 (HC Deb 26 November 1986 vol 106 cc291-2). Questions emerged equally from members who appeared against the 1967 Act or any future liberalization (the question above from 1985, for example came from Rev Smyth, Ulster Unionist Party MP, and appeared an intentional comment on the lack of 'back-street' abortions in NI) and those who wanted to prompt a discussion about NI's unique position (Mo Mowlam, later Secretary of State for NI, asked several pointed questions in the early 1990s, which appear directed at the provision of sexual health services for young people in the province – HC Deb 30 January 1995 vol 253 c487). Most of the questions regarding NI and abortion during this period were not from key political players, nor were they asked with any level of regularity, which suggests that abortion was never a pressing topic.

Furthermore, members of successive Westminster governments were eager to point out that they did not wish to change the law in NI and were conscious of what they perceived to be differing public sentiment around the issue in the region. Asked in 1986 of the potential for an extension, the then Under-Secretary of State for NI Richard Needham said that 'The legalisation of abortion in Northern Ireland was last reviewed in 1985. At that time, it was concluded that any change in the law would be opposed by an overwhelming majority of the population. I believe that remains the case' (HC Deb 12 November 1987 vol 122 c537). A similar response was provided in 1994, by the then Secretary of State for NI, Michael Ancram (HC Deb 25 May 1994 vol 244 c200). For the duration of this period, successive governments, Conservative and Labour alike, appeared reticent to change legislation, using public opinion as a justification. Moreover, when Northern Irish MPs specifically did talk about abortion in Westminster, they were quick to point to the perception that there was no support in the region itself for any change. Speaking during the debate around the Abortion (Amendment) Bill in 1988, the Reverend Martyn Smyth MP said 'by and large, the bulk of people in Northern Ireland, irrespective of their religious outlook or political convictions, have no desire to see the 1967 Act extended to Northern Ireland' (HC Deb 05 July 1988 vol 63 c252).

The dominant portrait painted at Westminster was one of a Northern Irish population who were happy to accept this legislative difference. The anti-choice voice was loud in Westminster, whereas pro-choice beliefs did not appear to be able to find representatives at the national level. In 1984, then Secretary of State Douglas Hurd MP confirmed that 'Since January 1981, representations have been received from eight district or borough councils, the Association of Local Authorities (NI), LIFE (NI), the 1982 Annual General Assembly of the Presbyterian Church, a Free Presbyterian Church and one private individual' (HC Deb 22 October 1984 vol 65 c461). Similarly, in 1993, it was confirmed in Commons debate that 'in the past 12 months, five representations have been received indicating that most people in the province would support the extension of the Abortion Act 1967 to NI. Twenty-one representations have been received indicating that many people would be opposed to such an extension and one that a majority of the medical profession would likewise be opposed' (HC Deb 05 July 1993 vol 228 cc38-9). This was equally represented in the actions of Northern Irish MPs: in 1995 the Secretary of State confirmed that in the previous three years the only representations from these MPs were to express opposition to extending the Abortion Act 1967 (HC Deb 25 May 1995 vol 260 c749). In 1995, an all-party delegation met the Prime Minister John Major to express distaste for any attempt to extend the legislation to NI (HC Deb 02 May 1996 vol 276 cc1281-2). This cross-party group meeting with the PM with a clear anti-liberalization message reflects the broader message of support for the status quo which was reaching Westminster from NI. The pro-choice voice was either not organized enough to target Westminster with its lobbying or could not find supportive voices to champion its cause in Parliament.

The rarity of reference to abortion in NI means the brief questions and responses concerned with it do not capture the ways in which the discourse around abortion more broadly in British society was changing. Sheldon argues that by the time of the 1990 HFE Bill, abortion had been conceptualized in two dominant ways: as a medical issue with 'an increasing reliance on scientific and medical knowledges' (Sheldon, 1997, p. 109) on both sides of the debate, and 'an acceptance of the foetus as a separate individual' (Sheldon, 1997, p. 114) without any ties to, or within, the maternal body. This polarization of the debate was fuelled in part by a growth in new technologies – the development of 3D and 4D ultrasounds which allowed for the first time 'access' to the baby in the womb (Palmer, 2009) – and several scandals around alleged 'botched abortions'. By the 1990s therefore, 'considerable ground had been lost in popular assumptions about abortion' (Sheldon, 1997, p. 122) with the social welfare-based discourse of Steel's original 1967 Bill now at a remove from public understandings of the procedure. In this more emotive environment, where foetal imagery was now readily being employed to indicate the alleged 'evils' of abortion, focussing the argument around any sort of woman-centred debate appeared difficult. Coupled with the absence of a pro-choice Northern Irish voice at Westminster, this did not make for a friendly environment for the liberalization of abortion laws.

'A special case': Devolution and abortion at Westminster

With a landslide Labour victory in the UK in 1997, major constitutional reform appeared inevitable. Devolution had been a key electoral promise of New Labour, and the creation of new political institutions in Belfast, Edinburgh and Cardiff was proposed. With electorates in Wales and Scotland voting positively for devolution in 1997, and the Good Friday Agreement gaining the support of the Northern Irish population in 1998, the road was paved to begin working out the process of devolution of power from Westminster.

During debates around the devolution of power to the Scottish Parliament and the Welsh and Northern Irish Assemblies at Westminster, the issue of abortion was raised briefly. In a debate in March 1998 an amendment was tabled by Dr Liam Fox, Conservative MP, to devolve power regarding abortion to the Scottish Parliament. As he pointed out, whilst abortion was being left with Westminster, the death penalty, euthanasia and human transplantation were all devolved to the new Parliament in Edinburgh. The British Government, however, was happy for abortion to remain at Westminster, as a matter which necessitated nationwide policy and legal control (HC Deb 31 March 1998 vol 309 c1109).

The contradiction of this position was quickly raised. Maria Fyfe, MP for Glasgow Maryhill, addressing NI said that 'It is impossible to know how many hundreds of thousands of women are forced to make the journey to mainland Britain' (HC Deb 31 March 1998 vol 309 c1099). Justification for the situation was provided by then Secretary of State for Scotland Donald Dewar's representation of the province as 'different' because of its tragic past, but how this corresponds to separate abortion legislation appears confused. When pressed on the issue, Dewar continued in a similar vein: 'The law in Northern Ireland is very *different*, because it *is a special case* ... The *special* social and political situation in Northern Ireland is not a reason for contemplating further differences in the United Kingdom (UK) in this sensitive area' (HC Deb 31 March 1998 vol 309 c1109, emphasis added).

In the wake of devolution abortion was thus subject to legal mismatch across the various territories of the UK. Abortion, central government argued, was too important to be devolved to Scotland, and was portrayed by them as a health issue which required national uniform standards. Yet, in the very same debate, NI was presented by the national government as 'different', 'special' and thus justified in its separate legal standing. This discourse is decidedly different from that seen previously around the initial introduction of the Abortion Act. Abortion was not a medical issue at the time of devolution, as it had been in the discourse of 1967, but an issue of separate cultural tastes.

'A dirty deal': Abortion at Westminster in 2008

As the lack of sustained interest regarding abortion in NI at Westminster suggests, political activism on abortion in the UK has been relatively muted. None of the main UK parties adopt a strong party line on abortion, nor do they whip votes on the issue. Political movement around abortion is cautious.

Yet, despite this, in 2008 a serious attempt was made at Westminster for the first time to extend the 1967 Act to NI. The Human Fertilization and Embryology (HFE) Bill was then passing through Parliament. In 1990, this Act had been used to lower the abortion time limit to twenty-four weeks, from twenty-eight. As such, several liberalizing measures related to abortion were proposed when the Bill was passing through the Commons in 2008, including extending the Abortion Act to NI. Doing so via a bill intended originally to deal with controlling the issue of human fertilization and embryology research presented a 'rather clumsy and convoluted mass of legislation' (Fox, 2009, p. 334) and suggests how toxic the issue of abortion was deemed to be politically. Unable to be discussed on its own terms, it had to be quietly inserted into a larger bill which was only tenuously related to terminations.

As O'Dowd Cross Bloomer (this volume) explain, NI pro-choice activists at the time were optimistic that the amendment would pass and were confident that change would finally occur. They were especially hopeful as this was the last time that Westminster could intervene on this issue, given the understanding that criminal justice powers were to be devolved to the province. Originally fronted by Emily Thornberry MP, she subsequently dropped the amendment which was then taken up by Diane Abbott MP. Abbott's presence as a long-established parliamentarian and senior figure within the governing Labour party meant that it maintained a key presence. However, the amendment was pushed down the running order, making it virtually impossible for it to be debated in the Commons. As a result, it was not on the agenda for discussion.

During the broader debate on the HFE Bill, Abbott raised the issue of NI and abortion. She framed her interest in the issue as resting on an understanding of equal rights, arguing that she could receive similar healthcare in any other area in NI, with the sole exception of abortion (HC Deb 22 October 2008 vol482 c328). Yet Northern Irish MPs were not persuaded by this line of attack. They presented the issue as a matter which was now under Stormont's remit. Jeffrey Donaldson (DUP) MP argued it would be 'entirely wrong for this House to legislate against the wishes of the parties in the Assembly' because Northern Irish political parties would then have to bring about a law they did not agree with (HC Deb 22 October 2008 vol481 c331). Leaders of the four main Northern Irish parties wrote to every member of the House of Commons, declaring that it should be an issue for Stormont and not Westminster. By accepting this interpretation, Westminster showed deference to the notion that this was an issue of regional sensitivity rather than Abbott's representation of a problem which required standardization across the UK.

Furthermore, the way in which Westminster succeeded in dropping the amendment suggested to Northern Irish activists that they could no longer hope for change to come via Westminster. It was strongly inferred in contemporary media[1] that the DUP had received assurances the previous month that were they to vote for the Government's proposed 42-day detention limit for terror suspects, then no attempt would be made by the Labour government to extend the Abortion Act. Indeed, Diane Abbott made this allegation directly in a Westminster Hall debate on abortion and NI the following July (HC Deb 15 July 2009, vol496 c89WH). Activists felt that this was the last opportunity for change from Westminster and were angered that this chance was thwarted via a backroom political deal. It demonstrated to NI activists that they could not rely on Westminster as the lever for change.

Furthermore, activists in NI were appalled at the idea that attempts to extend abortion legislation would derail the peace process, apparently used by both Northern Irish MPs to stop action from the Government, and by the Government to stop the amendment being tabled by backbenchers. As activists described it, members of national government concurred with the understanding presented by Dewar at the time of devolution that NI is 'different' and 'special':

> [Northern Ireland] is known as a quirky little place and people don't really understand it so they kind of want to leave us well alone. So, if you tell them something like abortion could put the peace process in jeopardy then they're inclined to probably believe them.
>
> (Pro-Choice activist, interview 2014)

UK MPs thus appeared willing to sign up to a simplistic understanding of contemporary NI (Thomson 2016a; Thomson 2019a). As such, an uncomplicated rendering of the province and its politics could be exploited by pro-life elements and political parties eager to avoid a controversial issue.

Post-Hillsborough Agreement: Can Westminster intervene?

The Hillsborough Agreement of 2010, agreed between the main political parties and the British government, devolved justice and policing powers. As such, the law relating to abortion was now under Stormont's jurisdiction. However, whether abortion in NI remains an issue for Westminster is contentious. According to the UK's ratification of the United Nations Convention on the Elimination of All Forms of Discrimination against Women (CEDAW), the case for clarification of existing legislation, or legislative change, may only rest at the national as opposed to the devolved level. As described by Cross O'Rourke Simpson (this volume) the UK government has continually evaded efforts by CEDAW to elicit clarity on abortion legislation. Despite its treaty obligations, Westminster appeared unwilling to intervene on this issue.

Contemporary Northern Irish MPs were aware that Westminster was unwilling to act on abortion (Northern Irish MP, private interview, 2013), whilst acknowledging that it could step in and enforce the rules if it so wished. Most MPs and MLAs, however, were steadfast in their assurance that the issue of abortion was one that could now solely be considered at Stormont:

> The decision on the abortion lies with the Assembly. I've spoken on abortion two or three times I've been here [Westminster] in the last three and a half years, my stance has reflected my party's stance. ... I'm glad that they don't get the last say in Northern Ireland. Because the people of Northern Ireland decide.
>
> (Northern Irish MP, private interview, 2013)

However, whilst other MPs interviewed acknowledged that abortion was now a devolved issue, they also suggested that it was more complicated than that:

> It is entirely a devolved matter, so the NI situation would not be discussed in Westminster virtually at all... my experience here is that *if people can hide behind devolution even where it isn't technically devolved*, they will. And if it is definitely devolved, they will not encroach on that in terms of expressing a view or an opinion. So, I don't think we'll get any lead on this issue coming from government in the UK. (Northern Irish MP, private interview, 2013) [emphasis added]

This suggestion that devolution is a useful reference point when Westminster does not want to discuss things that are too controversial has many other exemplars in contemporary Stormont-Westminster relations. It echoes both events in 2008 described above, and more recent criticisms from the shadow Health secretary regarding Health Secretary Jeremy Hunt's insistence that it was the Stormont Health Ministry's prerogative as to whether or not they continued a ban on gay men donating blood. Devolution often appeared as a fluctuating point in discussion around abortion and NI, and at times a useful diversion from calls to action (Moon et al., 2019).

2017 onwards: Liberalization at last

Change from Westminster in the wake of the failures of 2008 seemed unlikely, with national government willing to hide behind an understanding of abortion as a devolved issue first and foremost, even in the first iterations of the Diana Johnson's UK decriminalization. However, unprecedented political circumstances from the 2016 Brexit referendum onwards forced Westminster to act on Northern Irish discrepancy around abortion laws.

Following the 2017 General Election, a Conservative minority government was elected. As Creasy and Sanquest (this volume) describe, Labour backbencher Stella Creasy seized the opportunity proposing an amendment to the Queen's speech to pressurize the government to enact change, ensuring that the cost of terminations for Northern Irish women travelling to England would be covered by the NHS.

This was the strongest move that Westminster had ever taken on abortion in NI. This sudden change of heart on the issue can be explained firstly by the slim majority that the Government had, meaning that it was more willing to compromise on a minor legislative issue to pass the Queen's speech. Secondly, the issue was still framed by Westminster as remaining primarily devolved and thus an issue for Stormont. The Government's letter stating the new framework for those travelling to England concluded with a reminder that:

> None of this changes the fundamental position that *this is a devolved issue in Northern Ireland.* It is for the Northern Ireland Executive and the Northern Ireland Assembly to decide on their policy going forward. This announcement does not change that position.
>
> (Greening, 2017)

This was echoed in the House of Commons debate, where the issue was framed as a devolved responsibility, with the Government and Creasy alike seeking to reassert that they were not acting beyond their deemed remit. Regardless, and despite the bizarre situation this now put women in NI in (with the financial cost of their abortions covered in England, but not at home), it represented a huge step forward in their rights and was the clearest movement yet made by Westminster.

In 2019 further change was initiated due to the suspension of the Northern Irish Assembly at Stormont in January 2017, following a scandal around a renewable heating scheme. Direct rule was never formally established, but the suspension of Stormont and the difficulties of establishing cross-party talks in NI, given the context of Brexit negotiations, meant that Westminster had a much greater sway in Northern Irish affairs. Two backbench MPs Stella Creasy and Connor McGinn (the Northern Irish born Labour MP for St Helens North) proposed a series of Bill amendments aimed at liberalizing abortion, introducing same sex marriage and creating a victims' pension scheme if Stormont was not re-established by October 2019. They passed overwhelmingly through the Commons, and October came and went with no reinstatement of the devolved administration. This meant that abortion, in line with the CEDAW Committee recommendations, had to be made available in NI by the end of March 2020.

The changes came into law from 1 April 2020 and represent hugely significant advances on women and girls' rights, as detailed in Campbell (this volume). What was unthinkable only a few years previously is now a legal reality. How was it made possible? Again, political impetus came from opposition backbenchers, allowing government distance from these changes. Furthermore, the political culture at Westminster had been changed enough that there was a groundswell of support amongst MPs for progress (Campbell, this volume). Indeed, there was a paradigm shift towards confusion as to why NI should differ on these issues. Several senior Conservative female MPs, including the Women and Equalities Minister, Penny Mordaunt, voiced strong support for change on abortion (Weaver and McDonald, 2019). Changing attitudes at Westminster, coupled with unprecedented circumstances (Brexit, the RHI scandal, the DUP supply and confidence deal), pushed the issue of abortion in NI into Westminster's remit and finally forced action.

Conclusion

Northern Ireland has always existed on the periphery of Westminster's attention (Bogdanor, 2001). On key social reform issues it was left behind – the decriminalization of gay sex, the abolition of the death penalty, divorce. For most of these socio-cultural issues, NI eventually gained the same rights and laws as the rest of the UK, yet abortion proved the hardest to amend. Although same-sex marriage was also only legalized in early 2020, same-sex civil partnerships were introduced in 2004 during a period of Direct Rule. Abortion, on the other hand, has routinely seen less engagement from Westminster. The province was ignored during the initial legislation in the late 1960s and was given scant consideration from the mainstream British parties since. There was little engagement from successive governments on including NI in the 1967 Act. Following devolution, abortion was understood to be an issue for Stormont (Moon et al., 2019; Thomson, 2019a), with Westminster resistant to involvement, despite its international human rights obligations, including CEDAW. Following the devolution of criminal justice powers in 2010, Westminster no longer viewed abortion as under its remit, until the actions of backbenchers and the peculiar set of circumstances following the Brexit referendum forced the issue onto the attention of the national government.

Northern Irish women and girls now, finally, have a legal right to termination of pregnancy although access remains precarious. As Campbell (this volume), Rowan and Simpson (this volume) and Allamby (this volume) detail, although an interim service is operational much remains to be done to see full enactment of the legislation, and equal abortion services for women and girls across the UK.

Note

1   'Legalise abortion in Northern Ireland', *The Observer*, http://www.theguardian. com/commentisfree/2008/oct/19/legalise-abortion-northernireland-labour. Accessed 13/11/2014. R. Prince and M. Beckford, 'Abortion plans for Northern Ireland abandoned due to peace process', *Daily Telegraph* (15th October 2008). See also Northern Ireland Devolution Monitoring Report 2009: Wilford, Rick and Robin Wilson (eds), *The Northern Ireland Monitoring Devolution Report*, UCL Constitution Unit, 2009. http://www.ucl.ac.uk/constitution-unit/research/research-archive/ni09.pdf. Accessed 24/12/2014.

6

The request for an inquiry under the CEDAW Optional Protocol

Judith Cross, Catherine O'Rourke and Audrey Simpson

Introduction

This chapter will focus on the request made jointly by AfC, FPA NI and NIWEP to the CEDAW Committee to conduct an inquiry into access to abortion in NI in 2010. The chapter will address the motivations for making the request, in the context of political apathy at Westminster and political opposition to abortion law reform in Stormont. The chapter will document the practicalities of working together to compile the submission to the CEDAW Committee, including efforts to engage the local human rights and women's sectors in the initiative. Finally, the chapter will include reflections and evaluation of the initiative, emphasizing practical lessons that can be useful to abortion rights advocates in other jurisdictions.

The authors of the request were involved in gender politics in various ways, through academia, public policy, service provision and legal routes as well as through involvement in the women's sector. They sought to challenge and effect change for women in NI across several fields such as poverty, childcare, equal pay, access to education and training and reproductive rights and used different avenues and levers to progress these areas, including international human rights instruments. Anne Marie Gray, a social policy academic, and Judith Cross, a public policy analyst, first worked together on the emerging Gender Equality Strategy from the Office of the First and Deputy First Minister. Audrey Simpson, director of the Family Planning Association instigated the judicial review against the Department of Health Social Services and Public Safety (DHSSPS) on the need for guidance on the provision of abortion services in NI and Catherine O'Rourke was a human rights academic who had previously contributed to some activities by AfC and NIWEP. The convergence of the authors at this time is a natural follow-on from the work that they were doing around effecting change for girls and women in NI.

The organizations

In 2009, when NIWEP, FPA and AfC first considered making a request to the CEDAW Committee to conduct an inquiry into access to abortion in NI, the local context for reform was grim. Liberalization of NI's abortion legislation seemed unachievable. There was political apathy at Westminster and, at times, vitriolic opposition by the NI Assembly. Anti-choice supporters claimed that there was widespread opposition to the introduction of more liberal laws. Such claims also ignored the findings of five independent opinion polls, carried out between 1992 and 2008 by Ulster Marketing Survey (1992, 1993, 1994, 1995) and Millward Brown Ulster (2008), which clearly demonstrated strong public support for a liberalization to NI's law on abortion. Furthermore, surveys carried out in 1994 and 2009 into the attitudes of gynaecologists indicated similar support amongst practising gynaecologists for law change (Francome, 2004, 2011). Anecdotally, support for liberalization of the law existed from cross-party MLAs as well as senior civil servants. Frustrated by the lack of progress in reform, three organizations coalesced to explore how they could together end the ongoing discrimination and criminalization of girls and women in Northern Ireland (NI) who chose to end their pregnancy. They were:

1. The Family Planning Association (FPA) in NI (reconstituted as Informing Choices NI in 2019). FPA was the leading sexual health charity and the only organization in NI to provide non-directive, non-judgemental counselling, information and support for girls and women faced with an unplanned or crisis pregnancy. Since 2001 the organization had been embroiled in ongoing legal proceedings in the NI High Court to affect change in the provision of abortion in NI.

2. The Northern Ireland Women's European Platform (NIWEP) is an umbrella body with a membership of national and local organizations and generalist and specific bodies. NIWEP worked to increase knowledge and use of the Convention on the Elimination of All Forms of Discrimination against Women (CEDAW) and had taken the lead in the preparation of Shadow

Reports to the CEDAW Committee. NIWEP representatives attend the examination of the UK government by the CEDAW Committee and monitor the implementation of the Committee's recommendations in the UK.

3. AfC was set up in 1996, emerging from the Women's Right to Choose Group, to encourage the then incoming Labour government to extend the 1967 Abortion Act. They have since campaigned for free, safe and legal abortion access in NI, an end to the criminalization of women.

The three organizations had extensive experience of lobbying, advocacy and campaigning at community, local, national and international level as well as working directly with women with an unplanned or crisis pregnancy. Acknowledging that there was clearly no 'official' appetite at Stormont for liberalizing NI's abortion law, they argued instead that for years the UK Government had ignored grave and systematic human rights violations of women's reproductive rights in NI. They agreed that the route with the most potential would be to analyse closely the Convention on the Elimination of All Forms of Discrimination against Women with regard to its relevance to women's reproductive rights in NI.

The three organizations, whilst different in their approach to the issue of abortion, had a common goal and that was to challenge or remove the existing legislation to enable access to safe, free and legal abortion services at home in NI.

The confluence of local and international dynamics

CEDAW was adopted in 1979 by the UN General Assembly and has three fundamental principles: non-discrimination, substantive equality and state obligation. It was therefore described as an international bill of rights for women (Freeman et al., 2012). The Convention has been ratified by 193 States Parties, including the UK, who are legally bound to fulfil, protect and respect women's human rights. Every four years, each state party must submit detailed self-monitoring reports on measures they have taken to implement the obligations of the Convention. Each report is considered by the CEDAW Committee, a body of twenty-three independent experts on women's rights established to monitor state compliance with the Convention. After consideration, the Committee addresses its concerns and recommendations to the state party in the form of Concluding Observations (Freeman et al., 2012).

Significantly in its 1999 Concluding Observations to the UK, the CEDAW Committee expressed concern that devolution of legislative powers from the UK Government in Westminster to a Northern Ireland Assembly (NIA) might result in the uneven protection of women's rights across the UK. Following the signing of the Good Friday Agreement in 1998 and the establishment of the NIA, legislative responsibility for health was immediately transferred to the Assembly but responsibility for criminal justice remained at Westminster. Therefore, as abortion was criminalized, the responsibility for change remained with the UK Government. The Committee specifically referred to women's reproductive rights and recommended that a process of public consultation on abortion in NI should take place. The Committee stated that:

> The Committee notes with concern that the Abortion Act 1967 does not extend to NI where, with limited exceptions, abortion continues to be illegal [...] The Committee also recommends that the Government initiate a process of public consultation in Northern Ireland on reform of the abortion law.

In its 2008 Concluding Observations the Committee again specifically expressed concerns over NI's inconsistent position on abortion. It recommended:

1. A process of public consultation on abortion should be initiated.
2. Abortion law should be amended so as to remove punitive provisions imposed on women who undergo abortion.
3. Health services should be delivered in a gender-sensitive manner to all health.

Despite the concerns unequivocally expressed by the CEDAW Committee, the UK Government consistently refused to acknowledge the grave and systematic violation of women's reproductive rights in NI. The three organizations concluded that the utilization of CEDAW's Optional Protocol procedure to urge the Committee to conduct an Inquiry offered the most potential to achieve decriminalization.

The request for an inquiry: Aims, process and substance

The aims of the Inquiry would be to brief the CEDAW Committee on the ongoing discrimination and inequality experienced by women in NI with an unplanned or crisis pregnancy; document and provide evidence of the grave and systematic nature of human rights violations under CEDAW, including a cross-section of case studies from NI; seek an end to human rights violations with regard to women's reproductive rights in NI as there were no remaining domestic avenues; to hold the state party, the UK, accountable for its actions; and ultimately, it was hoped, bring about structural change.

Using the Optional Protocol, a mechanism that had been in place since 2000, was discussed with a representative from NIWEP at the 2009 UK Periodic Review hearing (O'Rourke, 2016). NIWEP approached AfC and FPA and sought to discuss this option. Against the political context – the failure of Westminster, the NIA and the devolution of justice on its way, it seemed there was nothing to lose. The practicalities of taking this work forward and the time it would require were thankfully unknown at the start. The initial meetings examined the risks of taking this forwards and O'Rourke (2016) outlines these clearly, namely the political costs in that the Committee may reinforce the dominant religious and moral views; the Committee could refuse to carry out the inquiry and or fail to find 'grave or systematic violation' of rights. The risks were different for each organization, but it was felt that a collective request to the Committee was best and allowed for the sharing of resources and expertise.

Substance of the submission

In terms of structure of the report, we followed the Articles of the Convention. Mindful that the inquiry procedure was reserved for 'grave or systematic violations' of the Convention, we had to ensure that we were able to establish evidence to meet this criterion.

We concentrated on violations of CEDAW article 1 (discrimination against women), article 2 (prohibition on discriminatory laws, policies and practices), article 5 (discriminatory social and cultural patterns), article 10 (discrimination in education), article 12 (discrimination in healthcare), article 14 (discrimination against rural women) and article 16 (discrimination in marriage and family relations). This gave scope to focus on the extreme restriction of abortion services, coupled with the lack of clarity and risk of criminal sanctions on women and health professionals. These articles also enabled a move beyond the strictly legal arguments and allowed a reveal of serious lapses by the UK Government across a range of areas by a range of state actors. Section 2 details the following CEDAW violations:

Article 2: Prohibition of discrimination
Article 2 (c): Duty to provide equal protection of the law

The criminalisation of women from Northern Ireland seeking abortion denied them:

Equal entitlement to healthcare: and

Equal protection of the law enjoyed by their British counterparts.

Article 2(d): Duty on public authorities to refrain from discrimination

CEDAW itself had clearly stated that:

It is discriminatory for a State Party to refuse to legally provide for the performance of certain reproductive health services.

Article 2(f): Duty to take all measures to modify or abolish discriminatory laws, regulations and practices

In 2008 the Committee recommended to the UK the removal of punitive provisions for women in Northern Ireland who undergo an abortion. Westminster chose to ignore this recommendation and consequently girls and women in Northern Ireland who chose to have an abortion were still being forced to raise between £600 and £2000 to pay for an abortion in England or other European countries and labelled and stigmatised as criminals.

Article 2(g): Discriminatory national penal provisions

This article requires all states to repeal all national penal provisions which constitute discrimination against women. Yet, the law on abortion in Northern Ireland was regulated by criminal statutes, principally the Offences Against the Person Act 1861.

Article 5: The obligation to modify discriminatory social and cultural patterns

The UK Government had consistently failed to modify discriminatory social and cultural patterns for several decades by the perpetuation of a culture of silence, stigma and denial on the basis of perceived consensus in Northern Ireland against more liberal access to abortion services.

Article 10(h): Non-discrimination in education

Research indicates that young people in Northern Ireland do not receive accurate and non-judgemental education about abortion in all schools throughout Northern Ireland.

Article 12: Non-discrimination in healthcare

It is discriminatory for health systems to refuse or fail to provide health services that only women need, such as obstetric care and safe abortion services. Furthermore, CEDAW's General Recommendation 19 articulates an obligation on States to ensure that women are not forced to seek unsafe medical procedures such as illegal abortion because of the lack of appropriate services in regard to fertility control.

Article 14(2)(b): The rights of rural women

FPA's sexual health helpline clearly demonstrated that women in rural areas have limited access to family planning clinics compared to women in urban areas and in particular to emergency contraception. Further because of the close-knit nature of rural areas confidentiality was an issue therefore women with an unplanned pregnancy were less likely to go to their GP or sexual health clinic. This combined with the overall stigma of abortion in Northern Ireland makes women in rural areas more likely to keep their pregnancy secret and thus susceptible to resorting to unsafe abortion practices.

Article 16(1)(e): Non-Discrimination in marriage and family relations

CEDAW noted that women bear disproportionate responsibility and burden of work in bearing and raising children. The Committee also recognised that the number and spacing of children have an impact on access to education, employment and personal development for women, to an extent that does not apply to men. The absence of legal, free and safe abortion in Northern Ireland infringes the right of women to decide on the number and spacing of their children.

For FPA, NIWEP and AfC it was clear that there were strong arguments and evidence which could be used in the drafting of a submission to demonstrate that the UK Government was in grave and systematic violation of the Convention. We made fourteen recommendations to CEDAW Committee based on the Articles noted above and several appendices complemented the report.

Contesting the 'cultural distinctiveness' defence

Previous UK Periodic reports showed that the UK Government sought to hide behind devolution and reinforce the cultural distinctiveness of NI to accord religion a privileged position in relation to public policy. For example, the UK Fourth Periodic report stated that:

> While there has been adverse comment in recent years on the state of the present law, there is also strong public opposition to any change in the law. The Government wishes to take a considered view before any decision on further action is taken.
>
> (UK, 4th Periodic Report, 1999, p. 136)

In order to counter the UK Government's cultural argument, it was important that evidence to the contrary was provided to the Committee. It was clear that the dominant religious and moral view of abortion was not the norm as supported by the Life and Times Surveys and other opinion polls, showing a more nuanced view on abortion. Further, the ongoing civil society pro-choice activism challenging the unacceptable violation of women's rights was detailed, as were the daily emotional, practical and financial implications for women of NI regarding reproductive health services. Case studies were also included in Appendix five of the report to highlight to the Committee the lived realities of NI's restrictive abortion law, consequences which most women in the rest of the UK do not experience.

Whilst these were documented in the main report, it was still felt that letters of support were important. A letter from the three organizations was sent to a range of stakeholders asking for their support in the form of a letter or a statement, for the request for an inquiry to examine the circumstances of abortion services in NI. However, getting support from some quarters proved problematic as they were either silent on abortion or openly hostile to the issue. Some women's groups found being openly supportive of abortion rights difficult, as many were reliant on state funding and worried that this could be jeopardized if they openly backed abortion rights. However, we got letters of support from the Women's Resource and Development Agency, a regional women's organization and a local women's group, Highfield, as well as Women's News and Choice Ireland. AfC had begun building alliances and partnerships with the trade union movement and student movement. This paid off as there was support from the main trade unions, UNISON, Unite and the Irish National Teachers Organisation.

The more visible human rights NGOs in NI, at this time, however did not address the issue of abortion and remained silent on this. Amnesty International in NI and the Committee on the Administration of Justice (CAJ) both campaigned openly on human rights issues and remained silent on the issue of abortion. The CAJ's shadow report submission in 2008 to CEDAW did not refer to abortion despite the concluding comments in 1999 as outlined above. O'Rourke (2016) notes that whilst Amnesty International changed its position on abortion in 2007, the Belfast office remained silent on this issue. Indeed, even those with statutory responsibility for the protection of human rights failed miserably by reinforcing that NI was so culturally distinct that violations of human rights could continue. For example, the position of the Northern Ireland Human Rights Commission (NIHRC) in 2001 in respect of abortion was as follows:

> The issue of women's rights in respect of reproduction, and especially the issue of abortion, has been one of the most controversial in the Commission's consultation to date. The Commission has concluded that it would be inappropriate for it to

suggest that the issue should be resolved by the Bill of Rights; it is best dealt with by specific legislation drafted by democratically elected representatives.

(NIHRC, 2001)

After the report was finalized and submitted to the CEDAW Committee Secretariat in December 2010, it was disseminated to key statutory stakeholders in NI such as the Ministers of health and justice as well as the permanent secretaries, the chief medical officer, the NIHRC chief commissioner and the chief executives of the main health providers in NI. The report was also sent to the Home Office and the Government Equalities office minister as well as a range of NGOs. The confidentiality surrounding the inquiry process created difficulties for civil society, not least the lack of information as to how the inquiry was proceeding, if at all, within the Committee. In early 2013, we received a request from the Committee for an update on developments since the inquiry request was first made. This was the first indication we received that our request was being actively considered by the Committee. We were also aware that the CEDAW Committee in the intervening years had introduced an additional level of scrutiny to the UK Government's inaction on the issues by means of the follow-up procedure. This indicated the seriousness with which the Committee now approached the UK's repeated non-compliance on the issues and gave a sense of reassurance. Nevertheless, the Committee's decision-making concerning the inquiry request remained unclear.

A letter to the report authors from the Committee Secretariat on 29 July 2016 indicated that the CEDAW Committee had decided, in cooperation with the State Party, to undertake an inquiry with respect to access to abortion services in NI. The visit to Belfast and London, between 10 September 2016 and 19 September 2016, was to be kept confidential and we were asked to facilitate meetings by compiling a list of relevant stakeholders including women who had been directly affected.

The Committee's visit

The organizations were invited to an informal meeting with the CEDAW Committee members and the Secretariat on Sunday, 10 September 2016. One of the inquiry team witnessed first-hand the ongoing protests outside the Marie Stopes Clinic which had opened in 2012. We identified and coordinated a list of people and organizations that the Inquiry Team needed to meet to ensure they got a full picture of the situation in NI, including key members of the judiciary and the police. Academics and civil society representatives were identified to speak to the Inquiry Team as well as key statutory officials from the areas of health and justice, including service providers and commissioners of health. We identified parliamentarians, from the NIA and Westminster, to speak to the Inquiry Team and this included political parties with anti-choice views. Due to locations and time constraints several individual meetings took place via Skype and Facetime. In parallel to this we identified and approached individual women prepared to tell their experiences, AfC offered support to women before and after their meetings.

One of the major challenges in coordinating the visit of the Inquiry Team was the need to keep this confidential and not hinder gathering of evidence. Our concern was that if the word got out that this would jeopardize and stall the inquiry. Thankfully, we maintained this throughout the visit.

Inquiry findings

On 23 February 2018 – more than seven years after the initial request to conduct an inquiry was made – the CEDAW Committee made public its inquiry report into access to abortion in NI. The Committee concluded definitively that the de facto and de jure limitations on access to abortion in NI constitute both 'grave and systematic' violations of the rights guaranteed under the CEDAW Convention. The global significance of this determination should not be understated. This was only the fourth time that the Committee found a state party to be in 'grave or systematic' violation of the Convention under the inquiry procedure, despite having the capacity since 2000. Moreover, it was the first time the Committee made such a determination with respect to abortion.

The Committee found the UK to be in violation of CEDAW articles 1, 2, 5, 10, 12, 14 and 16. The Committee determined that the 'deliberate maintenance of criminal laws disproportionately affecting women and girls, subject[ed] them to severe physical and mental anguish' constitutes 'gender-based violence' and 'may amount to cruel, inhuman and degrading treatment', in violation of articles 1 and 2, read together with articles 5, 12 and 16 (para 72a). Further, the Committee found that the laws criminalizing abortion rendered abortions inaccessible in NI, irrespective of their legality, due to clinicians' fear of prosecution (para 73), constituting a violation of article 12. In addition, school discretion over the substance of relationship and sexual education in NI, which permits 'poor quality sexuality education for youth and anti-abortion and abstinence ethos indoctrination' constitutes a violation of articles 2, 12 and 16 (para 75). Moreover, the iniquitous impact of the law on 'rural, migrant, asylum-seeking, refugee women and women in situations of poverty' violates CEDAW articles 2, 12, 14 and 16, in 'dereliction of [the UK's] public health duties'. Also, the Committee found violations of article 10 and 12 due to the State party's failure 'to protect women from harassment by anti-abortion protestors when seeking the sexual and reproductive health services and information' (para 72e). Finally, the Committee determined that the UK's 'failure to combat stereotypes depicting women primarily as mothers exacerbates discrimination against women' and violates article 5, read with articles 1 and 2.

Importantly, the CEDAW Committee only makes public the findings from its inquiry procedure in situations in which it determines 'grave or systematic violations' of the Convention. In the NI case, the violations were held to be 'grave' due to the situation faced by women in cases of severe or fatal foetal impairment, and victims of rape or incest, who are compelled by the criminal law to carry pregnancies to full term. The resulting 'severe physical and mental anguish, constituting gender-based violence against women' therefore met the Committee's threshold of gravity (para 73(a)). Further, the violations were held to be systematic because the criminal law and public policy compels women with unviable or unwanted pregnancies either to carry those pregnancies to full term, to travel outside NI to undergo an abortion or to self-administer abortifacients (para 73b).

Implications and learning

In terms of its local significance, the inquiry report by the CEDAW Committee was the clearest possible statement that restrictive access to abortion in NI, and the underpinning criminal law and public policy was a manifest and ongoing human rights violation. The inquiry report was impressively detailed and sensitive to the local context in which restrictive access to abortion prevails. The Committee correctly and robustly identified the negative gender stereotypes that inform – and are reinforced by – restrictive laws and policies on abortion in NI. They named and evidenced the full range of state and public actors who perpetuate such stereotypes. The strength of the Committee's determinations meant that the issue could no longer legitimately be denied or marginalized by those (state actors, civil society organizations and political parties) who formally avowed a commitment to human rights and gender equality. It was no longer tenable for such actors to obfuscate and dissemble on the issue of abortion. The report thereby constituted an important call to action to advance gender equality in NI. Finally, the report was clear – in the strongest possible terms – that devolution was no justification for the UK's failure to comply with its obligations under CEDAW to women in NI.

In its response to the inquiry report, the UK worryingly relied heavily on devolution to justify its continuing inaction (UK Government, 2018). The response focused on disputing some findings of fact, redirecting responsibility to a range of actors outside of its direct control, and attributing overall inaction to devolution. Nevertheless, at the time of the report being published, it was clear that in light of the ongoing suspension of devolved institutions, and the growing prospect of direct rule, such defences by the Westminster government were sounding increasingly hollow. The time to remedy the manifold violations identified in the inquiry report had come.

Certain dynamics that were specific to the NI context, in particular concerning the suspension of the devolved Assembly and Executive, meant Westminster's authority to legislate was clear. The CEDAW Committee's damning findings were vital to convincing Westminster that inaction was no longer acceptable and that deference to the devolved government was not a neutral position; rather it was perpetuating what had been determined by the CEDAW Committee to be the 'grave and systematic' violation of the rights of women in NI. Whilst the dynamics surrounding the Westminster legislation are more fully discussed elsewhere in the volume (Thomson, Creasy Sanquest), the framing of the Westminster intervention as very clearly around ensuring human rights compliance reveals the CEDAW significance. Immediately following the publication of the CEDAW Inquiry report, the Westminster Women and Equalities Committee commenced its own inquiry into abortion law in NI, citing the CEDAW Committee findings in its justification for doing so (WEC, 2019). Further, in the highly significant Westminster legislation, the CEDAW recommendations were central to the rationale and parameters of reform. Section 9 of the 2019 Northern Ireland (Executive Formation) Act was titled 'Abortion etc: Implementation of CEDAW recommendations' and provided inter alia that:

> The Secretary of State must ensure that the recommendations in paragraphs 85 and 86 of the CEDAW report are implemented in respect of Northern Ireland.

Despite the specifics of the NI case, there are nevertheless clear points of learning for abortion rights activists in other jurisdictions. These pertain most significantly to the importance of valuing the process, and not just the ends of making an inquiry request. Given the very long timelines in securing success through the inquiry route, it is important to identify and maximize benefits from the process of collaborative working and evidence collection involved in compiling the submission to the CEDAW Committee. Most importantly, the opportunity to work across organizations with shared goals around decriminalization, though not necessarily with a history of collaborative working, yielded ready dividends from the process. Ultimately, these relationships of collaborative working were beneficial for positioning abortion rights activists to organize and exploit the opportunities presented by suspension of the devolved political institutions.

Second, the documentation of the manifold human rights violations ongoing due to restrictive access to abortion was an important output of the process. The submission requesting an inquiry was, in-and-of-itself, the most detailed, comprehensive and robustly evidenced documentation of the legal, political and social contexts of access to abortion in NI, as well as the material, emotional and political consequences of the restrictive abortion regime. Documentation of human rights violations is an essential advocacy strategy, that had hitherto been largely unexploited due to resistance from local human rights organizations to advocate on the issue of abortion access. The submission requesting the inquiry therefore evidenced the value of the collective endeavour and enterprise of its authoring organizations, who were able to pool their service provision and advocacy expertise in order to produce this unique submission.

Third, regarding the process benefits of the inquiry request, actively seeking out support for the inquiry request across civil society organizations was arguably the first time local human rights actors were called to account for their inability to advocate for abortion rights. Whilst it is necessarily a speculative point, the process around compiling the inquiry request, and the failure of the key 'mainstream' human rights organizations to support the request despite repeated adverse findings by the CEDAW Committee in its Concluding Observations, appeared to soften the ground for subsequent change by challenging those actors and organizations on their own terms. In 2014, the Belfast office of Amnesty International UK launched a pro-choice campaign. In 2015, the NIHRC commenced important strategic litigation challenging the human rights compliance of access to abortion. Further, in 2017, the Committee for the Administration of Justice adopted a clear pro-choice position, after decades of silence on the issue. In hindsight, the dynamic of actively calling to account local human rights actors and organizations for their unwillingness to support the inquiry request might have been more strategically exploited at the time of compiling the submission. It is notable, and in many respects regretful for them, that one of the most effective advocacy campaigns ever to engage an international human rights body to remedy ongoing violations in NI proceeded without the involvement and support of any of the established local human rights organizations.

Finally, the ongoing nature of the CEDAW engagement and scrutiny remains beneficial. The inquiry report required a state party update from the UK on its activities to remedy the violations within six months of publication of the inquiry report. However, this ongoing scrutiny goes well beyond that initial response. The Committee is free to request updates at regular intervals. Critically, this issue will remain prominent in all CEDAW Committee engagements with the UK's periodic reporting to the Committee long into the future, if the UK continues to be a state party to the CEDAW Convention. Political resistance and challenges to rolling out the new legal framework have become especially acute with the COVID-19 pandemic. In order to get to a point of free, safe, legal and local, abortion ongoing scrutiny by the CEDAW Committee and other international human rights actors will be necessary. In many respects, the CEDAW inquiry initiative was successful well beyond even our most ambitious expectations, nevertheless, substantial implementation challenges persist. Whilst the legislative framework has changed, those political actors and key institutions cited by the CEDAW Committee as responsible for the violations remain in authority. We are hopeful that the CEDAW Committee will continue to be an ally in this ongoing campaign for rights.

7

Working within Westminster

Stella Creasy and Cara Sanquest

The Abortion Act 1967 introduced legal conditions for access to abortion for women in England, Wales and Scotland. Following this, supporters of reproductive rights from all political parties have defended them by seeking to avoid the matter being debated again by the Parliament. Nowhere have the consequences of this approach been felt more keenly than in NI – where until 2019 access to abortion was limited to a handful of exemptions. This chapter will consider how and why abortion rights of women in NI were 'off limits' for over half a century, and what it took for this to change. In doing so, it explains how NI came to have the most progressive abortion laws of any nation in the UK – and why, despite this victory, the fight for reproductive rights continues.

Don't rock the boat: The history of abortion rights in the UK Parliament

Abortion legislation across the United Kingdom is rooted in the Offences against the Person Act 1861 (OAPA). This criminalized abortion – putting it on equal footing to 'placing gunpowder near a building, with intent to do bodily injury to any person', 'assaults with intent to obstruct the sale of grain, or its free passage' and 'inflicting bodily injury, with or without weapon' (UK Government, 1861). This Act not only criminalized those who sought an abortion at any stage in a pregnancy, but also those who helped. In 1967 a private member's bill proposed by Lord David Steel, then MP for Roxburgh, Selkirk and Peebles, provided exemptions from prosecution in Scotland, England and Wales provided the pregnancy was less than twenty-four weeks along and that 'termination is necessary to prevent grave permanent injury to the physical or mental health of the pregnant woman' (UK Government, 1967).

It was the fourth parliamentary attempt to legalize abortion access between 1951 and 1967. Public opinion had changed following widespread press coverage of the risks of backstreet abortions and evidence that by the mid 1960s unsafe abortion was the leading cause of avoidable maternal deaths. Then came the thalidomide controversy, with the severe birth deformations experienced by those who took this drug, and the heart-breaking choices open to their mothers as a result. For over fifty years this bill, and by definition OAPA which it modifies, defined access to abortion in England and Wales, despite medical developments such as abortion pills. Thus, in 2020, abortion is still formally illegal in England, Scotland and Wales, except for those who are exempted from prosecution under this Act.

NI was not mentioned in Lord Steel's bill – excluded from exemption by omission, rather than explicit requirement (Thomson, this volume). Yet the effect of this – and so leaving OAPA to be applied there unamended – was to keep in place some of the most oppressive laws on abortion in the world. Women who had been raped, became pregnant and sought a termination as a result could face a longer prison sentence than their attackers. Those with foetal abnormalities were forced to carry their child to term despite the diagnosis (UK Supreme Court, 2018). Prosecutions for seeking an abortion were a reality, with police raids on activists and those who had bought abortion pills online and the prosecution of a mother who had sought an abortion for her fifteen-year-old daughter in 2017 (McDonald, 2017).

In 1990 Harriet Harman MP attempted to extend the exemption to NI – with Lord Steel admitting he couldn't even 'remember exactly why the 1967 Act was not extended to Northern Ireland, but I suspect that one reason was that in those days Stormont still existed' (Hansard, 1990). It met vigorous opposition in Parliament, with concerns 'unmarried women' (Paisley, in Hansard, 1990) might access abortion, that it should be a matter for Stormont – although not in service at the time – and that it was the will of the people of NI to prevent all abortion access.

This episode reinforced the perceived wisdom amongst campaigners and parliamentarians alike that extending abortion access to NI was in the 'too difficult' box and would remain so. This did not stop many from seeking to raise the issue. Glasgow Maryhill MP Maria Fyfe consistently advocated for women in NI to have equal abortion access, tabling questions and speaking on the subject through the 1990s. In 2008 Emily Thornberry MP tried to amend the Human Fertilization and Embryology Bill (HFE Bill), reportedly leading to a 'row' between the then Leader of the House of Commons, Harriet Harman, and Prime

Minister Gordon Brown (Hennessy, 2008). The bill was delayed, and then when it came the time to debate Thornberry's amendment, the Labour Government introduced a programme motion which effectively prevented it (Thomson, this volume).

Diane Abbott MP sought to pick up where Thornberry left off, and tabled a cross-party amendment with the backing of the British Medical Association, the Family Planning Association and the British Pregnancy Advisory Service and others (Hansard, 2008). Yet again, the amendment was not debated because of what Abbott termed a 'shabby manoeuvre' by Ministers (Hansard, 2008b). It was reported that Catholic Labour MPs were seeking a free vote on amendments in the HFE Bill regarding embryo research (BBC News, 2008a), and there was a by-election looming in predominantly Catholic Glasgow East (Hennessy, 2008). The government had also recently secured the support of nine DUP MPs to extend the period terrorists could be detained without charge to forty-two days on a parallel piece of legislation. Eager to ensure this legislation passed and the by-election won, the rights of the women of NI were an easy bargaining chip for those tasked with parliamentary and political management. When Mo Mowlam left office as Secretary of State for Northern Ireland, she said that her biggest regret was that she had failed to find an appropriate time to extend the Abortion Act to NI (Sheldon et al., 2020).

Between 1967 and 2017, most discussion of abortion rights in Parliament was led by those who wanted to roll back the rights the 1967 legislation provided through debates on term limits, sex selection and the role of counselling (BBC News, 2008b). With a powerful and well-funded anti-choice lobby active, campaigners for reproductive rights reacted by seeking to close down all discussion of abortion as the best tactic to prevent their success. The consequence was little legislative progress on abortion rights.

In March 2017, Diana Johnson tabled a ten-minute rule bill to decriminalize abortion in England and Wales. Although the bill did not extend to NI and had no chance of becoming law, it was a brave move to test the appetite of MPs for removing criminal law as the underpinning of abortion rights in the twenty-first century. Yet when the bill only passed 172–142, the slim majority reinforced the view that when it came to reproductive rights it was best not to rock the boat and raise the matter at all. This in turn defined the willingness of many on the issue of rights for NI itself. As Sally Sheldon documented, 'UK governments have charted a course of studied inaction, which has been apparently unaffected by political party, the personal views of relevant ministers, or the locus of legislative competence for abortion law and policy' (Sheldon et al., 2020, p. 761).

It took a perfect storm of events between 2017 and 2019 to change these conditions. The collapse of the Stormont executive, the hung parliament and sustained campaigning forced UK representatives to address the issue directly. At the same time, Supreme Court rulings (UK Supreme Court 2018, 2017), desperate and tragic personal stories (BBC Newsbeat, 2017; BBC News 2019b), international human rights breaches (UN CEDAW, 2018) and an historic referendum in Ireland contributed to a situation where no longer could any politician argue that the threshold for the required level of suffering of women and girls in NI which would prompt action had not yet been reached.

A return to the chamber: The 2017 Queens Speech

On 8 June 2017, a snap general election returned a hung parliament, forcing Theresa May to broker a confidence and supply agreement with the Democratic Unionist Party in return for their ten votes. A political party previously ignored by many in UK politics suddenly moved centre stage, as the power brokers of the fate of a government which had squandered a majority with an ill-advised election.

Parliament began considering May's Queens Speech on Wednesday, 21 June 2017. It was dominated by Brexit. Yet, just a week after the election on 14 June 2017, the Supreme Court had handed down a judgement discrimination in the case of a fifteen-year-old girl. She was a UK citizen who travelled from NI to England for abortion and had to pay £900 for treatment, funded by a charity, the Abortion Support Network, rather than access it free on the NHS (UK Supreme Court, 2017). Her argument was supported by five abortion rights organizations, barristers from Caoilfhionn Gallagher QC and Jude Bunting QC acting in the case. Using concern over the prospect of the DUP defining the Government's agenda, a cross-party group of MPs led by Stella Creasy proposed an amendment that would require women from NI to be able to access abortion services in England and Wales as part of the NHS.

Many parliamentarians admitted they were unaware that women from NI, despite being UK taxpayers, were charged to access NHS services if they came to England or Wales for an abortion. In turn government ministers, expecting a fight on Brexit, were blindsided by a debate on reproductive rights and struggled to respond to questions about why such discrimination occurred.

Traditionally only opposition front benches can propose an amendment to the Queen's Speech which is selected for consideration. However, in 2014

Speaker Bercow had set a controversial precedent which allowed the speaker the flexibility to pick additional amendments for votes which could show they had substantial backbench and cross-party support. Stretching the limits of parliamentary procedure would become critical to parliamentary activity between 2017 and 2019. With a hung parliament and an active champion of backbenchers as speaker willing to challenge precedent, many saw opportunities for a wide range of causes. Recognizing this, a strategy was developed which recognized securing abortion rights in NI would be a marathon not a sprint; that repeated pressure through amendments and votes and incremental change would eventually bear fruit.

Initially government ministers tried to argue access to abortion for women from NI was still a devolved matter (Green in Hansard, 2017a), but soon found this untenable. Stormont had not been sitting since 9 January 2017 following the collapse of the power sharing agreement making it impossible for the Assembly to act (Kingsley, 2017). Two days later, Jeremy Hunt, Secretary of State for Health, tried to placate campaigners with the offer of a consultation stating, 'I agree that all women, in all parts of the United Kingdom, should have the same rights to access healthcare' (Hansard, 2017b). That evening, the front page of the *London Evening Standard* led with 'Abortion Vote Chaos Hits May: PM Fights to Avoid Queens Speech Defeat as Pact with DUP Sparks Crisis' (Murphy, 2017).

Campaigners rejected the offer of consultation and threatened to force a vote, leaving the Government with no option but to act or else risk the unthinkable – that a Queen's speech bill would be amended and so perceived a failure. In total, over 100 MPs including former Government ministers had co-signed the amendment (Elgot and McDonald, 2017). On 29 June, the Chancellor announced funding to cover the costs for women from NI to travel to England for abortions in return for its withdrawal. Governments in Scotland and Wales soon followed suit, and the British Pregnancy Advisory Service, who had long provided for women from the island of Ireland to access abortion in England and advocated strongly for a change in the law, were given a tender to run a government funded Central Booking Service where women in NI could call to book a UK government funded abortion in all three countries. To avoid sensitivities around devolution, the scheme was funded by the Department of Women and Equalities rather than the Department of Health and Social Care. In the first three months of the scheme, 342 women accessed abortion – the equivalent of 4 every day (Hammond, in Hansard, 2017c).

The scheme was not perfect – lack of provision for the transport of foetal remains, means tested travel grants and the requirement to travel to access healthcare, all meant that it was not a solution for many women. However, the policy itself undermined the government position that the denial of basic healthcare to women in NI was nothing to do with the UK Government. Defying wisdom not to raise reproductive rights in Parliament, the amendment brought the battle for reproductive rights back to the heart of Westminster and set the stage for further progress.

2018: The year abortion access became a human right

The United Nation Committee on the Elimination of Discrimination against Women (CEDAW) had often criticized the UK's inaction on abortion law in NI. Followed sustained efforts by civil society to force the pace of change a request was made for an inquiry by CEDAW by AfC, the Family Planning Association NI and the Northern Ireland Women's European Platform (O'Rourke, 2016; Cross O'Rourke Simpson, this volume). Published in February 2018, it concluded that NI's abortion laws resulted in 'grave and systematic' violations of human rights, and that the UK was the state party responsible; crucially it stated devolution was no excuse for this situation (UN CEDAW, 2018). This was only the fourth time that CEDAW found such a breach had taken place, having only carried out three other inquiries of this nature.

Despite being found to have breached the human rights of its own citizens, the UK Government remained silent, refusing to respond to this report in any meaningful way (UN CEDAW, 2018). It was not until 25 May 2018, when the Republic of Ireland voted resoundingly to lift the abortion ban, that parliamentary attention returned to the issue (Campbell, this volume; Roberts, volume 2). With celebrations around the world and in the UK, this referendum result dismantled assumptions that 'Catholic Ireland' would not support reproductive rights and threw attention back to the situation in NI.

When parliament returned a week later, campaigners used the SO24 parliamentary process to call an emergency debate on the consequences of the Irish referendum result on women in NI. This process required at least forty MPs from across parties to stand up when a proposal was made to the Commons to secure the debate. Abortion has traditionally been considered a matter of conscience and not one to which a party whip could be applied, so the call to action generated substantial attention. Several sitting Conservative Government ministers including the Secretary of State for NI Karen Bradley, International Development Secretary Penny Mordaunt and the Environment

Secretary Michael Gove stood to show their support for change – much to the surprise of both campaigners and government whips alike.

The subsequent debate showed how discussion on abortion access had begun to change following the intervention of the UN to put human rights concerns at its centre. Speaking in the debate Stella Creasy said 'Devolution, even if functioning, does not relieve this place of our responsibility to uphold human rights, whether in Northern Ireland or elsewhere' (Hansard, 2018a). SO24 debates did not provide for legislative amendments, but the debate itself was ground-breaking. Heidi Allen MP spoke about her own abortion and asked 'Are people seriously telling me that, in a civilised world, rape, incest or a foetus that is so sadly deformed it could never live, are not sufficient grounds for a woman to have the power to decide for herself – that she should not make that decision? No. Enough'. Jess Philips MP read stories from women in NI and shared that she had had an abortion as well, stating 'I and the hon. Member for South Cambridgeshire (Heidi Allen) are not criminals'. The response from those opposed was furious. Sammy Wilson MP argued he was 'not embarrassed about the legislation in Northern Ireland' and '100,000 people are alive in Northern Ireland today who would otherwise have been killed before they were even born' (Hansard, 2018a).

In the same week as this SO24 debate, the Supreme Court ruled on the question as to whether women who had a fatal foetal abnormality or were victims of rape in NI should be able to access abortion services at home (Allamby, this volume). Sarah Ewart, an incredibly brave campaigner, had shared her story of a devastating diagnosis of foetal anomaly publicly as well as in the courts, becoming a powerful advocate for reform (McKay, this volume). The Supreme Court had ruled that a human rights breach had occurred, but as the case against the UK Government had been brought by the NI Human Rights Commission and not a direct victim of the policy, it could not compel action to redress the injustice caused by a lack of access to abortion rights (UK Supreme Court, 2018). Creasy secured an urgent question to the Secretary of State who claimed 'that we do not want women who are victims of the situation having to come to court and make the case themselves' (Hansard, 2018b). Despite these words of concern, it would become clear the Government could not – and indeed would not – act to prevent such a scenario for fear of antagonizing their coalition partners in the DUP.

With renewed parliamentary interest MPs sought to find ways to channel this into action. Alongside debates and questions in the chamber in September 2018, the cross-party Women and Equalities Committee launched an inquiry into abortion in NI (House of Commons Women and Equalities Committee, 2019). So too, the British-Irish Parliamentary Assembly (BIPA) launched an inquiry into the cross-jurisdictional implications of abortion policy. The report of the Committee noted the divergence in abortion legislation between Ireland and the UK and how this had 'implications for their reproductive rights' (BIPA, 2019). Building on this, in 2018, Creasy coordinated a letter signed by 170 parliamentarians from across the UK and Ireland, which highlighted the promise of rights equivalency in the Good Friday agreement and contrasted this with the lack of comparable reproductive rights for women in NI (BBC News, 2018).

Yet as the matter rose up the parliamentary agenda, so opposition to change also strengthened. In January 2019 the government's long-awaited draft of the Domestic Abuse Bill was published – this legislation had been previously widely seen as a vehicle by which OAPA could be repealed (Hellen and Wheeler, 2019). In previous correspondence with the Home Secretary, MP Stella Creasy had raised the need for women in NI to have access to equal rights – in terms of access to abortion rights and legal recognition of coercive control – to enable the legislation to be compliant with the Istanbul Convention. Yet this latest draft published in January specifically restricted the territorial extent of the bill, thus removing from it anything that could impact on NI. Following press reports that this had been done to appease the DUP, another Urgent Question was granted to question Ministers about this change (Creasy in Hansard, 2019a), and in July 2019 when the bill was revised again, NI was included (Hansard, 2019b).

The Executive Formation Bill and same-sex marriage: An equal partnership

A second vein of parliamentary opportunities for action had opened due to the failure to reconvene Stormont. Without the Assembly in place, the UK Government was forced to bring forward legislation to cover the management of the NI Executive – bringing into parliamentary scope the provision of public services as a result. Through their joint membership of the Council of Europe, Conor McGinn MP and Stella Creasy MP had developed a partnership in seeking to promote human rights in NI and in October 2018 they proposed a new clause on equal rights to the Northern Ireland (Executive Formation and Exercise of Functions) Bill (Hansard, 2018c).

This was the first time both issues had been formally joined together – the campaign to extend same-sex marriage to NI was well established within

Parliament, with strong cross-party support including from some who strongly opposed abortion rights. McGinn had long been working with Lord Robert Hayward in the House of Lords to build support for same-sex marriage rights to be extended to NI. The Creasy and McGinn partnership led to both abortion and same-sex marriage campaigners working together at the Council of Europe itself, and in amendments in the UK Parliament. This willingness to work with the abortion campaigners was critical – resisting encouragement that one issue may be traded for the other by some (Dodds in Hansard, 2019c), their collaboration helped boost the chances of progress on both issues.

Government whips were caught out by both this partnership and the proposed amendment. What was intended to be uncontroversial technical legislation to address the lack of a functioning legislative assembly in NI suddenly became a hotbed of political, constitutional and moral traps. A furious behind-the-scenes effort ensued, with ministers and whips arguing such proposals were not in scope of the bill and so should not be permitted. When this failed, in an echo of the 2008 HFE Bill, the government sought to redraft parliamentary rules – tabling a last-minute amendment to remove the ability of backbench MPs to make amendments which could be voted upon to legislation. Unlike in 2008, in 2018 the speaker allowed a manuscript amendment by campaigners to restore these rights, chastizing the government for such behaviour (Creasy in Hansard, 2018d).

Although officially a matter of conscience given the subject matter, the government privately urged MPs to oppose the amendment, arguing it undermined devolution. For other political parties, the matter brought different challenges. The shift from treating abortion as non-partisan enabled Labour to formally back the amendment (Butler, 2018). The SNP had avoided taking a position previously on the subject, for fear of undermining their position on devolution and independence for Scotland. Yet, with the debate shifting to human rights, pressure was building for them not to absent themselves. Those opposed to both argued not only for the 'moral' case against abortion and same-sex marriage but also that it was precisely the absence of local decision-making processes that meant parliament would breach the democratic rights of the people of NI were it to intervene (Little-Pengelly, in Hansard 2018d).

In the end the SNP again abstained from voting for or against the proposal. Despite this, the amendment was passed, defeating ministers, and requiring the government to report on what action it was taking to uphold the human rights of the people of NI in the absence of an Assembly every three months (Bradley, in Hansard 2019d, 2019e). Whilst the reports mattered little themselves, this meant the Secretary of State was forced to come to Parliament on a regular basis to explain both the lack of progress in reconstituting the Assembly and on protecting the human rights of the people of NI. This in turn guaranteed parliamentary attention to the subject would continue and facilitated campaigners to start legal action on the basis that no progress was being made (The Journal IE, 2019).

With government ministers and whips aware that campaigners would try to table amendments to any form of legislation around NI, attempts were made to try to see off further proposals. In March 2019 an amendment was proposed to the bill for the budget for NI which stopped funding for any prosecutions for abortion. It was withdrawn when the government implied it would commit to reviewing such prosecutions (Hansard, 2019f). Yet, when the Secretary of State spoke, she reneged on this pledge (Bradley, in Hansard, 2019g) confirming to campaigners that change could not be won in partnership with the government, only despite them.

Having failed to placate campaigners, the government reverted to redrafting legislation to try to prevent further amendments. Yet the prevailing political mood was one for change – helped by public outrage at the measures introduced in Alabama in May 2019 which outlawed abortion except where the life of the mother was at stake (Crockett, 2019). Faced with evidence that the law in NI was more severe as it criminalized women as well as doctors, the debate returned again to Parliament.

With stalemate on the future of the Assembly in NI continuing, ministers were again forced to request emergency UK legislation to cover the provision of public services in July 2019. Again, Creasy and McGinn worked together – this time tabling amendments demanding action to uphold human rights in NI if the Assembly was not reconstituted by a deadline. They were not the only ones who saw opportunity in this bill, with pro-Remain campaigners also tabling amendments to try to frustrate a 'no deal' Brexit. The stage was therefore again set for multiple confrontations.

Creasy's amendment on abortion explicitly sought to strengthen the human rights obligations already outlined in the NI Act 1998, requiring the Secretary of State to ensure the rights the CEDAW ruling conferred on women in NI were realized. It required action only if the Assembly in NI could not be restarted; yet it also clarified the requirement of the UK Government under the Good Friday Agreement to ensure that the Assembly, whether sitting or not, upheld equal rights for all UK citizens.

Faced with widespread public support, many Conservative MPs who previously expressed reservations joined the call for progress – Maria Miller, the

Chair of the Women and Equalities Select Committee, told parliament 'If the women in my constituency were facing the prospect of having to carry a baby that was going to die, I would man the barricades to change that law' (Miller, in Hansard, 2019c). So too, the SNP finally agreed to back the legislation, bringing a brace of votes to the parliamentary arithmetic. Ian Blackford, Leader of the SNP in Westminster, tweeted on the day of the vote 'While the SNP will always defend the principle of devolution, there are a specific set of circumstances in NI where there has been no functioning assembly for an extended period. In these circumstances, we believe it is right to give MPs a vote on these important human rights issues' (Blackford, 2019) with Nicola Sturgeon noting that 'there is no functioning Assembly in place just now and this is a human rights matter' (Sturgeon, 2019). The DUP expressed severe dismay that legislation intended to maintain the status quo for public service provision was now the locus of far greater change. Their Leader Nigel Dodds stated, 'the purpose of the Bill is simply to maintain the status quo by moving two dates to allow talks to continue, with no election in the meantime. However, that has now been effectively hijacked by a number of Members who want to introduce measures to override the Assembly, which I think is wrong' (Dodds, in Hansard, 2019c).

The Executive Formation Bill itself had been drafted to try to prevent it being a vehicle for the legislative changes being proposed. Again, the willingness of the Speaker and the Deputy Speakers to select amendments that had widespread cross-party support overrode demands both amendments on abortion and same-sex marriage be ruled out of scope. As a free vote was given, many government ministers found their own voice on the matter and voted for the amendments, leaving ministers no choice but to promise to honour the outcome. Both amendments passed with substantial majorities on 9 July 2019, marking the culmination of two years of intense lobbying and advocacy both within Parliament and with NI.

Yet attempts were made to dilute the legislation as civil servants and ministers panicked about legal challenge and political consequences. Efforts to challenge Brexit via the Executive Bill also meant a deal was done between the House of Lords Labour and Conservative Front benches to ensure the legislation itself passed before the end of the parliamentary term. This was used to pressure supporters into accepting changes to the abortion proposals to lengthen the time for implementation, and to require implementation to be undertaken by a public consultation. These changes in themselves opened the door to legal intervention in the decision to extend abortion access to NI. With the parliamentary clock ticking on the government, and a new Prime Minister Boris Johnson waiting to take over who could abandon the whole Bill, campaigners had little choice but to accept them. The Bill received royal assent on the same day as Johnson became leader of the Conservative Party.

Even after legislation passed, abortion rights were still being floated as bargaining chip in talks regarding the future of NI (Proctor and Steward, 2019). Stella Creasy, by then heavily pregnant, was also targeted by anti-choice protestors in her constituency angry at the enaction of the legislation itself (Creasy in Hansard, 2019h). The legislation – covering the details of how abortion would be accessible in NI to meet recommendations set by CEDAW and removing OAPA as the foundation for abortion regulation – was finally fully enacted via a statutory instrument on 25 March 2020 – eight months after the amendment passed in parliament. It allowed for abortion on request up to twelve weeks, on health grounds similar to those in England and Wales between twelve and twenty-four weeks, and post twenty-four weeks in the case of severe foetal anomaly or where there was a risk to the health or life of a woman. The regulations drew on the model implemented in the Republic of Ireland and argued for by Caoilfhionn Gallagher QC to the Women and Equalities Committee – with an on-request model found to be the only effective way to ensure access to abortion for those who are victims of sexual violence (Gallagher, 2019).

NI now has the most progressive abortion laws in the UK – with abortion decriminalized in contrast to England and Wales. It remains to be seen whether decriminalization of abortion for the rest of the UK will be possible. Following the 2019 election, the conditions which made change in NI possible have changed substantially. However, in winning the case for access to abortion as a human right, and not solely a matter of health service provision, two years in the UK parliament of debate upended fifty years of silence. Where once NI was synonymous with oppression of reproductive rights, campaigners elsewhere in the UK now cite NI as what to follow. For those opposed to such change it is a bitter pill to swallow; for those in favour, a fitting tribute to the hard work of all concerned in making it happen.

8

The supreme team

Susan McKay

When a crew filmed Sarah Ewart and Grainne Teggart, perched on the edge of a sofa, riveted by the TV screen in the corner of the room, it was their perfect stillness that was compelling. Each had their hands clasped as if ready to let them fly up to cover their faces. They were watching live coverage of proceedings at Westminster, waiting for the vote on the Act that would, if passed, decriminalize abortion in NI.

The cameras zoomed in. Speaker John Bercow ready to declare. 'The ayes have it', he said above the clamour of the chamber. 'The ayes have it'. The women drew apart, and without a word flung their arms open, clasped each other tight and hugged and rocked. 'It was like an out of body experience', Grainne recalled of that moment in the Belfast home of Sarah's Mum, Jane Christie. Interviewed afterwards, Sarah said she felt as if a huge weight had been taken off her shoulders. 'It has been a long six years', she said, and smiled a carefree smile never seen before by people who did not know her before a private tragedy turned her into a public figure.

As other chapters in this book demonstrate, it took a lot of brave and passionate people decades of hard campaigning to liberate NI from the outworkings of the 1861 law that forbade abortion in almost all circumstances. Generations of feminists had to pit themselves against entrenched misogynistic prejudices that permeated society, and that kept being replenished. This chapter sets out the extraordinary contribution to the struggle that was made when daughter and mother, Ewart and Christie, joined forces with Teggart, NI campaign Manager with Amnesty UK and the leader of its abortion rights campaign. Together they became a formidable team, combining – with utter determination – the personal and the professional, the strategic and the intuitive. (Unless otherwise stated all material is drawn from interviews with the author in August 2021.)

Sarah was happy when she got pregnant in 2013, shortly after her marriage to Jason. She was 23. The couple wanted a family. Everything was exciting, including going for a private scan at nineteen weeks to find out the baby's gender. But instead of leaving the clinic talking baby names, they left numb and devastated. The foetus Sarah was carrying, their daughter, had a condition called anencephaly. Neither the brain nor the skull would develop. After reading accounts by other women of their traumatic birth experiences, she made the difficult decision to have an abortion. She would later say: 'I am an ordinary woman who suffered a very personal family tragedy, which the law in Northern Ireland turned into a living nightmare' (Amnesty UK, 2015).

The nightmare when she learned she could not have an abortion in NI, the only part of the UK to have rejected the radical reforms in the 1967 abortion law. A woman had to prove that continuing the pregnancy put her life at risk or would permanently destroy her health. 'Basically, everyone turned us away', Ewart told me. One consultant, she said, banged her files on the desk and said, 'I'm not going to prison for anyone' (Gentleman, 2016). She learned that medical professionals were afraid because guidelines published that year reminded them if they performed an abortion or helped someone 'procure' one, they could be jailed for life (Hughes, volume 2; Morgan McLaughlin Kavanaugh Kirk, volume 2).

Her mother wrote an impassioned letter to senior local politicians urging them to deal with her daughter's 'horrendous ordeal' and show some compassion – her daughter was being made to feel guilty about a painful situation over which she had no control. Christie also contacted the Nolan Show on BBC Radio Ulster, and in October 2013 Sarah went on the programme. Conducted with sensitivity by Nolan this interview was public service radio at its best (BBC Radio Ulster, 2013).

Ewart sobbed as she spoke about her pregnancy. 'There is nothing they can do to make this baby live', she said. 'This baby is brain dead'. But she also conveyed her anger and bewilderment at the cruelty of a system that expected her to carry the baby until its heart stopped beating in her womb, or to deliver it at full term, and watch its death. Nolan asked her about her rights. 'There doesn't seem to be any rights for the mother', she said. 'That's just it' (BBC Radio Ulster, 2013).

Ewart described what had happened when she went to the Family Planning Association. 'There were protesters outside, and they were pushing leaflets in our faces', she said. Inside, she got the information required for organizing an abortion in England. She would have to go immediately. It would cost over £1,000 plus flights and accommodation. She sobbed again describing how as she left the building she faced the angry crowd again. 'We had a protester shouting in our face … followed us to the car shouting that I was ruining a child's life. I'll never forget it' (BBC Radio Ulster, 2013).

She said Stormont had to change the law. 'There's people out there who don't have the supportive family I have and can't afford these prices'. She said that before this had happened to her, she had not agreed with abortion. Now she was less inclined to judge. She knew that sometimes people did not have choices (BBC Radio Ulster, 2013). At this time surveys showed the population almost evenly divided on whether abortion should be allowed in cases of fatal foetal abnormality, with just under a quarter undecided.

Teggart heard the interview. Around Ewart's age, she joined Amnesty in 2009. 'I am only interested in human rights law when it effects people in their everyday lives', she said. 'I knew this interview was a defining moment. It changed the narrative. I felt devastated for Sarah and her family. It was exceptionally brave of them to put their heads above the parapet on this issue – and I also felt a bit of fear for them'.

The pro-choice movement had received a boost in 2013 when the UN's Committee on the Elimination of Discrimination against Women (CEDAW) found NI's abortion law to be discriminatory, but the new Attorney General John Larkin was militantly anti-abortion. In 2008 he had said 'If one is prepared to contemplate the destruction of a highly disabled, unborn child in the womb, one should also be prepared to contemplate … putting a bullet in the back of the head of the child two days after it is born' (*Belfast Telegraph*, 2012).

Teggart asked the Nolan team to pass her details on to Ewart. 'I knew the machinations of government and how to get things moving, and Amnesty had a lot of legal expertise. I felt we could work together', she said. 'When I met Sarah and Jane, I could see they were facing into hostility and difficulties. I said that Amnesty would back them if they wanted that support, and I left it with them'.

Christie and Ewart had written to all 108 MLAs. Hardly any even replied. Justice Minister David Ford of the Alliance Party was open to limited changes to the law. However, Health Minister Edwin Poots took the view that 'hard cases don't make good law' (Sweeney, 2013). Initially he said guidelines clarifying the law would suffice but following a meeting with Ewart and Christie he admitted in personal correspondence to them that 'a change to the criminal law would be necessary' if more options were to be open to a woman in Ewart's 'difficult and emotional circumstances'.

Then Jim Wells took over as health minister. He had compared abortion to the Holocaust. 'The meeting with him was a train wreck', said Christie. 'He told Sarah that consultants got things wrong and that she had destroyed a baby that could have survived. All I could do was just stand my ground with her'. They also met with First Minister Peter Robinson and Deputy First Minister Martin McGuinness. 'Robinson said he would have a hard job persuading some of his colleagues in the DUP', Christie told me. 'McGuinness got it'. 'He always made time for us', said Ewart. 'He said to me, "You know what Sarah? A dog would have been treated better than you." We are Protestants and what we got from him is not what we expected'.

Amnesty's new campaign, 'My Body, My Rights' was launched in October 2014 to coincide with the Justice Minister's public consultation on the abortion law. An accompanying Amnesty poll showed that a year after Ewart had told her story, 60 per cent of people believed abortion should be available in cases of fatal foetal abnormality. Speaking at the launch, Teggart said, 'Northern Ireland's abortion laws are not only out of line with international human rights standards, they are also utterly out of line with public opinion' (Amnesty UK, 2014).

Ford's consultation reached a similar conclusion and had been discussed by the executive. In May 2015 he recommended the law be changed. It was discussed on BBC NI's The View. Christie and Ewart were watching, feeling something like hope. Then Robinson spoke. He said the plan was 'doomed' and guidelines were the way forward. Ford accused the First Minister of making 'a complete U turn'; pointing out that guidelines explain the law as it stands (Amnesty UK, 2021). 'That was a very low point for us', Christie said. 'Grainne picked us up and carried us'.

Teggart now had a bold proposal that would shift Sarah's campaign into the legal domain. 'We knew that the Northern Ireland Human Rights Commission (NIHRC) was proceeding with a judicial review of the laws here, arguing they breached women's human rights under the European Convention in cases of rape, incest and serious/ fatal foetal anomaly' she told me. 'We knew the case would benefit from including the lived experience of our abortion regime'.

Amnesty and Ewart would intervene, with Ewart's personal story a crucial part of the evidence. 'We were so naive we had to google what a judicial review was', Christie said. 'But we trusted Grainne. She was very confident, very focused and she had a lot of hope. We wouldn't have done it with anyone other than her. We knew this was the way to go'. 'I was over the moon when they came back to us', said Teggart. 'I'd seen them get the run-around and I felt a very protective instinct towards them'.

Announcing their decision to work together, Teggart pointed out that 2000 women each year were leaving NI to get abortions elsewhere. 'That reality is a damning indictment of the Executive's failure to prioritise women's healthcare', she said. Ewart said the politicians had failed her and many others like her. By refusing to change the law, 'they have left me with no option but to go to the courts on my and other women's behalf' (Amnesty UK, 2015).

The case was heard in the High Court in June 2015 (Allamby, this volume). The NIHRC argued that the women had been subjected to cruel, inhuman and degrading treatment. In November 2015 Mr Justice Horner's judgement was delivered. NI's abortion law was incompatible with the Human Rights Act. It was now up to the Executive to sort this out. Health professionals welcomed the ruling.

The Attorney General, however, said he was 'profoundly disappointed' (Amnesty UK, 2021). At Stormont, in February 2016, the Alliance party proposed an amendment to the law in line with the ruling. Trevor Lunn MLA spoke about the importance of Ewart's intervention in 2013. Before that, he said, 'few if any people dared to speak about this issue'. The DUP opposed the amendment, its MLA Emma Little Pengelly claiming that 'there is no such thing as fatal foetal abnormality' (Amnesty UK, 2021). The amendment was defeated. The DUP pronounced 'rushed law could turn out to be bad law' and said that it was establishing a working group (Amnesty UK, 2021).

The Attorney General appealed against the High Court ruling. The case was heard in June 2016. A year later the Appeal Court delivered a judgement which Teggart described as 'absurd ... an insult to women and girls' (Amnesty UK, 2021). The three judges found that NI's laws did not breach human rights standards and were a matter for the Executive and not the courts. They had, Teggart said, let down another generation. Ewart called it 'a dark day for women's rights'. There was further bad news when the Supreme Court ruled that NI women were not entitled to free abortions in the rest of the UK – though an intervention by Labour MP Stella Creasy mitigated this by providing funds (Creasy and Sanquest, this volume).

'Sarah had become a focal point for the anti-choicers', Teggart told me. The night she came back from having the abortion she was tagged on a social media page with gory photos purportedly of abortions. These images on huge placards were a mainstay of the 'protests' that took place at Stormont, and outside the courts with each significant development. Ewart found Larkin's commentary particularly difficult. Teggart recalled one occasion when 'I was fuming, Sarah was fuming, and Jane was fit to be tied'. On another, 'I remember just reaching my hands across the table to them to say, leave it, don't worry'. Ewart remembered one prominent anti-abortionist who used to sit right behind her during hearings and meetings. 'We could smell her perfume as she approached', she said. Teggart also got abuse. 'I got miraculous medals and graphic images and threats that I would burn in hell', she said. 'There would be days when you'd think, "this is a bit shit"'.

But no one would ever get close enough to shove a leaflet in Ewart's face again. She was always flanked by Teggart, Ewart blonde and in white trousers, Teggart dark in a pink coat. Christie was always close by. She wore heels for one big day in London. 'By lunchtime she was walking into a media building in her stocking soles', said Teggart. Ewart went through two tumultuous pregnancies during the campaign. There was always a fear that anencephaly would recur, and she had frequent scans, injections and appointments – as well as court hearings, media interviews and meetings with government ministers, human rights organizations, and lawyers.

Teggart felt a huge weight of responsibility. 'I knew I had to keep things steady', she said. Christie described her as our 'oracle'. 'We knew we were alright so long as she wasn't panicking'. It was physically exhausting – often the women would be up at 4 am to catch the early flight to London, arriving back home after 9 pm. Teggart was pregnant with her first baby during the High Court case in 2016. 'Certain people would say that I must have no heart to be campaigning for abortion and me pregnant. I said, it is not about me'.

The NIHRC appealed the appeal court ruling to the Supreme Court. Ewart was again an intervenor alongside Denise Phelan, who was also with Amnesty, and Ashleigh Topley, who was supported by AfC (Topley, this volume). Both of these women were forced to carry pregnancies involving FFA until almost full term, when the baby died, after which they had to give birth. 'The judges of the Supreme Court have a unique chance to put right centuries of human rights abuse', Teggart said at the time. Ewart said, 'We have been abandoned by our government ... I hope the Supreme Court will bring about the change that I and other women so desperately need' (Amnesty UK, 2021). Teggart had invited the brilliant young solicitor Darragh Mackin to join what Christie was now calling 'the Supreme Team'. Mackin was also involved with Amnesty in the case of a woman who was being prosecuted for obtaining abortion pills for her teenage daughter who had got pregnant in an abusive relationship.

Mackin described his first meeting with the women. 'Jane said to me, do you know how anencephaly works? Then she produced a photograph. I was shocked but it was a very powerful way to show me what the state was forcing people to go through'.

I will never forget the feeling of energy in that room, the momentum, and the solidarity among them; the powerful love Jane brought to Sarah, the forensic attention Grainne brought to their strategy, the sheer courage and commitment Sarah had. They were dealing with horrendous levels of toxic disrespect. They were all intimately involved in all the decisions that were taken. They were formidable.

The case was heard in October 2017. Mackin and Teggart got sight of the judgement just before it was published in June 2018. In his Supreme Court judgement Mr Justice Kerr had referred to his admiration for the courage of the women who had added their testimony. 'The nature of their suffering and the trauma of their experiences are by no means irrelevant to the unravelling and resolution of the issues to which this appeal gives rise' (UK supreme court, 2017). (On his retirement Mr Justice Kerr described the case as the most important of his career.)

However, the court found while NI's laws breached women's human rights, the NIHRC lacked standing to bring the case because it was not itself a victim. 'I said to Darragh, how are we going to look Sarah in the eye and tell her we have won, and we have lost at the same time?' Teggart said. The case needed a victim to take it forward. 'We knew Sarah be that woman', Teggart said. Mackin, Teggart and Counsel worked on papers overnight. They all travelled to London the next morning. Ewart told the media that the case was not over. In January 2019, she brought her case to Belfast's High Court, with Amnesty as an intervenor. The campaign was entering its final phase, operating at full tilt at both legal and political levels.

The Executive at Stormont had collapsed in 2017 and Amnesty was now lobbying Parliament to intervene and as Teggart put it to me, 'drag Northern Ireland into the twenty-first century' (Teggart and Rowan, this volume). A 2016 opinion poll had revealed a dramatic rise in public support, with almost 60 per cent believing abortion should be decriminalized, while 70 per cent believed it should be available for women who had experienced rape, or fatal foetal abnormality. A further Amnesty poll in 2018 found that 65 per cent of NI people believed abortion should be available in some circumstances while 66 per cent believed that in the absence of the Executive at Stormont, Parliament should legislate (Amnesty UK, 2018c).

In May 2018 the Repeal the 8th Campaign in the Republic of Ireland had triumphed when Irish people voted in a referendum to remove a clause in the Constitution designed to outlaw abortion in all circumstances. Northern campaigners had helped (Roberts, volume 2). The campaign to ensure 'the North is Next' was now underway. Mackin commented that the tables had turned in that pro-choice crowds chanting support for Ewart and other women were now drowning out those declaiming that abortion was murder. A 2018 UN CEDAW report noted that 'the situation in NI constitutes violence against women that may amount to torture' (UN CEDAW, 2018; Cross O'Rourke Simpson, this volume).

Prime Minister Boris Johnson insisted that abortion was a matter for the devolved authorities, but Ewart, Teggart and Christie had met with Penny Mordaunt, the Women and Equalities Minister and welcomed her statement in July 2019 that Parliament would intervene if the High Court ruled in Ewart's favour. 'The paucity of care that women have endured in Northern Ireland is the most appalling thing', she said. Ewart said the situation was archaic and she should not have had to fight emotionally draining court battles to have her basic rights to healthcare. Amnesty got 62,000 signatures on a petition demanding abortion rights had it delivered to the NIO by twenty-eight women with suitcases, symbolizing women travelling for abortions.

Labour MP Stella Creasy also intervened again, reminding the government of its human rights obligations under the Good Friday Agreement. She told me in a 2019 interview that she was 'in awe' of Ewart. 'She is an amazing person who has been brave enough to come forward; it is extraordinary what she has achieved'. Abortion was not a devolved issue, she said: 'It's a fundamental question of freedom. Devolution is not segregation. Human rights are not devolved'. In July 2019, Creasy's amendment to the Northern Ireland Bill decriminalizing abortion came before Parliament. Ewart and Teggart took their places on the sofa. In the chamber at Westminster, Creasy watched cross-party MPs line up to vote for her amendment. 'I could see something magic was happening', she said. The bill was passed by 328 votes to 65. Unless Stormont reconvened by 21st October, abortion would cease to be a crime in Northern Ireland. The DUP MP Ian Paisley said it was 'an outrage to common decency'. But the ayes had it.

On 3 October, in Belfast's High Court, Mrs Justice Keegan ruled that NI's existing abortion law was not compatible with the European Convention on Human Rights. The onus was now on the British government to ensure that free, safe and legal abortion services were introduced. The DUP tried to re-convene Stormont in a last ditch bid to stop the new law but failed to get the support of other parties. The churches too intervened – a move that Ewart and Christie found particularly offensive. 'We are people of faith', Christie said. On 22nd October pro-choice campaigners gathered outside Stormont. Ewart, Christie and Teggart joined Denise Phelan and others behind Amnesty's banner with massive lettering that read in bold letters: 'Decriminalized'.

With Stormont back, the new law has stalled. UUP health minister Robin Swann refuses to commission services, the DUP vows to have it repealed. Teggart continues to campaign and is 'not remotely worried'. The Supreme Team WhatsApp group still exists but these days is mostly used to exchange photos of new babies and searing commentaries on Love Island. Ewart said if there is more for her to do, it will do it. 'It took a hell of a lot of work to get this, and I am not going to let it get lost', she said. 'We haven't gone away. Just because we're quiet for now – don't be fooled'.

9

Law reform and decriminalization delivered: Westminster and strategic litigation

Grainne Teggart and Ruairi Rowan

Stormont was never going to deliver abortion reform; this was clear to anyone working on reproductive rights in NI. Decades of political inaction (Lo and Thomson, this volume), a failure to institute even basic reform and a hostile political majority to full human rights compliant care held it back. The political collapse of Stormont would provide the opportunity for change (Campbell, this volume). Westminster intervention, propelled by strategic litigation proved critical to overturning the abortion ban and delivering CEDAW compliant law (Creasy and Sanquest, and Enright, this volume). This chapter gives an outline of key Amnesty and FPA moments towards the historic victory for reproductive rights.

An Amnesty report in 2014 detailing barriers to abortion in law, policy and practice (Amnesty, 2014) sparked a high-profile campaign that moved public debate and political consideration for reform. It worked with victims of NI's near total abortion ban, along with human rights expertise and advocacy. The partnership with FPA, Sarah Ewart and Denise Phelan proved a compelling combination.

In December 2014, the Northern Ireland Human Rights Commission (NIHRC) lodged a legal challenge on abortion (Allamby, this volume). Amnesty communicated with Sarah Ewart and her mother Jane Christie (McKay, this volume). Sarah had bravely shared the harrowing experience of receiving a fatal diagnosis with her first pregnancy and was forced to travel to London. Amnesty approached Sarah about her experience with the Northern Ireland Assembly (NIA) to change NI's archaic regime and suggested working together, beginning with an intervention in the NIHRC proceedings, to ensure the court was appraised of the lived reality.

In November 2015, the High Court ruled that NI's abortion law breached the human rights of women and girls (Allamby, this volume). As a result of the case and the public and political advocacy around the case led by Amnesty and Sarah Ewart, several Alliance Party MLAs attempted to amend the Justice (No 2) Bill to provide for abortion in cases of fatal foetal abnormality, rape or incest in February 2016 (BBC News, 2016a). Although defeated, this was the first occasion that the NIA debated widening abortion provision.

In March 2016, the NI Executive agreed guidance for Health and Social Care Professionals on termination of pregnancy in NI (O'Dowd Cross Bloomer, this volume). The guidance document highlighted early medical abortion pills accessed online and stated:

> There is no way of determining the extent of the use of such services in Northern Ireland, however, it is likely that they are being used. Their use to secure a miscarriage in Northern Ireland is likely to be an offence under the Offences Against the Person Act 1861.
>
> (DOH, 2016)

Less than two weeks later a 21-year-old woman was given a suspended prison sentence after pleading guilty to procuring her own abortion from medication she had purchased on the internet (BBC News, 2016b).

In January 2017, a woman and man accepted formal cautions for the same offences (BBC News, 2017a). The judge banned identifying the woman due to the heightened risk of suicide from any publicity. Later that month another woman launched a judicial review against the decision taken to prosecute her for supplying abortion medication procured online for her then fifteen-year-old daughter (McDonald, 2017). Amnesty immediately intervened in the case to bolster the human rights challenge and worked closely on the judicial review and advocacy at Westminster. The prospect of a criminal trial and prison sentence added to the urgency of engagement and messaging at Westminster. FPA also intervened in the case and stated:

> The criminal law on abortion in Northern Ireland is unclear. The law … on when it is necessary to disclose personal information to prosecuting authorities is unclear and unhelpful. The risk of criminal prosecution seems increasingly high. If that risk increases any higher, it will become difficult for charities such as FPA to continue to provide services.
>
> (FPA, 2017)

Amnesty, as well as intervening, ensured the mother (who had been anonymized to protect her daughter) had her voice heard in joint media statements issued at critical moments. The mother told Amnesty she was put through 'five years of agony' and explained how 'painful' it has been to have the prosecution hanging over her head 'every single day of my life, and I try for the sake of my family to keep my head above water'. Amnesty described this case as a 'cruel injustice'. The judicial review was heard in November 2018; when the daughter was used as a tool in her mother's prosecution it made a significant contribution to advocacy work on the decriminalization of abortion.

The shadow of Brexit was now threatening the stability of the UK Government with the DUP holding the balance of power. This heightened focus across the UK on the DUP and their policies, in particular their opposition to abortion law reform and equal marriage (Creasy and Sanquest and Campbell, this volume). That attention increased in June 2017 when the Supreme Court ruled in *R (on the application of A and B) (Appellants) v Secretary of State for Health (Respondent)* that it was lawful for women travelling from NI to be denied free access to abortion services in England. However, the court highlighted that the Secretary of State for Health had the power to change this policy decision if he so wished.

That ruling sparked an attempt by Labour MP Stella Creasy two weeks later to amend the Queen's Speech to enact this policy change. In tandem with this FPA, supported by Amnesty, BPAS, the Royal College of Obstetricians and Gynecologists (RCOG) and the Royal College of Midwives (RCM) coordinated an open letter to the Health Secretary signed by a cross-party section of politicians. The letter stated:

> We would like to highlight the court's ruling which states that, as Secretary of State, you hold the legal authority to change your policy on funding abortion services in England for women normally resident in Northern Ireland. We urge you to use this authority and reduce the significant financial burden women travelling from Northern Ireland face.
>
> (Elgot, 2017)

Signatories from NI included future party leaders, Doug Beattie, Naomi Long and Clare Bailey, alongside People Before Profit MLA Gerry Carroll. The letter was also signed by Conservative MPs Nicky Morgan, Dan Poulter and Sir Peter Bottomley. Further Conservative politicians expressed their support and fearing defeat in Parliament Government Ministers agreed to the change.

An urgent meeting was set up the following week with the Minister for Women and Equalities, Justine Greening, to discuss how the policy would operate. Stella Creasy attended the meeting alongside service providers and campaigners. Further engagement ensured there were no additional barriers for women and pregnant people from NI accessing free treatment in England. As a result, interim arrangements were agreed with service providers and a central booking system operated by BPAS was launched (DHSC, 2018). NI abortion seekers could contact a single telephone number which arranged travel and treatment with a healthcare provider in England.

Immediately prior to the launch of the new booking system CEDAW (Cross O'Rourke Simpson, this volume) released their report stating that thousands of women and girls were being subjected to grave and systematic violations of rights due to the law in NI (UN CEDAW, 2018). Following the CEDAW report and the ongoing threat of prosecution for accessing abortion medication online, Amnesty and FPA worked at pace to secure cross-party political support for decriminalization at Westminster and amongst local political parties. This sent a strong signal to UK political parties that, in the absence of devolved Government, decriminalization and law reform could be done with their express support. An initial step was to demonstrate the changing political attitudes towards abortion reform in NI and support for decriminalization within local political parties. Without a functioning Assembly and Executive, Belfast City Council as the largest council provided the best opportunity to highlight this. Amnesty and FPA drafted a Motion and worked alongside politicians in all parties to maximise support. The Motion was proposed by Alliance Party councillor Kate Nicholl and seconded by Sinn Féin's Mary Ellen Campbell. Following an amendment proposed by the SDLP the Motion read:

> This Council notes the increasing number of women who are accessing abortion pills via the internet, which leaves them vulnerable to prosecution.
>
> The Council further notes the impact on healthcare professionals who, under Section 5 of the Criminal Law Act (Northern Ireland) 1967, may have a duty to provide information to the Police Service. Therefore, if a woman requires medical assistance after accessing these pills, the threat of prosecution and life in prison is likely to act as a real deterrent, thus potentially having a detrimental impact on her health.
>
> Accordingly, the Council believes that this is a healthcare issue not a criminal justice issue. Women or health care professionals who care for them should not be treated as criminals.
>
> (Belfast City Council, 2018)

Both Rowan and Teggart addressed Council before the debate, and it passed with overwhelming support. In the two months that followed both the SDLP and Sinn Féin updated their party policy on abortion, and the Eighth Amendment was repealed by a landslide referendum vote in Ireland (Campbell, this volume).

This boosted the campaign for change and added impetus to Westminster engagement which was at times now biweekly and quickly amassing a strong constituency of support amongst key UK political parties.

In November 2017, the Supreme Court heard the appeal from the NIHRC and in July 2018 ruled that NI's abortion law breached the human rights of women and girls (Allamby, this volume). FPA, a group of service providers, AfC and reproductive health charities formed one intervention. Amnesty and Sarah Ewart formed another. FPA instructed Leigh Day and were represented in court by Dinah Rose QC and Jude Bunting, who had represented the charity in all strategic litigation throughout this period and provided valuable counsel. FPA's focus was on the changing attitudes in NI to the provision of abortion services and the impact on women of the breaches of their human rights (Rowan and Simpson, this volume).

Amnesty and Sarah Ewart jointly intervened to put the spotlight the harm from the rights breaches created by the law. Affidavit evidence in support of Amnesty and Sarah's arguments also came from Denise Phelan, who was forced to continue a pregnancy that had received a fatal diagnosis and resulted in her delivering a foetus which had died inside her. Ashleigh Topley also submitted affidavit evidence supported by AfC. There was huge media spotlight on the case, Sarah Ewart and Amnesty had a compelling media presence locally and internationally and Westminster eyes were on this case.

While the Supreme Court found the law was in breach of human rights, they also found that the NIHRC did not have standing to bring forward the proceedings as a victim (Allamby, this volume). Therefore, a declaration of incompatibility could not be issued. In an unprecedented move owed to the testimony of Sarah, Denise and Ashleigh the court went on to issue a judgement.

The win and a loss of the Supreme Court made it clear to Amnesty and the legal team – Darragh Mackin of Phoenix Law, Adam Straw BL and Monye Anyadike-Danes QC that it would be necessary for a victim to progress litigation. Following a briefing meeting with Sarah and her mother Jane Christie, they decided to take the challenge back to Belfast High Court. This announcement was made to a large crowd of waiting media at the front of the Supreme Court immediately following the judgement being handed down. Sarah Ewart and Amnesty sent an important signal to Westminster that the matter was not over.

Building on the court ruling, with Sarah's case now progressing through Belfast High Court represented by Adam Straw and Darragh Mackin and the changing political attitudes in NI, Amnesty and FPA arranged a drop-in event at Westminster to brief MPs and Peers the RCOG, BPAS and human rights barrister

Jude Bunting and enable them to show their support for the decriminalization of abortion. This was also attended by Labour MP Rupa Huq and was attended by almost fifty parliamentarians. An anti-choice event scheduled for the same time and taking place further down the corridor struggled to attract more than a handful. During this time Amnesty, Sarah and Denise continued Westminster strategy meetings with Labour Shadow Cabinet and key MPs within SNP. Darragh Mackin, of Phoenix Law, who worked with Grainne and Sarah also attended various meetings at Westminster. These meetings with key committee chairs and a core group of parliamentarians were paying off with a determined focus to stand up for women in NI and deliver change.

Frequent engagements at Westminster became commonplace over the coming months to brief MPs and grow cross-party coalition of support. Following the summer recess two visits to NI were arranged in September 2018 with Conservative MPs. One taking place in private, the other in public. These meetings built on a previous Labour Party delegation visit in February 2018 also hosted by Amnesty and FPA that involved meetings with healthcare professionals, legal professionals, local politicians, civil society groups and individuals impacted by the law.

On 7 September 2018 Maria Miller MP, who chaired the Women and Equalities Select Committee, and her party colleague Vicky Ford MP, travelled to NI for private meetings with Amnesty and FPA. They met Denise and her husband Richard Gosnold who shared their ordeal. It was clear both Maria and Vicky were impacted by what they had heard.

Shortly after, on 20 September 2018 the Women and Equalities Committee announced an inquiry into abortion law in NI (Gallen, this volume), and the visit to NI helped shape those terms of reference. On 28 September 2018 Conservative Party MPs Nicky Morgan, Anna Soubry and Huw Merriman travelled to NI in a visit that received widespread media attention. Conservative MP Heidi Allen was also due to attend but had to withdraw because of a family emergency.

To coincide with this visit a joint letter, coordinated by Amnesty and FPA, was published signed by Sinn Féin, Vice President, Michelle O'Neill, SDLP leader, Colum Eastwood, Alliance Party leader, Naomi Long, and UUP justice spokesperson Doug Beattie. The letter included the following statements:

> We are concerned about the harm being caused to women living under the existing Victorian era legislation which makes abortion illegal in almost every circumstance.
>
> We agree with the recent ruling of the UK Supreme Court that abortion law in Northern Ireland is in need of radical reconsideration.

> We call on UK Government to decriminalise abortion by repealing sections 58 and 59 of the 1861 Offences Against the Person Act and to ensure a human rights compliant framework governing access to abortion.
>
> (Amnesty International, 2018a)

During the visit three weeks earlier, Maria Miller had commented that there was a perception at Westminster that only the smaller parties in NI supported abortion law reform and this joint statement served to decisively counter this misconception.

On 23 October 2018, support for the decriminalization of abortion was tested in the UK Parliament through a Private Members Bill being taken forward by Labour MP Diana Johnson to decriminalize abortion. This was the second of such Bills brought forward by Ms Johnson but significantly, for the first time, the scope was extended to include NI because of several meetings with Amnesty and FPA. BPAS also played a key role with this bill and joint meetings were held with Diana as the text evolved and was finalized. The Bill passed its first reading with 208 in favour and 123 opposed.

Throughout the previous few years Amnesty, as well as the *Northern Ireland Life and Times Survey* (Gray, volume 2) had regularly tested public opinion in relation to abortion. In the lead up to the vote Amnesty published a new poll which found that 65 per cent of people living in NI believed that having an abortion should not be a crime and 66 per cent believed that in the absence of a devolved government, Westminster should reform the law. Seventy-eight per cent of people surveyed in Great Britain stated that abortion in NI should be decriminalized (Amnesty International, 2018a). This again made headlines and kept minds focused on building momentum.

A launch of Diana Johnson's private members bill was held in Parliament on 21 November 2018. Alongside this Amnesty published an open letter to Prime Minister signed by sixty female celebrities including Kate Beckinsale, Claire Foy, Jodie Whittaker and Olivia Colman. The letter urged Theresa May to give time to the Private Members Bill to be heard in Parliament with the celebrities stating that:

> We're counting on you and your government to stand with women and decriminalise abortion. Give us choice and control over our own bodies. Show women from Northern Ireland that you won't stand for them being governed by one of the harshest and cruellest abortion laws in the world. Show us that you value and champion the rights of all women, no matter which part of the UK they're from.
>
> (Amnesty International, 2018b)

At the end of 2018 and beginning of 2019 the Women and Equalities Select Committee travelled to NI as part of their inquiry. During their visit in January 2019, they heard from various organizations including Amnesty who provided oral evidence in public and FPA who met with the Committee in private. Prior to this they spoke directly with individuals who had been adversely impacted due to the denial of local abortion healthcare including Sarah Ewart whose intervention was vital and preceded the hearing of the judicial review in her case. This case served to be another critical defining moment in delivering law reform.

With pressure building, in February 2019, Amnesty organized the hand in of its 60,000+ strong petition to the NIO in London calling for the decriminalization of abortion. A suitcase march made up of twenty-eight women – representing the number of women who travelled to GB for abortion healthcare each week – was led by Siobhan McSweeney and Nicola Coughlan of television show Derry Girls. Cross-party MPs, activists and women impacted including Denise Phelan. Denise then spoke courageously outside the NIO's Westminster office, declaring that she and other women, were not criminals for seeking healthcare (BBC News, 2019c).

The petition hand in was followed with same day meetings with the Secretary of State for NI Karen Bradley and Women and Equalities Minister, Penny Mordaunt. The writing was on the wall, law reform was coming, and it was a matter of when and how rather than if.

The when and how quickly followed in the Northern Ireland (Executive Formation etc.) Act 2019, a Bill not designed for the purpose, it would ultimately serve as the vehicle to deliver abortion law reform and equal marriage to NI. The key amendments to the Bill regarding abortion were spearheaded by Stella Creasy MP who had worked tirelessly throughout this period to deliver law reform to NI (Creasy and Sanquest, this volume).

All the intense lobbying and relationship building paid off. Regretfully, FPA as an organization was not around to celebrate this historic change after being placed into voluntary administration in May 2019. Therefore, it was left to Amnesty and other organizations with Stella Creasy to negotiate the final framework and crucial moratorium on the application of criminal laws concerning abortion and cease all related arrests, investigations and criminal prosecutions. This would prove critical to the mother and daughter abortion pill case. The legislation received royal assent on the same day Boris Johnson became prime minister and included a clause that the proposals would not be enacted if the NI Executive was restored before 21 October 2019.

In the lead up to the October deadline the High Court gave judgement in Sarah Ewart's case which confirmed that the law in NI violated rights (BBC News, 2019b). Following this there was a desperate last-minute attempt to restore the NIA on 21 October so the new law would not take effect. Whilst this futile charade played out inside Stormont, outside Amnesty, Sarah Ewart, Jane Christie, Denise Phelan, lawyers Darragh Mackin, Ciaran Moynagh, FPA's successor ICNI and Amnesty activists who had spent years campaigning and supporting litigation came together, convened by Amnesty to create a now iconic 'decriminalized' image at Stormont and speak to waiting media. At midnight, the new law took effect and history was made.

The effects of the new law were felt the following day with the charges against the mother facing prosecution for buying abortion pills for her daughter dropped. Amnesty who had briefed the mother's legal team on the moratorium once secured, and ICNI, were in court to witness the jury being sworn in and the case dismissed. Reproductive rights in NI had finally been dragged out of the Victorian era and into the twenty-first century. Abortion was no longer a criminal justice matter, but a healthcare matter and the relentless campaigning, committed activism and strategic litigation had delivered real and substantial change (Cafolla, 2020).

10

Alliance for Choice as agents of legal change

Máiréad Enright

In October 2019, abortion was finally decriminalized in Northern Ireland (NI). For over 150 years, it was a crime to terminate one's own pregnancy, or assist a pregnant person to terminate theirs (Bloomer, 2020). No exceptions were made for rape, severe foetal anomaly or all but 'real and serious' 'long-term' health risks (O'Rourke, 2016). Avoiding this law meant travelling to England or illegally using abortion pills supplied by online providers (Bloomer et al., 2018). Today in NI abortion is newly legal on request, up to twelve weeks' gestation. From 12 to 24 weeks, abortions are permitted on health grounds. Thereafter, abortion is only permissible to avoid risk to the woman's life or grave and permanent risk to her health or following a severe or fatal foetal anomaly diagnosis (NIACT, 2021). Despite these restrictions, Northern Irish abortion law is now more liberal, in some respects, than that its English or Irish counterparts. Unlike the UK Abortion Act 1967, the NI Regulations permit access to abortion on request up to twelve weeks, without the need to show grounds, and on the approval of one doctor, rather than two, The 2018 Irish law permits abortion on health grounds only if the risk to health is a risk of 'serious harm. Abortion is not permitted on health grounds once the foetus has reached viability and is not permitted on foetal anomaly grounds except in a subset of fatal foetal anomaly cases. NI's abortion figures had dropped from fifty-one in 2012/2013 to just eight in 2018/19. In the six months after decriminalization, over 650 women terminated pregnancies in NI. Recent legal changes have been significant, dramatic and hard-won.

Most legal scholarship on these developments has focused on Stormont, Westminster, courts and international human rights bodies. Much less has been said about grassroots organizers' role in winning and embedding legal change. AfC is a feminist, affected-led collective campaigning for 'free, safe and legal' abortion access in NI. Rather than presenting AfC's work as ancillary or subordinate to 'formal' law-making, this chapter foregrounds them as key agents of legal change. As well as discussing AfC's formal lobbying and advocacy, it focuses on their essential 'critical community building' and 'service work', situating these activities within a pluralist account of legal transformation.

Alliance for Choice: An institutional story

Before Stormont's suspension in January 2017, the story of Northern Irish abortion law was one of deadlock. Despite growing public support for abortion reform, the main parties at Stormont were hostile to pro-choice advocacy (Campbell, 2018; Sheldon et al., 2020). Conservative law-makers traded in foetal rights tropes familiar from the global anti-choice movement, and cast themselves paternalistically as the protectors of presumptively vulnerable or misguided women (Pierson and Bloomer, 2017). Two bouts of strategic litigation failed to generate significant change. The first, led by the FPA NI (NIQB, 2003) was modest: it established a duty on the part of the Department of Health to issue guidance clarifying the scope of the existing abortion law (Sheldon et al., 2020). The aim was to address 'chilling effects' which drove doctors to interpret the already restrictive health ground even more narrowly than necessary (Rowan Simpson, this volume). However, 2009's counter-litigation from SPUC (NIQB, 2009) and resistance within Stormont meant that valid guidance was not published until 2016. Even then, the guidance emphasized criminalization of errant doctors and did little to improve implementation of the law. More importantly, the judgements, issued in 2003–2004, did not centre pregnant people's rights; instead, they pursued a medicalized account of abortion which undermined women's autonomy (Fletcher, 2005). The legal status quo remained in place (Bloomer and Fegan, 2014).

By 2017, however, two new, potentially more expansive, legal strategies were in motion. First, in 2010, a pro-choice collective invited CEDAW to investigate the position of Northern Irish abortion law under international human rights law. Then, in late 2015, litigation organized by the Northern Ireland Human Rights Commission (Allamby, this volume) bore fruit in the High Court when Horner J. held that the criminalization of abortion in cases of rape and fatal anomaly violated women's European Convention rights to private and family life. Both tactics marked a shift in legal activism around abortion, framing it as a matter of women's human rights. However, there was little reason for optimism at Stormont. The Department of Justice did not bring forward legislation in response to the High Court judgement. Instead, both the Department and the

Attorney General lodged appeals. Department of Justice efforts to legislate narrowly for both rape and fatal foetal anomaly exceptions were repeatedly blocked in the Executive (Sheldon et al., 2020, p. 785). However, when Stormont collapsed, the three-year hiatus allowed campaigners to make progress elsewhere.

Historically, the major parties at Westminster avoided action on NI's abortion law. Health is a devolved matter under the Good Friday Agreement. Refusal to intervene on human rights grounds was often explained by reference to NI's unique post-conflict political arrangements and supposedly distinctive 'cultural norms' (Thomson, this volume). However, CEDAW's intervention, the NIHRC's litigation, and a sustained campaign by pro-choice MPs at Westminster combined to reshape MPs' understandings of the relationship between devolution and human rights. Stella Creasy's office advanced a flurry of legislative projects (Creasy and Sanquest, this volume). Two were successful. The first required Westminster to take policy responsibility for low-income women living in NI by funding their abortion travel. The second, amending the Northern Ireland (Executive Formation) Act 2019, extended that responsibility by requiring Westminster to act on pressing human rights issues while Stormont was suspended. AfC participated in all three highly visible legal strategies. They were part of the group that invited CEDAW to investigate the shortcomings in NI's abortion law (Cross O'Rourke Simpson, this volume). The Committee confirmed that the law fell short of international human rights standards and made thirteen recommendations for change. AfC seized on these as a clear framework for future legislation. AfC also intervened in the NIHRC litigation and an AfC member, Ashleigh Topley, was amongst the women who gave evidence of lived experience of the restrictive law. When the case reached the UK Supreme Court, the majority drew repeatedly on the CEDAW report, and held that Northern Irish abortion law fell afoul of Article 8 of the European Convention (O'Rourke, 2016). Finally, AfC were part of the collective of pro-choice organizations working on Stella Creasy's parliamentary agenda. They not only ensured that parliamentarians heard Northern Irish women's stories (House of Commons, Women and Equalities Committee, 2019) and mobilized their supporters to lobby MPs, but also consulted on the shape of key legal provisions, resisting restrictive compromises where possible.

It is tempting to think of this institution-bound advocacy as AfC's 'real' contribution to legal change. However, we should not ignore everyday, less public, but equally valuable forms of legal agency (Enright et al., 2020). Drapeau-Bisson analysed Derry-based AfC members' account of a period of 'abeyance' around 2014, when Stormont's intransigence sapped motivation for formal lobbying (Drapeau-Bisson, 2020). Accordingly, she argues, AfC changed tactics in two ways. First, rather than focus energies on the state, the Alliance concentrated on building 'critical community' where new thinking on reproductive justice could flourish. Second, responding to the increased availability of 'abortion pills' they pursued 'service work', informing women about the best ways to access and use pills (O'Brien, Campbell this volume). Rather than think of 'critical community' and 'service work' as strategies pursued when legal work is not possible, I want to think about each of them as 'feminist law work' (Enright et al., 2020) which continues while formal legal change is ongoing and drives that change forward.

Jurisdiction and legal pluralism: What counts as legal agency?

The word 'jurisdiction' – the right to 'speak the law' (Dorsett and McVeigh, 2012) – describes the authority to judge an action's legal status: to interpret the prevailing law and apply it to lived events. Jurisdiction also encompasses the power to act upon or enforce such a judgement. Usually, we associate jurisdiction with the state. For example, the state asserts jurisdiction over women's reproductive lives by criminalizing abortions. However, jurisdiction is not state-bound. Rather it describes a range of social practices that bring law into being. To be effective, authoritative interpretations of the law must be received by ordinary people who integrate them with their 'situated knowledge' (Flynn, 2016, p.105) and apply them in their daily lives. Along these lines, Margaret Davies writes that:

> law is discursive, performed, assumed, located, relational and material. It is emergent in social space – through performances, intra-actions and material relations, and also through the imaginings, narratives and self-constructions that inform and are informed by these things … .
>
> (Davies, 2017, p. 89)

From this perspective, jurisdiction operates horizontally as well as vertically (Davies, 2017, p. 33): it is not only produced in state discourse and actions, but co-produced in how we engage with law in our encounters with one another (Graham et al., 2017). Everyday engagement with jurisdiction can be eventful; as when women are reported to police by people they trusted, and this leads to prosecution. However, jurisdiction is not always eventful. Sometimes it is upheld in private spaces when doctors refuse or do not offer certain treatments. Sometimes, it is maintained by passivity; as when women know not to even ask for an abortion. Rather than imagining jurisdiction as present only in the moments and spaces where officials assert or enforce it, it may be better to think of jurisdiction as mundane (Flynn, 2016, p. 105) albeit starkly visible when the state gets involved. From this pluralist perspective we can think of AfC's 'critical community building' and 'service work' as 'law work' (Enright et al., 2020).

'Critical community'

Stable jurisdictions emerge from repetition of certain authoritative interpretations of law, dispersed across whole populations, over time (Davies, 2016, 105). State jurisdiction has force because groups of people recognize it, agreeing to defer to its accounts of what is legal/illegal. However, this is a complex process. We know – not least from the example of AfC – that state performances of jurisdiction are received differently by differently situated audiences. People bring their other normative expectations and commitments – medical, social, religious, political – into their engagements with law (Hendry, 2019). Official legal pronouncements are often flexible or open-ended. For these reasons, Margaret Davies argues that law is:

> intrinsically plural – differentiated by different knowledges, subjectivities, locations, performances. It is also solid and fluid – predictable, merely probable, but also contestable and transient.
>
> (Davies, 2017, p. 89)

If law is intrinsically plural, then the force of jurisdiction depends on shared interpretations. Interpretation is generally inter-subjective: done together – other people, or with other people in mind. Harding and Peele use the term 'polyphonic legality' to explain how 'lay' people work together to co-construct legal meaning (Harding and Peel, 2019). We ask one another for explanations, opinions and resources. We may choose from competing alternatives. For example, an abortion-seeking woman may work out what the abortion law means for her through conversations with friends, family, doctors and other advisors. Law, on this interpretation-centred view, is

> a permanent interplay of ideas and principles in peoples' minds, gleaned from innumerable sources, that resolves into 'the law' for any one person in any one situation.
>
> (Anker, 2016, p. 187)

AfC built a 'critical community' within which abortion access was destigmatized and normalized (O'Dowd Cross Bloomer, this volume). Core strategies included adult community education (Bloomer et al., 2017), outreach, values and destigmatization workshops, conferences, information stalls, protests, pageants, clothing, theatre and music. AfC also worked in solidarity with other social movements including marriage equality campaigners and Repeal campaigners in the Republic of Ireland (Gallen, 2018). They established one of the few Northern Irish spaces where it was always safe to speak about abortion. Emma Gallen wrote, for example, of her work on AfC's street stalls:

> I have heard heart-breaking stories of abuse, told to me in daylight on the street because they know we won't judge, in a country that's been shrouded in shame.
>
> (Gallen, 2018)

In 'critical community' with others, AfC's members could learn the law, connect it to their own experiences, identify its shortcomings and strategize about how to change it. AfC took law out of its ordinary institutional and medical spaces, politicizing it and opening it up to peer-to-peer education (Fletcher, 2018, p. 236). What Drapeau-Bisson has called 'critical community', scholars of legal pluralism sometimes call nomos: a shared set of values, customs, habits and lifestyles; a backdrop of alternative social norms that shape their community's attitudes to law. Critical community is the environment in which activists can co-produce, share and pursue subversive interpretations of the abortion law, defying existing legal categories and imagining or perhaps demanding alternatives (Kleinhans and Macdonald, 1997, p. 25). Over time, in critical community AfC fostered radical approaches to law which animated their activism and advocacy. Here are some of its key features.

First, AfC privileged personal autonomy over national sovereignty. Whereas Stormont and Westminster emphasized abortion law as an arena of national self-determination, AfC sought to address the law's impact at the level of the individual body. In part, this attitude is a product of AfC's need to address identitarian divisions within a political system which assumes that nationalists and unionists have no shared concerns. AfC addressed both conservative unionist insistence that human rights were a nationalist issue, and nationalist reluctance to demand changes to 'British law' at Westminster. AfC became a cross-community organization where members put 'their social identity before their national one' (Cafolla, 2019). This meant that AfC could push beyond legal solutions built around a cautious approach to devolution. For example, in 2017, Westminster presented its fund to enable Northern Irish women to access abortions in England on the NHS as a compromise: offering some support to women while respecting Stormont's right to decide the abortion issue on its own terms. AfC immediately used this compromise to strengthen the argument for change; reasserting its insistence that devolution did not justify unequal access to healthcare. If Northern Irish women could access abortions in another part of the UK, why not at home? (Horgan, 2017)

Second, AfC were sceptical of liberal demands for 'law reform'. They did not necessarily think of law as empowering or protective (Enright et al., 2020). Often the tone of their legal commentary was sarcastic or playful (Campbell, 2018; 2016). Quoting Rosa Luxembourg in a 2018 article, Kellie O'Dowd associated law with violence:

> What presents itself to us as bourgeois legality is nothing but the violence of the ruling class, a violence raised to an obligatory norm from the outset.
>
> (O'Dowd, 2018)

AfC is committed to 'free, safe and legal' abortion. This means tolerating as few restrictions as possible on people's reproductive choices. That commitment partly explains AfC's essentially anti-carceral approaches to abortion access. It also informs AfC's critical approach to established liberal legal modes of abortion regulation. For instance, AfC shifted some years ago from demanding the extension of the Abortion Act, 1967 to NI to a more radical demand for decriminalization. This was because AfC objected to the 1967 Act's continued criminalization of women, and its unnecessary emphasis on medical oversight in early pregnancy. Similarly, although they engaged vigorously with CEDAW, AfC's critical community was not exclusively built around rights discourse (Pierson and Bloomer, 2017). In part, this is because international human rights law tends to be most useful in advocating for the so-called 'hard cases', and less useful where everyday entitlement to access early medical abortion is concerned (Fletcher, 2018, p. 236).

The work of critical community continues even when law reform has apparently been achieved. Following eventual decriminalization in October 2019, the NIO opened a consultation on the shape of future abortion regulations. AfC immediately mobilized the techniques of critical community; producing a page-by-page guide to encourage individual women to respond to the consultation (Alliance for Choice, 2019b), and running 'consultation cafes' where they offered assistance in responding effectively to the consultation questions. The original consultation encouraged respondents to choose between tightly defined options. Many of these assumed restrictions which were eventually included in the final regulations, including time limits, restrictions on who may offer abortion care, and controls on where it may be provided. AfC's guide asked women to ignore the prescribed 'tick boxes' and instead write to support alternatives which were closer to CEDAW's recommendations and to AfC's own commitment to 'free, safe, legal' abortion. Although its arguments were not reflected in the legislation's final text, AfC used the consultation to educate participants on the flawed policy arguments underpinning the restrictive dimensions of the consultation.

'Service work' in critical community

In a 2019 letter to pro-choice activists in Alabama, AfC summarized the service work they were doing to circumvent the abortion law. They put women in touch with the Abortion Support Network, which funds abortion travel, and with the online abortion pill providers Women on Web and Women Help Women (Yanow, volume 2; Atay, volume 2). They worked at the boundaries of legality. Even talking to women who had performed DIY abortions and declining to report them to the police was law-breaking (Fletcher, 2018, p.236). AfC wrote:

> You will have to become the people – instead of clinicians, that offer advice and help to women and pregnant people who need abortions, you will have to find ways of sharing the information that helps the most people without getting yourselves into trouble… [Y]ou and the people you help might actually get arrested, you might have your homes searched and your workplaces raided… .
>
> (Alliance for Choice, 2019a)

AfC's work made the law survivable for women otherwise denied abortions. Service work for survivability is often necessary, even where abortion access is legal. Many AfC members knew this from their time as clinic escorts, enabling women to access limited legal services at Marie Stopes Belfast (Biernat and Johnston, volume 2). However, illegal service provision is also 'work to make the law unworkable' (Press Association, 2016). From this perspective, its illegality, or what Duffy might call its anarchism (Duffy, 2020), is central to its success. Illegal 'service work' is necessarily often clandestine and cautious. Sometimes, however, it can ground public protest. For example, in 2015 when a woman was prosecuted for obtaining abortion pills for her daughter, over 200 AfC members wrote to the Director of Public Prosecutions admitting to offences relating to assisting women to have abortions, and demanding that police 'take us all on rather than picking on a single person' (McDonald, 2015). The woman prosecuted remained anonymous, while AfC members able to risk prosecution put themselves forward. They publicized their transgressive service work in order to challenge the law's legitimacy. In highlighting their own apparent immunity, they emphasized that the most vulnerable people were the law's real targets (Cahill, 2015). In early 2016, when another woman was prosecuted for terminating her own pregnancy, AfC protested in solidarity, reporting that they were considering handing themselves in to police (McDonald, 2016a). They argued that, had the young woman been able to afford travel, she could have avoided prosecution. They also insisted that the pills she used were safe: indeed, they were taken by many women accessing NHS care in England. That same year AfC members Diana King, Colette Devlin and Kitty O'Kane, all retired professionals, presented themselves at Derry's Strand Road Police station and asked to be arrested, confessing to offences related to assisting women to terminate pregnancies with pills (O'Brien, this volume). In addition to insisting that she had no duty to obey an unjust law, King claimed a defence (King, 2016). The law referred to procuring a miscarriage with 'poison', but King argued that the pills she had provided to women were 'essential medicines'. The activists were not arrested.

This action shows that 'critical community' and 'service work' are intertwined in several ways. First, over time, people's capacity to envision and enact alternative legal regimes in 'critical community' may undermine the legitimacy of the state's legal order, reinforcing their willingness to disobey (Cooper, 2019). In turn, service work is a constant reminder of repressive law's human costs and inspires often-complex critique. As AfC wrote in 2018:

> We [...] deal with people who access pills first-hand, indeed some of us have taken those medications ourselves, yet we are not criminals, we are just citizens who deserve to be treated with equanimity and compassion.
>
> (Alliance for Choice, 2018)

It was not necessarily safe for AfC members who had themselves taken pills to openly and individually disclose this. Second, experience of service work confers authority on some claims made in critical community. For instance, when AfC insisted that abortion pills were not 'poison', they advanced an alternative legal interpretation, developed in 'critical community' and drawing on their own intimate knowledge of the pills as safe medication. Third, illegal 'service work' may perform aspects of the kind of law imagined through the jurisdiction of 'critical community' and give it material presence. It is 'world-making' work (Delaney, 2010, p. 161). By assisting women to access abortions without medical or state permission, AfC showed, in practical terms, that things could be different. They offered themselves up for prosecution, and nothing happened; the police could not, at least directly, punish their disobedience. Their precarious immunity borne of critical community and its solidarities. As Fionnghuala Nic Roibeáird observed, 'If you touch one of us, you touch all of us' (Eric-Odorie, 2015).

These relationships between the defiance of illegal service work, and the alternative legality nurtured in critical community establish AfC's alternative jurisdiction over abortion. Others' interpretative efforts did not produce the same effects. For example, there was a time when some doctors in NI would terminate pregnancies for reasons of severe foetal anomaly (Side, 2006, p. 100). This practice depended on legal interpretation, since the letter of the law made no exceptions for foetal anomaly. Perhaps doctors implicitly understood that requiring a woman to continue such a pregnancy would expose her to the kinds of severe health risks which did justify an abortion under law (Rebouche and Fegan, 2003, p. 227). This medical engagement with law differed from AfC's work in two ways. First because doctors aimed, or were required, to obey the law, their flexible practice was readily extinguished once obedience was policed with more forceful threats of criminalization. Second, and more importantly, the practice was not publicly presented as transgressive, or rooted in a desire to alter the law. Indeed, the question of doctors' engagement with abortion law was subsequently presented in terms of clarity and confusion around rather than in terms of a principled desire to interpret the law more liberally. The dual ingredients of transgression and community ground AfC's jurisdiction.

Today, despite significant changes in Northern Irish abortion law, AfC activists continue to pursue service work in critical community with one another. From October 2019, when abortion was decriminalized, until Stormont re-opened in January 2020, anti-choice MLAs made some symbolic efforts to halt decriminalization and alter the new abortion regulations, but the content of the new abortion law was out of their hands (Moriarty, 2020). Implementation, however, was the Executive's responsibility. The new UUP Health Minister, Robin Swann, has obstructed implementation of the new regulations (Yeginsu, 2020). Formal services were not in place when the regulations took effect in late March, as COVID-19 swept across Europe. It seemed that, despite the change in the law, women would still be required to travel for abortions. With air travel suspended, some went to Liverpool by freight ferry; an eight-hour journey (Yeginsu, 2020). In April, under growing pressure, Robin Swann permitted willing trusts to go ahead with plans to provide early medical abortion on an emergency basis (Cafolla, 2020). However, this did not improve the position for many women who still needed to travel within NI or abroad during the pandemic. Some trusts are still providing early medical abortion, but services are precarious (NIACT, 2021). At the time of writing, no provision has been made for telemedicine, and it is extremely difficult to access an abortion in NI after ten weeks' pregnancy (NIACT, 2021). In February 2021, Paul Givan introduced a Bill in Stormont attempting to remove fatal foetal abnormality as a ground for termination under Northern Irish legislation. He has since been nominated as the DUP's candidate for First Minister. It is difficult to know when we can expect normalized legal abortion services in NI (Allamby, this volume).

AfC remains the first port of call for many women needing abortions (Higgins, 2020). As well as demanding that the government make establish abortion telemedicine services for the duration of the pandemic (McHugh, 2020), AfC continues to organize service work in critical community. Their website currently directs abortion-seeking women who are less than twelve-weeks pregnant and unable to access abortions in NI to the most appropriate online provider. It also offers a mobile phone number that women can call if they need advice when self-inducing an abortion. The NI regulations did not permit at-home use of mifepristone. This activism carefully negotiates the boundaries of the criminal law, though the stakes are now somewhat lower. Women themselves can no longer be prosecuted for using abortion pills. However, a health professional found to have 'procured' the termination otherwise than on the restrictive grounds provided for by law may be fined.

Conclusion: Co-producing law?

This chapter argues that AfC can be understood as actively producing legal change and reshaping the established boundaries of formal law-making authority in NI. Even if we only acknowledged AfC's repeated engagement within law-making institutions, we could read their influence in recent changes to NI's abortion law. However, it is their service work in critical community that radically challenges inadequate law. In this chapter, I have argued that AfC have established a kind of jurisdiction over abortion in NI; the power to articulate shared interpretations of prevailing law and give it (or deprive it of) everyday force). They are authoritative interpreters of state law, but they are also defiant and transgressive in how they apply that law in their 'critical community building' and legal 'service work'. Service work, especially, challenges boundaries between legality and illegality, confers authority on alternative interpretations of the law and materializes feminist possibilities for healthcare that the state might prefer to suppress.

Critical community and service work continue to be part of AfC's efforts to address unjust laws. AfC recently piloted an abortion doulas programme, 'Lucht Cabhrach'. An eventual network of doulas is intended to supplement the limited statutory framework for abortion in NI by advocating for abortion-seeking women and support legal abortion 'self-care' (Campbell et al., 2021). This formalization of AfC's service work represents a potential new departure; working the space created by decriminalization of self-induced abortion and infusing a legal experience with the ethos of autonomy, solidarity and tolerance of necessary disobedience that has characterized AfC's critical community. The new law is not everything AfC would have wished for. Writing in 2020 as co-convenor of AfC, Naomi Connor spoke directly to those still obstructing abortion access:

> We will not be silenced. We will not be deterred. We are here, standing strong in our rightful place.
>
> (Connor, 2019)

Their ability to seize that 'rightful place' is at the root of their radical legal agency.

Theme 2

Campaigning and activism

11

Blazing the trail-campaigns: The earlier years

Lynda Walker

This chapter identifies organizations and individuals who campaigned to change the abortion law in Northern Ireland (NI), highlighting some of the achievements and difficulties they experienced. It reviews some of the published material from that time, as well as reflections from key people in organizations.

In 1967 the Northern Ireland Civil Rights Association (NICRA) was established to campaign for rights in NI which were taken for granted in Britain. However, despite the passing of the 1967 Abortion Act, which was not extended to NI, this did not become part of the NICRA agenda. Women with unwanted pregnancies were prevented from accessing free, safe, legal abortion in NI and had to journey to England, Scotland or Wales, have a 'back street' abortion or continue with the unwanted pregnancy. In response, several organizations and campaigns formed to address the needs of women.

The Ulster Pregnancy Information Service was established in 1971, later called the Ulster Pregnancy Advisory Association (UPAA) (About 1971/72). Whilst it was not a campaigning organization, its stated aspiration was to change the law:

> The UPAA hopes there will come a time when the women of Northern Ireland can expect the same help from their hospitals as can their counterparts in Britain. In the meantime, they do what they can to prevent the unhappiness or outright tragedy that follows when there is an unwanted pregnancy.
>
> (UPAA leaflet undated)

The UPAA closed in 1999 after attacks on its office, the Family Planning Association later assumed its work. Intimidation started with picketing offices and at the home of a local counsellor. The demonstrators waved placards bearing images of aborted foetuses and the addresses of the women they accused of being killers. On 13 July 1999, the UPAA's office was attacked by arsonists. Two weeks later, the office closed, the staff were too scared to continue with their work. 'Precious Life, and the Northern Irish affiliate of Youth Defence, welcomed the UPAA's closure, calling it a "great victory for direct action"' (Holland, 1999, p. 4). This combination of campaigning for legislative change and provision of practical support for abortion access was a constant feature of the work of various organizations and individuals. In Derry, the activist Goretti Horgan was involved with Derry Women's Right to Choose Group from 1987 to 1996 and was a founder member of AfC Derry. She explains that:

> We mainly fundraised to help women get to England. This was virtually a full-time job as we had social workers and GPs from as far away as Belfast phoning us looking for financial help for desperate women.
>
> (Horgan, personal correspondence, 2020)

The women's movement

The women's movement was late coming to NI as politics was dominated by civil rights struggles, state violence and paramilitaries and the conservative influence of the church (Walker et al., 2019; Davis et al., 2020). In the 1970s the issue of women's rights started to surface. Organizations including the Northern Ireland Women's Rights Movement (NIWRM) and the Socialist Women's Group (SWG) began to campaign on a range of issues, including the extension of the 1967 Abortion Act to NI.

The NIWRM was formed in 1975. It received support from civil rights activists, Women's Aid, SWG as well as trade unions including: National Union of Public Employees (NUPE) now Unison, Amalgamated Transport and General Workers Union (ATGWU), NI Public Service Alliance (NIPSA) Belfast and District Trades Union Council, Queen's Student Union, Newtownabbey Labour Party, Communist Party of Ireland and the Workers Party. Women's Aid left after a few months because the NIWRM was not a 'women only' organization and the SWG, also left over political differences.

In 1975 at one of its first meetings in Transport House Belfast, the NIWRM adopted a seven-point Women's Charter. They included:

1. Equal opportunities in education, training and work.
2. Equal pay and condition.

3. Legal and social rights relating to social security, mortgages, hire purchase and so on.
4. Improved maternity leave and childcare facilities.
5. Parity of rights with women in Britain on a number of legal issues, rights to family home and divorce.

Improved family planning services was called for, as was recognition for non-working women to legal and adequate support. The call for abortion was contained under point 5: 'Parity of Rights for women in Northern Ireland with Women in England and Wales'.

The NIWRM members supported the campaigns through activism and conferences. My own interest in abortion law reform began when I moved to Belfast, it was clear the position of women in NI socially, economically and politically was much worse than in Britain. In 1974, I carried out research which outlined aspects of this discrimination as well as civil rights issues. This included comparison with some legislation in Britain that did not apply here, including abortion law. This was produced in booklet form for Queen's Students Union (QSU), Welfare Committee. The secretary of the committee at the time was Bronagh Hinds – soon to become the first woman president of QSU. The booklet was presented to a NUS conference in 1974, in Britain, on behalf of QSU. The research was also used for a feature article in the *Morning Star* where I drew attention to the political situation that women faced and outdated legislation which included divorce and abortion law:

> For many who want to terminate a pregnancy well it is just hard luck, only in extreme health cases are women allowed abortion: the 1967 Abortion Act does not apply to Northern Ireland. It is conservatively estimated that 1,000 go to England each year to obtain an abortion.
>
> (Walker, 1974, p. 4)

Other NIWRM members took part in pro-choice actions as well as supporting women's campaigns for contraception and support for the Anti-Amendment campaign in the Republic of Ireland. This was central to solidarity, and it also enabled women here to raise the issue publicly. The campaign was opposed to the Eighth Amendment of the Constitution Act 1983 which inserted a subsection into the constitution of Ireland, dangerously recognizing the equal right to life of the pregnant woman and the unborn child.

Defend the Clinics Campaign was formed in Conway Mill on 5 April 1987; it drew support from a wide range of people and organizations. The purpose of the campaign was to fight the decision of the High Court in Dublin which ruled that the Dublin Well Women's Centre (and others) could not give advice to pregnant women on all their options, abortion being the main issue (ni Phental, 1987, p. 3).

A Woman's Right to Choose was a central call for the SWG formed in October 1975 'by women from the Queen's University Women's Liberation Group and groups on the Trotskyist left – People's Democracy, the Revolutionary Marxist Group and the Irish Workers' Group, to fuse socialism and feminism' (Ward, personal correspondence, 2019). The SWG manifesto, launched on International Women's Day 1976, called for a Woman's Right to Choose and other demands which remain relevant today. The SWG folded in 1977 but many activists went on to form the Women and Media group who in turn supported the Northern Ireland Abortion Campaign (NIAC). SWG members also formed the Belfast Women's Collective. Margaret Ward was a key activist and along with others helped to organize the Belfast Women's Collective conference on 'Childbirth, Contraception and Abortion' in 1979 (Ward, personal correspondence, 2020).

The abortion debate was brought into sharp focus in 1980 prompted by the death of 21-year-old Charlotte Hutton as a result of a 'back street' abortion in Belfast. NIAC was formed holding their meetings in newly opened NIWRM Women's Centre in Donegall Street which became its base. The groups in Derry also used their Women's Centre 'which was one of the first Women's Centre to adopt a pro-choice position – as early 1990s' (Horgan, personal correspondence, 2020).

Women and Media booklet. A Woman's Choice 1980. Argues the case for free legal abortion

In 1980 three months after the formation of the NIAC, Women and Media produced a comprehensive booklet, *A Woman's Choice*, it explained the law in NI, gave information about organizations like the UPAA and NIAC and other contacts, about 'going to England', the different types of abortion and contraception. This was a campaigning booklet which also drew on women's experiences.

In October 1981 NIAC got the attention of the Members of Parliament (MP) at Westminster, when activists Marie-Therese McGivern and Marilyn Hyndman delivered 624 wire coat hangers to the MP's: 'As a NIAC member I helped with putting BA tickets on wire coat hangers and actually getting sufficient hangers – 624. Each of these had a facsimile of a British Airways ticket with the message, "these are the two ways in which Northern Ireland women get an abortion"' (Ward, 1984, p. 15). This action was an imaginative feat, which secured media attention, but not the required reform.

In April 1982 NIAC carried out a survey amongst 442 general practitioners throughout NI, drawn from the Yellow Pages Telephone Directory. Some 78 (16 per cent) completed the questionnaire. The results showed that 57 per cent of the sample was in favour of changing the present legislation to allow a termination of pregnancy to be made easier and 14 per cent were in favour of more restrictive practices.

Nuala Quiery who was active in NIAC said:

> We succeeded in drawing attention to what was a hidden issue. Awareness raising was therefore one outcome as also was helping reduce the shame felt by women who had had abortions and who were silenced by this. There were strong negative religious based responses, and it was hard to convey the notion of choice and personal agency, and the bigger picture of factors influencing conception and the awful circumstances women found themselves in. It was seen as a problem for individuals with no interest in the contribution of lack of sex education and contraceptive services, poverty, subjugation and exploitation of women.
>
> (Quiery, personal correspondence, 2020)

On 29 February 1984 the Northern Ireland Assembly (NIA) debated abortion legislation. NIAC reported on Rev Ivan Foster's motion opposing the extension of the 1967 Abortion Act or similar legislation in NI. In his speech he said,

> Adolf Hitler had more charity in him than the abortionist because abortionists would seek to put to death child with no defects, a child who is perfectly formed.
>
> (Women's News, 1984)

The motion was passed by twenty votes to one (Mr Morrow of the Alliance Party). NIAC dissolved in 1984 in order to broaden its campaign to draw in professional people and others who would be influential. During its four years, it helped raise awareness of the need for abortion law reform using several campaigning methods. Undoubtedly the coat hanger trail was the most striking but,

All the actions were important in bringing to the public attention the need for abortion reform. We started leafleting in Cornmarket and had joint events with feminists in Dublin.

(Ward, personal correspondence, 2020)

Northern Ireland Abortion Law Reform Association

The work of NIAC paved the way for the establishment of Northern Ireland Abortion Law Reform Association (NIALRA) in 1985. NIALRA continued the campaign to have the 1967 Abortion Act extended to NI; it was made up of women's rights campaigners, people from the legal, medical and educational professions. (Note NIALRA as an organization had existed in the late 1960s but had disappeared by the 1970s; Horgan, 2009.)

In 1987 NIALRA organized a major International Tribunal on Abortion in the Europa Hotel, it was huge and the first international tribunal of lawyers, doctors and academics who heard evidence from local women, women's groups, community support organizations and medical and legal professionals. Gabriel Scally, Madge Davison, Margaret Ward, Goretti Horgan, Bill Rolston and Anna Eggart all attended.

> The legal evidence as it pertained to Northern Ireland was presented by Madge Davison, Law Lecturer at QUB and medical evidence was presented by women with experience of pre-natal screening for foetal defects by general practitioners and by the Consultant Medical Geneticists for Northern Ireland (in absentia).
>
> (Women's News 1989, pp. 16–17)

The Tribunal considered that there were five specific issues to consider:

1. Women from NI are having abortions, but they are not having them in NI.
2. Women from NI must pay for their abortions in Britain; this discriminates against women who are economically disadvantaged. Those who cannot travel must endure an unwanted pregnancy or resort to a 'backstreet abortion'.
3. As a result of the legal situation, certain ante-natal tests, which are commonly available in Britain, are not routinely offered to women in NI.

4. Women in NI are prey to isolation, fear and loneliness to a greater extent than are women elsewhere in the UK.
5. The European Parliament proposed that abortion travel should stop and in 1981 urged the European Council 'to ensure that every woman who finds herself in difficulty can obtain the necessary assistance in her own country' (Clark Glass, 1995, pp. 2–3).

Bill Rolston also recollects that:

> We met regularly through those years, we were involved in picketing at times, in letter writing – to MPs, GPs, others. We also pursued briefly the possibility of direct action, establishing abortion facilities in Belfast, but that came to nothing.
>
> On a number of occasions Anna Eggert pushed for an action like they had had in Germany. There 100 prominent women who had had abortions acknowledged this publicly… The subsequent public debate contributed to a change in the law, but she never persuaded enough women here to rise to the challenge.
>
> The main problems we encountered were apathy tinged with censorship. We managed to get British politicians, including Secretaries of State, to reply occasionally to letters but British governments would not legislate above the heads of local politicians.
>
> (Rolston, personal correspondence, 2020)

Gabriel Scally was one of the medical professionals involved in NIALRA; he writes:

> While I was working as a public health physician in Belfast I joined the Northern Ireland Abortion Law Reform Association, which had been formed in 1985, and spoke at a public meeting on reform. The general atmosphere, whilst not reflecting support for an alteration in the legal position regarding abortion in Northern Ireland, did not display any overt hostility to those who were either advocating liberalisation of the legal position or, quietly, providing assistance to women seeking a termination. This all changed with the inception of a young people's sexual health service in Belfast provided by a local organisation which had been created as an affiliate to Brook Advisory Centres in London. I received death threats, I also received demands, particularly from the Democratic Union Party, for my resignation, but the momentum created to open the Brook clinic could not be halted.
>
> (Scally, personal correspondence, 2020)

His involvement in NIALRA in turn helped to change the policy of the British Medical Association (BMA). He writes:

> Whilst a medical student at Queen's University Belfast in the 1970s I was aware that abortion was available under limited circumstances within the health service in Northern Ireland. The most widely known area of medicine where termination of pregnancy was performed was in the realm of congenital abnormalities.

The NIALRA booklet carried information about the motion that was moved by Gabriel Scally, at that time a doctor in NI, who had studied at Queens University.

> It was also common knowledge amongst medical students and staff that some consultants would carry out terminations of pregnancy on women in the early stages of pregnancy and the surgical procedure would be treated as dealing with menstrual irregularity. As a junior doctor in a small hospital outside Belfast I came across less sympathetic attitudes when a woman decided to have a termination of pregnancy because of a recently diagnosed cancer. She was immediately shunned by many of the nursing staff on the ward and had to be transferred as soon as possible to another hospital where she would be treated more sympathetically.
>
> (Scally, personal correspondence, 2020)

In 1984, as a delegate to the Annual Representative meeting, Dr Scally succeeded in getting a motion passed committing the BMA to support the extension of the 1967 Abortion Act to NI. There was active opposition to progress this but at meeting the following year, 1985, he 'succeeded in getting a motion passed that committed the BMA "actively to pursue" the extension of the Act. This appeared to have the effect of ending the opposition within the BMA and enabled the organisation at UK level to press for extension'. (Op cit.)

NIALRA petered out in the mid-1990s 'on the basis of not having made progress on a single issue. That said there was also the beginning of a number of other – younger – groups and individuals active on the issue, so I believe our contribution was to have kept the flame lit during the lean years' (Rolston, personal correspondence, April, 2020). His view that no progress had been made is clearly an underestimation.

The Committee for the Administration of Justice (CAJ) produced a handbook 'Civil Liberties in Northern Ireland' some of which outlined the abortion law in practice on abortion. It highlighted that some abortions were carried out lawfully in NI but that, 'doctors receive no guidance from the DHSS and the medical teaching profession has had to draw up its own guidance on the interpretation of the law for the benefit of medical students'. They concluded that a woman is 'effectively faced with the choice of a trip to England or recourse to a back street abortion here' (Dickson and Davison, 1990, p. 194). The lack of clarity regarding the law was to become a major issue that the FPA took up throughout the 1990s and 2000s (Rowan and Simpson, this volume).

This initiative of the NIALRA International Tribunal motivated the FPA NI to invite the Europe Region of the IPPF to co-facilitate a one-day symposium on the abortion law in NI. This was held on 12 December 1994 in the Slieve Donard hotel in Newcastle, County Down. In June 1993, the Standing Advisory Commission on Human Rights (SCAR) issued a public consultation document on the issue, written by Simon Lee, Professor of Law at Queen's University Belfast, it observed that:

> The law on abortion in Northern Ireland is so uncertain that it violates the standards of international human rights law. It could not withstand a challenge before the European Court of Human Rights at Strasbourg.
>
> (Glass, 1995, pp. 2–3)

Northern Ireland Women's Coalition

Northern Ireland Women's Coalition (NIWC) was established in 1996 to ensure that women were included in the peace process and governing bodies (Fearon, 1999). As a coalition it came with all the inherent problems of broad politics, meaning the NIWC did not highlight the contentious issue of abortion. Kate Fearon notes it was a topic for canvassers in elections, but that did not come up on the doorstep:

> The NIWC as a whole did not feel pressurised to have a strong liberal-leaning policy on this simply because it is politically active group of women. The priority in this election was women's participation, and campaigning on reproductive choice would not have contributed strategically to that end. The NIWC's official position was thus accurate: there were differing voices in the subject within the NIWC, just as there were differing voices on the constitutional question. The NIWC nevertheless acknowledged the reality that some 1,800 women a year travel from Northern Ireland to have their pregnancies terminated. This reality would have to be addressed rationally.
>
> (1999, p. 27)

The Manifesto for the 1998 elections gave priority to the implementation of the Good Friday/Belfast Agreement. A policy was formed that embraced the need for improved sex education, enhanced healthcare regarding contraception, better affordable childcare facilities along with a women's right to choose. It was a comprehensive policy that took into account the need to prevent unwanted pregnancies as well as to provide for abortions.

There were criticisms inside and out of the NIWC. Some felt that the campaign for abortion law reform was inadequate, and others outside the organization used mention of abortion to denigrate the NIWC. Political parties were smarting that the NIWC would take their support away. Ironically, the DUP initiated one of the first discussions in the NIA on abortion law reform, when party member Jim Wells moved a motion that opposed the extension of the Abortion Act (1967) to NI (Pierson and Bloomer, 2018).

Monica Williams of the NIWC proposed an amendment which would have referred the matter to the Health, Social Services and Public Safety Committee. Joan Carson Unionist Party (UU) Mary Nelis-Sinn Féin (SF), Eileen Bell and Alliance Party (AP) Jane Morris (NIWC) all addressed the need to improve healthcare for women in NI. However, the 'debate was memorable for the fact that Joan Carson Ulster Unionist (UU) and David Ervine of the Progressive Unionist Party (PUP) spoke in favour of the extending the Abortion Act to Northern Ireland' (Rossiter, 2009, p. 178). Monica McWilliams explained:

> My address in the Assembly was to take the speeches off the floor of the Chamber and set up an enquiry in the Health Committee on terminations for fatal foetal abnormalities and rape and other crisis pregnancies. Some in the NIWC did not think that was enough and it was a tough issue to debate at that time. I got hell at the doors for that speech when I went out to canvas so times have changed.
>
> (McWilliams, personal correspondence, 2020)

In fact, this reflects the earlier comment that the NIWC was never able to please everyone. There was a framework of equality, human rights and inclusion, a policy that was agreed and the method of having a collective discussion over time, it was one that the NIWC could be proud of, but not all members embraced it.

Support V campaigning

The combination of campaigning for legislative change and provision of practical support for women in need of an abortion was a constant feature of abortion activism. In Derry, Goretti Horgan was involved with Derry Women's Right to Choose Group from 1987 to 1996 and was a founder member of AfC Derry. She explains:

The move from the Woman's Right to Choose Group to Alliance for Choice (1996) – an upfront campaigning group was about ending the fundraising which we felt put a band aid over a gaping wound and to move to campaigning to get abortion rights for NI.

(Horgan, personal correspondence, 2020)

Marie Mulholland summarizes her involvement which was a combination of campaigning and support for women, actions

Were mainly practical giving financial support to women needing abortions by helping them to access services in Britain; organising their travel, linking in with Irish and British feminists to meet them and accompany them when possible, raising funds for their travel and accommodation and cost of the abortion.

(Mulholland, personal correspondence, 2020)

Activism also included engaging with trade unions. Unison like some other unions was a British based-union, which had a right to choose policy, but getting action and commitment from unions in Ireland North or South was difficult. She writes:

I was involved in NUPE/UNISON and was the coordinator for Women's Support Network (WSN) it had a Women's Right to Choose policy which we developed in the mid 1990's. I attended lots of meetings to get the policy through in the WSN, likewise NUPE/Unison. Conferences where motions on supporting a women's right to choose were debated including one very difficult Irish Committee of Trade Unions (ICTU) women's conference in the mid 80's where the motion failed because of opposition from major Republic of Ireland unions.

(Mulholland, personal correspondence, 2020)

Extending the campaign

Kate Fearon noted

As a student officer at QUBSU from 1991–1993 I was campaigning on abortion rights, and sexual health particularly HIV/AIDS. Amongst other things, we provided information to individual students who needed to travel to England for abortions. Together with Alison Ahern I started AfC, which aimed to change the laws, starting with a legislative review. Audrey Simpson of the Family Planning Association was a mentor. I moved to Dublin where I was involved in then SPUC vs. Grogan case on abortion rights. Back in Belfast, in 1995, AfC targeted decision-makers, such as Mo Mowlam. Once the NIWC started I simply didn't have time to continue to be involved in AfC. I don't recall that we formally dissolved it, and in a few years, I know that other activists took up the name and were campaigning, which was great.

(personal: Fearon, correspondence, 2020)

Goretti Horgan in 1998 records that Derry AfC was part of the new Voice for Choice (VfC) the UK-wide umbrella organization of pro-choice groups that campaign for improved abortion rights. Between then and October, AfC in Derry gathered signatures for a civil society open letter asserting that the political parties did not speak for the majority in relation to abortion. The letter was signed by the leaders of all the main trade unions in the North, many leaders of the community and voluntary sector and some politicians – including Eileen Bell, first speaker of the Stormont Assembly, it was sent to Gordon Brown.

From 1998 to 2008, AfC Derry worked closely with VfC and the All-Party Sexual Health Group at Westminster to try to get the 1967 Act extended to the region. At a public meeting in Belfast in 2008 with speakers from trade unions, politicians, activists and the FPA, Dawn Purvis predicted that when Stormont got responsibility for criminal law, we would never get a change in the abortion laws and that would be the end of the campaign (O'Dowd Cross Bloomer, this volume). However, she could not foresee the consequence of Stormont going on leave for three years, or the force that AfC would become, along with the increased support from MPs' and some section of the media in Britain (Campbell, this volume). Marie Mulholland (2020) notes: There was hostility, silence, fear, anger, hypocrisy entrenched attitudes, the vicious judgements on women in need, the invisibility of so much pain endured by generations of women and the dismissal of our realities.

Nuala Quiery said:

I do remember that I was one of the very few who felt able to speak publicly about my views on the plight of women in the North in regard to abortion. I did an hour-long radio interview in the early 1980s on Radio Ulster with a GP about the need for reform. My mother didn't speak to me for a month after the radio interview, but she eventually came to understand that abortion is not something anyone would seek to promote but rather it is a fact of life and the lack of power and autonomy in women's lives, and that women should have the right to choose.

(Quiery, personal correspondence, 2020)

Bill Rolston reflects:

Odd to look back on – I was a middle-aged man, a 'respectable academic' and parent, and yet frequently hid from cameras or under pseudonyms in case my mother would find out what I was doing! I would also argue that similar self-censorship was part of the reason Anna failed to persuade a group of women to publicly acknowledge they had had abortions in order to start a public debate.

(Personal: Rolston, correspondence, 2020)

And in the 1980s: I was a member of a management committee of a Youth Training Centre in Andersonstown after I did an interview on television about the Right to Choose, some of the members resigned from the committee (Walker, 2020).

Margaret Ward adds to this:

For a time, I worked as women's officer in Community Services Dept of Belfast City Council I couldn't speak publicly on the subject for fear of consequences for Community Services, which was generally disliked by Unionist members of Council. This did not prevent me continuing to work as an activist.

(Personal: Ward, correspondence, 2020)

The difficulties that were encountered reflect the tough experiences of campaigners who along with those who had abortions were considered criminals. Some of the problems that they and their families faced are revealed in this chapter. Workers at the UPAA lost their jobs and like Gabriel Scally were faced with the threat of physical violence, for others hostility meant self-censorship.

Conclusion

This chapter can only tell part of the story so many actors are excluded. I also think that the role of the media requires a story of its own, the mass media, political party papers, and the smaller women's papers and magazines. Through the years the support for abortion law reform grew which is thanks to the many people who took up the baton despite problems such as the political situation, moral views, violence, lack of democratic rights, sectarianism and those who did not want a British law to be introduced. However, it is the British Government who must bear the overall responsibility for the lack of reproductive rights until 2019 (Walker, 2017; Davis et al., 2020).

In the last fifty years a whole range of women's organizations, women's centres, some trade unions and rights organizations did not campaign for abortion law reform – it was an issue too hot to handle, though gradually this changed. Initially it was left to those organizations who were specifically established to campaign on abortion like NIALRA and or who dealt with women's rights, reproductive rights and health issues, like the UPAA, FPA NI and some women's organizations like the AfC, NIWRM, SWG and WSN, who took up the fight (Rossiter, 2009, p. 180).

The long struggle and many years of campaigning have eventually achieved the unthinkable for women in NI the decriminalization of abortion. However, the service has yet to be commissioned and a word of caution is needed against those who might take this from us; what we have, we must defend.

A total of twelve people were contacted and eight responded. I wish to thank those sent me useful information.

Horgan Goretti: Academic, socialist and trade union activist from Derry. AfC.

McWilliams Monica: Former Member of the Local Assembly for the NIWC. Academic and women's movement activist. NIWRM.

Mulholland Marie: Women's movement and trade union activist from Belfast.

Purvis Dawn: was active from the early 1990s until the present day. She was involved in the Progressive Unionist Party, being the Party Spokesperson leader after David Ervine, on the Board and Chair of AfC, Belfast, was the NI Director of Marie Stopes International, and Trustee/Treasurer FPA NI/Informing Choices NI.

Query Nuala: Women's Movement activist, NIAC.

Rolston Bill: Academic, NIALRA

Scally Gabriel: NIALRA; Brook Advisory Centre Gabriel Scally is visiting professor of public health at the University of Bristol.

Ward Margaret: Women's Movement Activist, historian, writer and academic Socialist Women's Group, NIAC, NIALRA.

12

Alliance for Choice new beginnings

Kellie O'Dowd, Judith Cross and Fiona Bloomer

This chapter will map the work of AfC from the summer of 2008 until December 2016, covering the period when the organization became re-activated (Walker, this volume) and up until the focus shifted to Westminster following the suspension of the NI Assembly (NIA) in January 2017 (Pierson, this volume; Campbell, this volume). It will chart how and why the organization renewed its focus in 2008; consider how it developed during the following decade, the challenges and barriers faced and its key achievements. It will reflect on the political landscape during this period, which Pierson details in her chapter, as well as the public policy agenda. We will document the ally-building across a number of sectors and the intersectional nature of the actions and programmes that were delivered by AfC.

AfC spent this period laying the building blocks of a social movement for change: we designed and created new conditions for engagement on abortion by framing it as a health, welfare and social justice argument. The resulting analysis highlighted the key challenges we would mount on the morally conservative discourse that dominated abortion in NI. This focus allowed women to create their own narrative based on their lived experience of the spectrum of sexual and reproductive rights.

AfC's mission was to turn religious, misogynistic and stereotyping discourse on its head using empirical and narrative evidence, and sheer determination to be heard. AfC built relationships with a wide range of allies such as the trade unions, women's organizations, political parties across three jurisdictions, national and international abortion rights activists, human rights organizations and academic researchers. We also challenged equality and human rights bodies to voice their concerns rather than ignore the issue or position it as 'too difficult'. We made abortion a key election issue in 2016 for the NIA and moved this pressure to Westminster when Stormont collapsed (Thomson, this volume).

Analysis of AfC in this period, its multi-faceted approaches and narrative development is crucial to understanding how groups at the shallow end of power relations in a morally conservative society can over a ten-year period turn legal reform from an aspiration into a reality.

The chapter authors Kellie O'Dowd (activist), Judith Cross (activist) and Fiona Bloomer (research adviser) were all involved with AfC from 2008 onwards. This chapter recounts our recollections of the work of the organization, drawing on documented sources where relevant.

Introduction

Alliance for Choice (AfC) was formed by Kate Fearon and Alison Ahern in 1996, and its purpose was to campaign for the extension of the 1967 Abortion Act to NI. However, as they soon became involved in other political issues at the time, as detailed in Lynda Walker's chapter (this volume), the organization lay dormant until 2008. Practical help for women and other lobbying activities continued quietly as the NI Peace negotiations involving The Good Friday/ Belfast Agreement and devolution took centre stage.

The context in which women and campaigners operated in relation to abortion law was referred to as an 'Iron Curtain' (Fegan, 2010); carefully constructed and policed to prevent women and the medical profession from getting accurate and non-biased information. This served to curtail women's entitlement to have an abortion should they be legally entitled to one. Furthermore, given the precarious funding of women's groups in NI, and their reliance on government grants to operate, those interested in the issue were too frightened to publicly state they were supportive of more progressive abortion legislation (Walker, this volume; Rowan and Simpson, this volume).

'Complete disregard', 'deliberate obfuscation', 'regrettable', 'missed opportunities', 'downright disgraceful' are the phrases that come to mind when looking back at the attempts by various statutory actors to prevent women in NI from accessing abortion services, despite GB-wide access. AfC felt that preventing access to abortion held us in a perpetual state of abandonment. The focus for them was on the protection of the foetus over the right to bodily integrity, including the Northern Ireland Human Rights Commission, a statutory body set up to promote and protect human rights. Others such as Amnesty International and the Committee on the Administration of Justice were silent on this issue during this period, inexcusable given their responsibilities to equality and human rights as this reinforced unfounded assumptions that NI was largely anti-choice (Cross O'Rourke Simpson, this volume; Pierson and Bloomer, 2017).

It would be remiss not to mention the silence of the women's sector in this debate prior to 2009. Whilst there is a long history of the women's sector in NI being comfortable around issues such as childcare, poverty, employment, political representation, the sector was silent on sexuality and abortion. This may have been due to a fear of funding as many relied almost entirely on the statutory agencies for financial support. It was also difficult to counter the aggressive approach used by the churches and anti-choice organizations at that time. Fegan (2009) argued that this was, 'due to a complex and government complicit cultural bulwark against information, understanding and change'. Bloomer and O'Dowd (2014) also argued that the ideological alignment between religious and many political leaders bolstered the anti-abortion lobby. It is therefore not surprising that the women's sector were curtailed in using their voice on this issue. They did however continue to provide practical financial support covertly for women who still 'had to go to England' (McVicker and Crickard, this volume).

The acts of betrayal

The Good Friday Agreement (1998) presented a key opportunity to address abortion policy, with its commitment to 'the right of women to full and equal political participation, and Section 75 of the NI Act, which purportedly put equality of opportunity at the heart of public policy'. Despite focus on equality and human rights, Fegan and Rebouche (2003, p. 222) noted that:

> … the language used to promote peace and social progress, when juxtaposed against that used to frame the abortion debate, shows how far the latter fails to address either women's reproductive agency or equality …

Despite a commitment in the Labour party's manifesto in 1997 to extend the 1967 Abortion act to NI and being in power for over 18 years, they refused to act on this. The amendment to the Human Fertilisation and Embryology Bill tabled by Diane Abbott, MP, was essentially blocked by Harriet Harman through the use of parliamentary procedures, as it would destabilise the peace process (Thomson, this volume).

This act of betrayal by the Labour party to women in NI made the euphoria that greeted their landslide election in 1997 short-lived – it was a kick in the teeth; but one of many which will be explored further in the chapter. False dawns as AfC were soon to learn were plenty.

The fight for women's reproductive rights in Belfast was reinvigorated when on 31 January 2008, Judith Cross and Kellie O'Dowd (Cross, O'Dowd) and others picketed an event at the Spires Centre Belfast, which was part of a UK wide anti-abortion speaking tour, led by Ann Widdecombe (UK Conservative Party MP) (Socialist Worker, 2008). Meanwhile, efforts by activists to raise the matter with the governing Labour Party reached fruition when first, Emily Thornberry MP and then Diane Abbott MP tabled an amendment to the Human Fertilization and Embryology Bill in July 2008, calling for the extension of the 1967 Abortion Act to NI (Thomson, this volume). The Bill was due to be debated and voted on in the Autumn of 2008. To begin building the campaign, activists joined forces with feminist and trade union activists, with people such as Brenda Callaghan and Barbara Muldoon and members of the Socialist Workers Party were amongst the first to join. Thus began the sustained efforts of AfC to bring about legal change.

Weekly meetings were held in the Belfast Unemployed Resource Centre, where discussions ensued on actions and strategies to raise awareness and gain public support for the amendment. Given the moral conservatism and the stigma surrounding abortion, coupled with a lazy and archaic media narrative, it was clear to all that this was not going to be an easy campaign. In the weeks that followed, activists wrote to all MPs in the UK, organized a petition and held weekly signing sessions in Belfast City Centre.

In early September 2008 AfC organized a large public meeting to provide a platform for the public with key stakeholders. Around 250 people attended, with speakers including: Bernadette McAliskey; prominent activist and ex MP; Taryn Trainor from the Unite the Union, Dr Audrey Simpson from the Family Planning Association NI, Dawn Purvis and Anna Lo; the only 2 publicly pro-choice MLAs out of 108 in Stormont, and Goretti Horgan representing AfC. At the meeting people were urged to contact MPs to ask them to support the amendment. Leading up to the day when the amendment was tabled (22 October 2008), activists continued with weekly petition signing sessions. On 22 October, representatives from NI travelled to London to present a petition to No. 10 Downing St.

Despite these efforts, women's rights in NI again were sacrificed on the altar of NI politics, and the 'armed patriarchy'. During the forty plus years of conflict, feminists referred to those involved in the conflict as the 'armed patriarchy' as victims of rape or domestic violence were silenced or were expected to keep quiet, and feminism was deemed irrelevant to the 'real constitutional issues'.

The amendment was filibustered (Thomson, Creasy and Sanquest, this volume). Rossiter (2009) documents the political powers at play during this time. A letter was sent in May 2008 to all Westminster MPs signed by all the main political parties represented at Stormont, with the exception of the Alliance Party and the Progressive Unionist Party, which stated that the leaders spoke for over 90 per cent of the population who did not want the Act extended and that to do so would damage the Peace Process. A similar letter was also issued by the leaders of all the Northern Irish Churches.

After the defeat of the amendment, attendance numbers at the AfC meetings dwindled as many activists moved on to other campaigns or agendas. The authors of this chapter were not those activists. It is important to acknowledge that whilst abortion is a prominent issue now, it was not always, and it was difficult to engage people in a sustained way in this early period.

Where next?

Following the Westminster defeat in October 2008, there was a realization that AfC had to be proactive in raising awareness, to inform, educate and set the agenda ourselves. A positive determination grew which brought in new activists young and old, from different spheres: community development, politics, academics, policy, legal, student movement and trade unions. There was a recognition that AfC had to reach into new areas, build partnerships with those not traditionally associated with this type of struggle. The visibility of the organization grew through a myriad of activities such as stalls at trade union conferences, motions at trade union conferences, engagement with the student movement, embracing social media, circulation of pro-choice information, marching at May Day rallies, pub quizzes as fundraisers. All of these activities brought in new members as well as raising the profile of the campaign. There was also an understanding growing, that even if the 1967 Abortion Act was extended to NI, there would be resistance to setting up services, as evidenced in South Africa (Bloomer et al., 2018). Changing the law without cultural readiness would still mean barriers to access.

Educate, agitate and organize

At an AfC planning meeting in February 2009, four pillars were identified – legal, activism, lobbying and funding, in recognition of the need to frame our own discourse, based on a feminist analysis of the particular circumstances in NI; otherwise, the dominant moral religious views would remain unchallenged and statutory bodies and decision makers would not be held to account.

Legal pillar: Policy and research

After the 2008 amendment failed, we realized that our legal pillar would need to pivot to the international arena and to begin legal and policy education amongst the activists. We did the former by using UN human rights instruments (Cross O'Rourke Simpson, this volume). We did the latter by hosting seminars aimed at the public on the Department of Health guidelines on the termination of pregnancy and inviting expert speakers to events such as Breedagh Hughes (Royal College of Midwives), Audrey Simpson (FPA NI) Eileen Fegan (legal expert) and Wendy Savage (specialist in obstetrics).

AfC utilized activist expertise to submit responses to public consultations by government bodies and organized letter writing campaigns to maximize our voice and reach. There was no illusion that such actions would have an immediate impact, but it was the start of raising awareness amongst statutory officials and to establish AfC as the expert voice on abortion in NI. For example, AfC submitted a response to the Health and Social Care Board in 2011 when they were undertaking a review of health and social care services, to remind them that abortion was legal in particular circumstances: we also wrote to the new minister when justice was devolved to NI in 2010 reminding him of his responsibility under both CEDAW, the European Court of Human Rights judgements and the need to decriminalize abortion (23 August 2010). His eventual response was that this was not something that he as a justice minister could conclude upon individually (30 October 2010).

Taking forward the legal pillar, AfC partnered with NIWEP and the FPA NI in using the optional protocol under CEDAW to highlight the grave and systematic violations against women (Cross O'Rourke Simpson, this volume).

We were also conscious of the need to use the human rights instruments at our disposal as another lever to draw attention to the continued breaches of human rights of women in NI and during this time responded to a series of international consultations which are detailed elsewhere in this volume (Allamby, this volume; Rowan and Simpson, this volume).

The opening of the Marie Stopes International clinic in 2013 (Biernat and Johnston, volume 2) led to further lobbying and a spike in social media activity by AfC, specifically against attempts by anti-abortion politicians to restrict the clinic (Pierson, this volume). Further, as explored by Enright (this volume), active involvement in court cases was exemplified in NIHRC judicial reviews which ultimately led to the UK Supreme Court case. As intervenors, AfC centred the lived experience of the restrictive law and the Supreme Court drew heavily on the CEDAW investigation, which we had played a key role in.

During this period of AfC development, we recognized that our work must be informed by an evidence base; yet aware that little existed, we invested time in identifying gaps and sought to produce a robust evidence base to inform critique of policy and inform our work (e.g. Bloomer and O'Dowd, 2014; Bloomer et al., 2017). Bloomer also co-founded the Reproductive Health Law and Policy Advisory Group (RHLPAG), a joint initiative between academics interested in reproductive health and rights, alongside Dr Kathryn McNeilly (QUB) and Dr Claire Pierson (University of Liverpool). RHLPAG produced ten briefing papers during 2016–2021, targeted at policymakers, hosted workshops for MPs and MLAs and provided evidence to inquiries. As Campbell discusses in the following chapter the role of RHLPAG proved particularly useful when engaging with the SNP at Westminster on the issue of devolution.

Alongside conducting research we also attended international conferences to present our research and learn from others. At the conferences we met with leading activists and academics, exchanging ideas and building international solidarity. This energized us, reducing a sense of isolation and enabling an expanded discourse of reproductive justice and the significance of creating cultural readiness which needed to run in tandem with legislative change.

AfC activists with their particular set of research and policy skills used every opportunity and policy instrument and consultation to raise the issue locally, nationally and internationally to highlight the breaches of women's rights and to remind statutory bodies of their responsibilities to deliver abortion services for women and girls. It certainly felt for some of us that this type of activism would never bear fruit, as it felt so far removed from the activism of marching on the streets and engaging with the public. It certainly made the decision-makers sit up and take notice, to recognize us as serious players and not just a bunch of 'feminists with an agenda'.

While engaging with the establishment to counter their denial of abortion as an issue, the broader engagement with policy and legal instruments gave us the knowledge and confidence to break the silence on abortion and to begin to dismantle the religious and conservative views by enabling the voices of real women to be heard.

Activism pillar: Education, protests, pints and comedy

Taking forward the activism pillar, we identified awareness raising and education as proactive measures, in contrast to the reactive activities against anti-choice protests and stigmatizing media discourse. What had become apparent since

2008 was the need to challenge the silence and stigma, to open people's hearts and minds; one at a time if required. We knew we wanted to run our own race, rather than being led by the opposition.

While many trade unions were supportive and had provided occasional funding, we needed other sources of support, to develop training materials and pay a community facilitator. Until then our annual budget was circa £300, largely raised from fundraising activities such as pub quizzes. In 2009 we applied to the Joseph Rowntree Reform Trust (JRRT) for funds to develop a community education programme. Our aim was to raise awareness of existing abortion law amongst women with a view to breaking the silence on abortion and raising awareness of the impact that the existing law had on them and their lives. We were granted the funding and undertook a feasibility study identifying existing international good practice in relation to information on abortion, taking account of the highly restricted legislative framework and moral conservatism in NI. This informed the content of the programme.

We piloted the materials with four groups across NI. What became apparent from the pilot, delivered by Eileen Fegan a legal specialist, was that women who have never had a conversation about equality and discrimination, gender stereotyping, misogyny and patriarchy may not be ready to dive straight into conversations around a discriminatory law and practice that stops abortion access; one of the most taboo subjects on the island.

What we needed was a consciousness raising programme. We knew that in order to bring about cultural, social and legislative change on abortion, women must have not only the knowledge but confidence to speak about this issue authoritatively. We wanted women to be as angry as we were about this injustice and to challenge decisions made about their lives by healthcare professionals, politicians and local representatives. We wanted to instil the courage to break the silence and to dispel the myths propagated by churches, politicians and the media, that no-one supported abortion in NI.

Following an evaluation of the first pilot programme and with further financial help from JRRT, we developed Challenges and Choices; a Woman's Guide to the twenty-first century. This was a six-week programme designed to contextualize abortion as a key element in the struggle for women's liberation. The programme was delivered by Eileen Fegan and later Felice Kiel who were both excellent in tailoring the workshops to the needs of the different groups. From these workshops we could see the confidence and articulation of the participants increase. The length of the programme meant being able to get busy women for six weeks uninterrupted by school holidays or work or other commitments was difficult. Nevertheless, we persisted, and we ran the programme successfully with twelve groups over a three-year period (2012–15). The programme was delivered during three watershed moments in the fight for abortion rights in NI: the opening of the Marie Stopes Clinic in September 2012, the tragic death of Savita Halappanavar in October 2012 and the BBC coverage of Sarah Ewart's abortion journey in 2013.

By the time AfC launched the Trust Women campaign in 2015 (Gallen and Campbell, this volume) which made abortion a key issue in the 2016 NIA elections: we had created enough discourse in the local media, that the workshops evolved into one-off three-hour sessions tailored to the participants; women, community, trade union, LGBTQ+, student, political parties and youth groups. The silence around abortion had been shattered and the narrative had changed enough for the workshops to be condensed and tailored.

These new workshops explored abortion through values clarification exercises, imagining what circumstances women should be permitted to have an abortion, influenced by the discussions happening in the media and in real life. Participants also considered the disparities in the law with the rest of the UK and the world which led to an understanding of women's individual experiences and the impact on them and their families when they were denied healthcare.

As momentum grew it became apparent that volunteers representing AfC in public, on the weekly stall in Belfast, in media interviews, at trade union or other events, needed to understand and embody the AfC mission and values. This was a key point in terms of movement building, the organization was growing so quickly we needed to upskill new volunteers. Therefore, specific volunteer training was developed, 'Let's talk about abortion', was compulsory for AfC activists to attend and largely delivered by chairs O'Dowd and Campbell and one recently trained activist. The sessions covered the law, information on abortion pills and their safety, unacceptable language (racist, homophobic, sexist, sectarian, etc.), and finally how to handle difficult questions around abortion. This also allowed activists to choose roles suited to their comfort zones, which gave them agency, depending on their own preferences and strengths. 'Let's talk about abortion' grew exponentially as impetus around the Repeal the 8th Campaign in Ireland grew and AfC recruited more volunteers for solidarity canvassing. As a result, AfC had now fostered a dedicated team and opportunities for new and enthusiastic activists to develop as organizers.

AfC's collaboration with the Open University and the My Body My Life project enabled more workshops in women's community groups based on a booklet about experiences of abortion across the UK (Campbell, this volume). AfC member Ashleigh Topley also managed a NI version of the successful Irish,

In Her Shoes abortion stories project (Topley, this volume). As a result of AfC's community education programmes, consciousness raising occurred around how much more difficult the experience of accessing abortion was for women North and South, due to the legal and geographical barriers faced, and how the stigma for these women was more prominent and pervasive.

AfC also imagined creative ways of engaging with the wider public and to bring some joy into the campaign. Activism can feel lonely, fruitless and exhausting when relentlessly challenging the patriarchy in a morally conservative society, which is also emerging from forty years of conflict and trauma.

In 2011, AfC organized a small festival to highlight the absurdity of the 1861 Offences against the Persons Act being on the Statutes for 150 years. The series was titled the 'Carnival for Sexual Rights and Freedom; Pro-Choice, Pro-Sexuality'. Our collaboration of activists came from AfC, Belfast Feminist Network, the Rainbow Project, and Irish Congress of Trade Unions Youth Committee. Although it attracted a small but dedicated audience, it marked the beginning of ally building and of a new set of conversations around bodily autonomy with progressive activists working together for change. As a framework for working together we agreed on three fundamental principles:

> Sexual freedom is the fundamental human right of all individuals to develop and express their unique sexuality.
> The right to personal autonomy; to bodily integrity, sexual dignity, privacy and consensual sexual expression without societal or governmental interference, coercion or stigmatisation.
> The right to exercise sexual freedom and choice over the most intimate and personal aspects of our lives.

Ongoing collaboration with Reclaim the Agenda (RTA); the organizing committee for the International Women's Day Rally and programme of events from 2012 onwards included AfC and the issue of abortion through talks and events and centred the issue in the women's sector. RTA is a collective of feminists, women, trade union and youth activists and individuals which was independently resourced and therefore could be braver and bolder than the women's sector on the issues it chose to highlight. AfC organized countless talks, film nights, quizzes, exhibitions and karaoke events to raise funds, and bring together activists in joyous ways. In 2014 as part of the International Women's Day programme AfC presented 'Stand Up For Choice'; a comedy gig in the Mandela Hall hosted by local comedian Gemma Hutton and featuring progressive award-winning comedians Mark Thomas, Josie Long, Robin Ince and Bridget Christie.

Alongside this work, AfC were organizing protests within the public realm, about women across the island of Ireland who had been denied abortions. In the Republic of Ireland; the death of Savita Halappanavar in 2012 and the inhumane treatment of Ms Y in 2014. In NI AfC organized protests against the treatment of the mother charged with procuring abortion pills for her daughter (A and B Case), the 21-year-old arrested for accessing pills online, as well as counter protests against the loud anti-choice lobby. We knew that many other human rights violations existed, and the balance between a woman 'going public' with her story always had to be weighed against her right to a private life and not being thrown to the media wolves in this village we call NI. As activists we never asked anyone to disclose whether they had accessed abortion healthcare. After all, as a woman of childbearing age, we all could be 'Spartacus'; what we wanted was to create an environment where those who wished to disclose publicly could do so in a supported way when and if they were ready to do so.

During this time AfC efforts to promote safe self-abortion at home developed, recognizing the benefits of Early Medical Abortion (EMA) in light of the failure of the state to provide statutory access to abortion. Beginning with stickers promoting Women on Web (WOW), and later Women Help Women (WHW), AfC brought about awareness of EMA on toilet stall doors, public walls, lamposts and even buses. Initial efforts brought apprehension; could an activist caught with stickers be arrested under the new guidelines on the termination of pregnancy? Fortuitously, confidence grew as relationships with legal experts became stronger. AfC built key relationships with WOW and WHW, hosting workshops with their team and developing information campaigns about medical abortion (Yanow, Atay, volume 2). Volunteers were trained on EMA to provide support to those who may need it, a key part of this was ensuring clear messages via social media that the medication was safe and effective.

In 2016 our public support for the 21-year-old woman charged with committing an illegal abortion, resulting in her being given a suspended sentence, and a second case involving a mother procuring abortion pills for her teenage daughter, was embodied at first by public protests outside court. These cases had been preceded by two public letters, the first signed by over 120 activists in 2013 (McDonald, 2013) and the second by over 200 activists in 2015 (McDonald, 2015) stating that they had taken or had helped supply abortion medication. Such public letters mirrored those used elsewhere, for instance France in 1960s which served as a symbolically powerful method of public support for abortion (Bair, 1991). A year after the 2016 letter, the workplace of one activist and home of another were raided by the police on International Women's Day, searching for medication (Enright, this volume; McVicker Crickard, volume 2). These cases and public protests garnered global media attention which in turn pivoted the local Assembly and Westminster towards the issue.

The ability to create and amplify our own narrative came with the explosion of social media especially from 2010. Abortion was no longer held to ransom by lazy journalism espousing narratives that were factually incorrect and lagged behind public opinion. AfC no longer had to put up with anti-choice zealots of mainstream media to satisfy the idea of journalistic 'balance' which meant that if you had a pro-choice opinion, it must be balanced with the counter view. Our relationship with the local television station Northern Visions TV and monthly feminist programme Reclaim the Agenda allowed AfC to take up feminist space uninterrupted for thirty minutes to explore, contextualize, dispel myths and inform viewers about abortion. These could also be viewed on demand and posted to social media sites for others to access. Of course, social media comes with its drawbacks, but the positives certainly outweighed the negatives at this juncture in the campaign.

Lobbying

AfC responded to the NIHRC strategic plan in February 2013 asking them to prioritize reproductive rights and to comprehensively respond to systemic human rights abuses. AfC used international human rights frameworks as the basis of our key tasks, as it was the only policy lever available at that time.

The Department of Justice in 2015 consulted on the criminal law on abortion: lethal foetal abnormality and sexual crime. The public consultation, whilst within a justice and not a health framework, was a positive development for us as it was another avenue for further dialogue on abortion (Enright, this volume).

Through responding to consultations on the guidelines for health professionals over the years, AfC consistently argued that clear information was needed for women to understand when they could access legal abortion services. In addition AfC argued that the Department of Health should also consult directly with women, as well as pointing out the flagrant disregard to international human rights standards. AfC took the opportunity in the spring of 2013 on the publication of *The limited circumstances for a termination of pregnancy in Northern Ireland: A guidance document for health and social care professionals on law and clinical practice* to gather the views of women. We held three sessions in May and June 2013 and reached over seventy-five women. AfC invited departmental officials to give an overview of the guidelines, but no-one was able to attend; however, the overwhelming view from participants was disappointment with the failure of the duty of care by the Department of Health by refusing to provide abortion services and that the guidance reflected the language and opinions of the religious right, which had no place in public policy.

Funding pillar

Funding for abortion campaigning was particularly difficult to access during this period. Locally, no funding source was open to our work bar small amounts donated by Trade Unions, which was usually paid back in kind in the form of workshops or talks. Unite the Union were always at hand to provide support for one-off funding requests such as travel costs to attend international conferences. Outside of NI the lack of awareness of the dire situation about abortion, and a lack of awareness of NI being a different legal jurisdiction to Ireland, meant there was an uphill battle in getting funders to recognize the need. An extensive amount of time was spent on preparing funding applications and sourcing potential donors, but we had more failures than successes, which was disheartening. One funder who became consistently supportive was the Joseph Rowntree Reform Trust who continue to support the work of AfC to this day. Smaller pots of unrestricted funds were accessed by the advent of our Local Giving fundraising platform, which allowed for monthly donations as well as one-off crowdfunding campaigns, it also raised visibility around an issue and was often used for proactive fundraising or for projects otherwise hard to support financially. AfC also developed evolving ranges of branded merchandise which offered some unrestricted funds, this allowed supporters to show solidarity in a range of ways.

Challenges

Whilst reflecting back on what has been achieved it is important to consider specific challenges that had to be overcome, not least the aforementioned funding issue.

The ethos of AfC has remained the same throughout and has won many allies, in the early days however AfC were perceived as 'too radical' and felt used for pulling in crowds to events but not regarded as a valued partner. One potential partner in the Carnival for Sexual Rights and Freedom withdrew when we advised we would be partnering with the LGBTQ+ community as they did not want their core message on abortion diluted. Such judgement did not deter us.

Politicians, aside from those already publicly pro-choice, were often wary of engaging with AfC, even if they personally wanted to, as the pressure of a party line was immense, even to be seen at an academic event discussing abortion policy was too risky for those whose party policy was anti-abortion. Others needed to be educated about the reality of abortion, having spent little time considering it, beyond the stereotypical rhetoric of 'young, reckless girls needing abortions'. The powerful testimonies of women such as Sarah Ewart and Ashleigh Topley helped change this, combined with our campaigning based on robust evidence, indicating the policy flaws, the extent of abortion travel, and the stigma associated with abortion (McKay, this volume). Whilst Sarah Ewart and her mother conducted extensive lobbying to raise awareness, cynicism was evident amongst some. At one event a senior political figure asked, 'could we get other women to speak out as politicians were growing bored of hearing the Ewart story again and again'!

Conclusions

The multifaceted approaches that AfC developed during this period (2008–16) came from a deep analysis not only of what the problem was in terms of lack of access to abortion rights, but a sound theory of change. During this period we remained focused on what we wanted to achieve – legislative change and challenging abortion stigma. We remained proactive, we did not allow distractions to move us away from the end goal.

The ability and sheer talent within the ranks of AfC allowed us to challenge the hegemony on abortion through legal, policy, research, education, media, protest, movement building and socializing. The grit and determination of a bunch of 'pissed-off' feminists in AfC made the establishment sit up and listen, by amplifying the lived reality of abortion to the point where we could no longer be ignored.

In the early days of May Day Rallies and Pride parades, people looked puzzled or unimpressed as we passed. The cautious AfC banner, with its strapline 'our bodies, our lives, our right to decide' and our name, omitted abortion. The same cannot be said of the support ten years later as we marched through the streets of Belfast at the Processions March in 2018 (a UK-wide celebration of one hundred years of votes for women). We formed the largest and loudest section of the parade; the movement building had paid off. AfC were applauded throughout the route and our reception as we entered the grounds of Belfast City Hall was emotional, welcoming and amazing.

The retelling of this decade is dedicated to every woman who ever had to think about having 'to get the boat' who 'went to England' or who 'couldn't get to England'; to all who felt shamed or judged at the hands of the church and the state, and to those who helped make it a reality by raising their voices and used their skills in a time when it would have been much easier to just shut up and ignore it.

13

Reflections of an activist

Maria Amélia Ponte Lourenço

First a little background about myself, I was born in Angola to parents from Portugal and Angola. We became refugees following the 1975 civil war. I moved to live in Portugal and Madeira, and then to England in 1995. In 2010, as a single mother with two young children I moved to Northern Ireland (NI). Before I came here, I knew nothing about the Troubles (the thirty-year period of civil unrest and violence). I only knew of Mo Mowlam (who was previously the Secretary of State for NI and the first woman to have held the post) she was such a great inspiration. After I settled in NI, I met many other women who became role models, Baroness May Blood (the first woman and the first working-class person to be given a life peerage and seat in the House of Lords) did such great work that with women's groups, her and I might differ in our views on many things but how she went about her work was amazing, she was so feisty, her work like many others as a woman was not valued properly. Bernadette McAliskey (a civil rights leader and former politician) falls into that category too; she has achieved so much. For the abortion issue Anna Lo (politician and previous MLA) also stood out, not because she was from an ethnic minority background, I felt a connection with her as she had our cause at heart.

When I arrived in NI, I became more interested in politics of the land, I have always been involved in trade unions, so I brought that experience with me. I became involved in campaigns such as Love Equality advocating for equal marriage for the LGBTQ+ community. I was so shocked when I found out that abortion was illegal in almost all circumstances in NI. As a single parent in a new country, I felt I was less than third class, that I was voiceless as a woman, as a member of the ethnic minority community. I realized I didn't have control over my body, the government did. I was worried how I would have coped if I became pregnant, how I would have found the money to travel for an abortion.

Through a connection with Clare Bailey (now the leader of the Green Party NI), I attended training organized by AfC. The training was delivered by legal expert Eileen Fegan and from her I learnt so much about the context here and the work that needed done to raise awareness about the dire access to abortion. Over the coming months I became involved in AfC. I attended events, joined marches and rallies. I met so many wonderful people, all with this passion for change. At one of these events at Ulster University I met Mara Clarke from Abortion Support Network (ASN), and we became friends, along with Ann Rossiter. Ann is such a fascinating woman; she immediately made an impact on me, her passion for the cause, her personal story about having an abortion, how much she has achieved. Mara works so hard on ASN, I am in awe of her work.

As my sons grew, I talked to them about abortion and the restrictive law we had here. They came with me to marches, they have their own minds, and I don't expect them to think just like me, but they are aware and understand what the issues are.

When I look back on the last ten years I can see how much has changed – I remember travelling to Dublin with a handful of people to the annual March for Choice, there were maybe a few hundred attending. In years that followed we would have had bigger numbers from Belfast travelling and the last march I was at there were thousands at it.

It has been wonderful to see the younger activists come on board; their energy is infectious. They are throwing off the oppression that we have been forced to live with.

Social media has been a real game changer. Through it we have met activists from around the world, shared our stories and learnt from each other.

For myself, in my own little way I am proud that I empowered others in the ethnic minority communities to reflect on the abortion issue – for them to think 'this could be me'. They have had the courage to say – 'can you help me' and if I have been able to alleviate the pain of one of my sisters then the pain has been worthwhile.

For me the main challenges have been making sure we as activists were safe. We have been verbally attacked at rallies, and once I came very close to physical harm. This is the price we had to pay. There are many problems in this society, I am a Health and Social Care Work sector employee, working with disabled children. I see the suffering the children and parents go through. I see how many children with disabilities are put in care. So many women are judged, as single parents, as ethnic minorities, we get labelled – I have raised two beautiful boys as a single parent living in NI. I am proud of that achievement.

My own mum had post-natal depression; the family tried to get her treatment, but this was in a context too of other family members using the words 'loony' to describe people with mental health problems. We still have a long way to go to understand how to deal with these issues and recognize that they all are interlinked. My mum died from suicide when I was nine, so for me this is personal issue too, the fight for access to abortion is part of wider issues that we need to address, to remove inequality in our society.

In summing up I would say the last two years have been emotional. I never once imagined we would be where we are now that we have decriminalization.

I remember that exact moment when I found out that Stella Creasy (MP) had brought about the legal change – it was amazing, to be part of the movement that helped bring about change. That day I had just finished a long shift at work. I went home alone, and I wished I could join all the activists in Belfast marking the occasion. A friend called around, we had a drink and then went to an old pub in Bangor; we ended up talking to the bar man about abortion, that was amazing, prior to that he would not have talked about abortion but here we were – we were all able to talk about it, without being afraid of being judged and attacked – that was so symbolic. I cried.

We need to pass on the message – if you feel something is wrong in society; you can step up, even it is not directly affecting you, you can bring about change. The journey can be tough, you need to know how to deal with setbacks; the highs and lows of activism; negotiating all of that is part of the journey. I have done my part and helped others. I have made so many wonderful friends, I have helped bring others in. I am so glad to have been part of the fight for changing abortion law in NI.

14

In Her Shoes – Abortion stories

Ashleigh Topley

In early 2014, I was denied an abortion. I was pregnant with my first baby, a girl, and at my twenty-week scan my husband and I were told that she had a fatal foetal abnormality and would die before or soon after she was born. Despite this, and because of the abortion law that governed at the time, my request for an abortion was denied, and I was forced to remain pregnant until my pregnancy naturally came to an end. It took fifteen agonizing weeks for that to happen and eventually my daughter Katy was stillborn when I was thirty-five weeks pregnant.

I became involved in activism a few months after I lost Katy. While I was still pregnant, I came across a video on YouTube of an interview with Dr Fiona Bloomer. I emailed Dr Bloomer, I explained my situation and asked her how I could get involved to support the campaign. She told me about AfC and suggested I come to a meeting later in the year. In August of 2014 I went to my first AfC meeting in Belfast. I was totally out of my comfort zone and awestruck by these activists who seemed so knowledgeable and passionate.

In December that year, I had heard about how the Northern Ireland Human Rights Commission were taking a judicial review (Allamby, this volume). I decided to apply to be an intervenor and wrote out my statement of evidence. At that stage I had never spoken publicly about my experience, so I asked my solicitor for assurances that I could remain anonymous. My husband and I were terrified by what could happen if our identities became known, as we were still in the early stages of our grief and we felt that there was a stigma that we had even considered having an abortion. Furthermore, we were frightened of any hassle from the anti-choice groups. I was accepted as an intervenor and the case was scheduled at the High Court in Belfast for June 2015. The case progressed through the courts and culminated at the Supreme Court in June 2018.

The final day of the three-day hearing in the High Court was the first time I shared my story in public. I gave approval to my real name being used rather than just my initials. I remember feeling sick with nerves but also immensely proud when the barrister spoke my name in court. Over the years that have followed I have been able to tell my story many times on various platforms, and each time I speak out it does get easier; however, I will never forget how nervous I was that very first time.

I believe that the sharing of our lived experiences is incredibly powerful and truly demonstrates the impact that the lack of abortion access had on so many of us in Northern Ireland. A first-hand account of what someone has gone through brings to life how awful it is and spells out things to the audience that they may never have considered. I have a deep understanding of how difficult it can be to speak out and share your story, even anonymously, so when the opportunity presented itself to get involved in In Her Shoes Northern Ireland I jumped at the chance.

In Her Shoes Northern Ireland

In Her Shoes Northern Ireland is the sister page to the In Her Shoes – Women of the Eighth Facebook page that was created by Erin Darcy in the run up to the 2018 referendum for the Repeal of the Eighth Amendment to the Constitution of Ireland, which had created an almost complete ban on abortion. The page anonymously shared private stories of the real and devastating impact of the Eighth Amendment and allowed undecided voters to place themselves in the shoes of the storytellers. By the time Ireland historically voted Yes to Repeal on 25 May 2018, the page had gathered over 100,000 followers and has since been credited with encouraging a national conversation on human rights that would change Ireland forever.

After watching the impact that In Her Shoes – Women of the Eighth had on both the successful campaign and opening up the conversation surrounding abortion, it was thought a page specifically for NI could have similar success. Erin worked with us to set up the page, gave us a crash course in how she ran the original page and then handed the reins over to us. In Her Shoes Northern Ireland launched on Facebook in January 2019 and now has over 8000 followers. We have also expanded to Twitter and Instagram and are growing our followers there.

I became involved in the administration of the page shortly before it launched. In January 2019 I was in Derry speaking to the Westminster Women and Equalities Committee for their inquiry into abortion. I was chatting to one of the other attendees who asked me if I would be interested in joining the WhatsApp group for the page. I agreed and discovered that the page was to be launched imminently which meant I had a lot to learn about managing a Facebook page and not much time to learn it.

In order to launch the page, we used stories specifically from people from NI that had been submitted to the My Body My Life exhibition and the Women and Equalities Committee Inquiry, with permission. Posting the very first story was nerve-wracking, and my heart was beating like a drum when I clicked the button to share it.

27 January 2019

I had been on the pill since after the birth of my sixth child.

We had already decided not to have any more children and my husband was considering a vasectomy when I became pregnant again. He had just become unemployed.

Our youngest was 10 months old and we were really struggling financially. We discussed our options and agreed we could not afford to have another child.

I went to my GP who told me that abortion was illegal in Northern Ireland so I could not have one.

The GP did not give me any information or offer to refer me to another doctor. He said he would book me into maternity services.

I was stunned.

We looked on the internet and rang a clinic in England. We were told the procedure would cost £600 and we would have to pay for our own flights and accommodation on top of that. When we checked flights, the cost went up to over £1000. There was no way we could afford that.

Even if I travelled by myself, we could still not afford it. The most we could scrape together was £200.

We did not know what to do, so we rang the clinic again and explained our circumstances. Then the clinic suggested we contact a support organisation which provided some support, but we still had to wait another two weeks and sell some items of furniture and some of our children's toys to get the rest of the money.

I travelled alone to England and came back the same day contrary to the advice of the doctor at the clinic because I couldn't afford the overnight stay. I had wanted to have my abortion in Northern Ireland, with my husband at my side, in a local hospital, without having to sell my children's toys to pay for the operation.

We were unsure what the response to the story would be, so we were poised and ready to moderate any comments. However, we shouldn't have worried because almost immediately the likes, comments and shares started mounting up. It was thrilling, and emotional, to watch. As more and more people interacted with that first post, the page follower count started to rise.

Two days after publishing the first story, the page received a new story through messenger. It was an emotional moment. I felt a strange mixture of emotions; I was saddened and angry that yet another person had been forced to suffer an unnecessary trauma, but I also felt incredibly honoured to be trusted to be their voice and to tell the world their story. In their account, the submitter wrote:

> The only person I could confide in for years was my best friend who was my rock through everything. My own mum still doesn't know, she kept saying at least you didn't have kids with him, or you would have been tied to him for life, I felt a pang every time she said that. I know it was the right decision for me, but I still feel I can't tell even my family for fear of being judged. My partner now knows everything and was amazing. He is so kind and supportive and we are very happy with a child of our own now. I feel it's about time I shared my story as so many women here in Northern Ireland have been through similar things.

As more stories were posted, more emails came through. Many emails and messages shared the sentiment that the submitters had kept their experience a secret because of the stigma they felt from society:

> To this day, they don't know, neither do my friends. I know they would all judge me. It's my deepest, darkest secret and it haunts me that one day it will come out and all because we were taught that abortion was bad.
>
> It's a horrible secret I keep to myself, I have no guilt, but I fear that society would be ashamed of me for not having that guilt.

Others said that they had read someone else's story and had a similar experience and they wanted to now share their own story:

> I feel the same as that story. I don't know who I can tell that I had an abortion last summer.
>
> Feels good to get that out. Thank you for what you're doing. I read a similar experience on your page this morning and that gave me the courage to share. Thank you, x.

Something that has been heart-warming is when people comment on the stories they write as if they are speaking directly to the person who has written the story.

> Thank you for sharing your story. There is no shame in what you did. You were brave and strong enough to make the best and right decision for you.

Thank you for sharing, you don't have to feel shame, we are so conditioned to it. I'm so sorry you had to travel alone and hope that life has moved on well for you. Best wishes.

I'm sorry you found yourself in that heart-breaking and tragic situation, and that you've had to endure the stigma surrounding abortion in NI. But I am very glad you found the help you needed and were able to graduate with flying colours as a result. People need to wake up and realise the impact of an unwanted pregnancy on a young person's life. 'Pro-life' is such a lie.

Overall, the comments have been supportive and positive. The moderating team are always on standby when a new story is posted so that we can monitor the comments, but we have rarely had to step in and act.

The sharing of lived experiences is so powerful because reading someone's story written in their words paints crystal-clear pictures of the people who need and have abortions. When people read the stories, they can easily imagine the type of person that the submitter could be, and they realize the words they are reading could be the words of their friend, colleague, sibling or parent. The stories can, and have, started conversations, be that between friends, at work, round the family dinner table and as a result the accounts of these real-life lived experiences have been able to challenge some people's preconceived notions of abortion seekers. The stories have also demonstrated the many different reasons why someone may need to have an abortion and once again have contributed to minimizing the stigma that has been attached to abortion for far too long.

In the run up to decriminalization, there was even more focus on challenging and erasing the stigma and shame that has traditionally been tied to accessing an abortion in Northern Ireland. The stories that were shared on In Her Shoes Northern Ireland laid bare the trauma and suffering that people have had to endure and really brought home just how awful it has been for people who have been denied or had to travel to have an abortion. The stories are not dramatized or embellished and are rarely even edited, so this gives a true sense of who the submitter is from the language they use and their writing style.

As 21 October 2019 drew closer and the topic of abortion gained more news coverage and became more prominent on social media, the posts gathered more traction than ever before. In Her Shoes Northern Ireland made it simple for people to show their support for decriminalization because they were able to interact with and share the stories on their own Facebook page. This allowed people who may not have been comfortable discussing abortion in public to show their support for the campaign virtually.

After decriminalization, several stories came in outlining that the submitter only felt comfortable sharing now they knew they were no longer able to be prosecuted.

The email exchange below happened between 21 and 24 October 2019 and really made it clear just how important a resource In Her Shoes Northern Ireland is not only for the campaign for decriminalization but as a support system for those who have been made to suffer from the lack of provision.

From: EE
Sent: 21 October 2019 18:36
To: In Her Shoes NI <ihsnorth@gmail.com>
Subject: Story

Hi,

I have a story to share, but my story involves me having an abortion not legally with pills purchased on the internet, I'm not sure where it stands if it's safe for me to share my story with your page or if I can be prosecuted for sharing it

Thanks for taking the time to do what you do, it's helped to know I wasn't alone when going through what I did.

From: In Her Shoes NI <ihsnorth@gmail.com>
Sent: 21 October 2019 23:10
To: EE
Subject: Re: Story

Hi,

I see you have emailed through your story now so I will take a read of it. As I'm sure you know abortion has now been decriminalised (!!!) so there is absolutely no risk of any prosecutions. Even had it not been decriminalised, all of the stories I receive are kept strictly confidential and anonymised.
Best wishes,
Ashleigh x

From: EE
Sent: 21 October 2019 23:22
To: In Her Shoes NI <ihsnorth@gmail.com>
Subject: Re: Story

Thank you so much!

Such a wonderful thing to see happen in our lifetime!

X

From: EE
Sent: 22 October 2019 10:00
To: In Her Shoes NI <ihsnorth@gmail.com>
Subject: Changed my mind

Hi Ashleigh, I think I've changed my mind about my story being shared. I've read enough opinions on Facebook the last few days to last me a lifetime don't think I can handle them on my own story. Thank you for taking the time to read it xx

From: In Her Shoes NI <ihsnorth@gmail.com>
Sent: 22 October 2019 10.03
To: EE
Subject: Re: Changed my mind

Oh EE, Facebook is going to be tough for a while. But just know that you are not alone, you are one of so many who have suffered. You have done nothing wrong and have nothing to feel ashamed about. There is absolutely no pressure to share your story, but you might actually find it helpful, the comments we get on the stories are always incredibly positive and supportive.
Sending you so much love,
Ashleigh xx

From: In Her Shoes NI <ihsnorth@gmail.com>
Sent: 22 October 2019 10.10
To: EE
Subject: Re: Changed my mind

And I've just now read your story. It is incredibly powerful, and I think it is a really important one to share if you feel able.
But I will do nothing without your permission.
You write so well and have covered so many issues.
Look after yourself,
Ashleigh xx

From: EE
Sent: 22 October 2019 16:21
To: In Her Shoes NI <ihsnorth@gmail.com>
Subject: Re: Changed my mind

Hi Ashleigh,

Thank you for your kind words, I think you're right and would like you to share my story.
Thank you so much
Xx

From: In Her Shoes NI <ihsnorth@gmail.com>
Sent: 22 October 2019 16:23
To: EE
Subject: Re: Changed my mind

EE,

There is absolutely no pressure to at all.
Yours is so well written that I would love to share it tonight though if you feel that would be too much I can hold off until you give me the go ahead.
I can empathise with how hard it can be to put yourself out there.
Ashleigh xx

From: EE
Sent: 22 October 2019 16:28
To: In Her Shoes NI <ihsnorth@gmail.com>
Subject: Re: Changed my mind

No, you're right I'm ready, the last couple of days will have been so hard for others who have gone through what I have, I hope they can take comfort in that they are not alone. Will keep an eye out for it.
Thank you xx

In Her Shoes – Northern Ireland

Published by Ashleigh Topley 22 October 2019 19:00

The discussions around abortion in Northern Ireland have always been turbulent, however in the past year and a half this has been even more so due the referendum in the ROI. As a result of this, it has made what was already an incredibly difficult time for me, significantly harder. I had to repeatedly read comments that I was a 'murderer' from Facebook friends or listen to debates in work or social circles that I'd killed my baby. Obviously, none of these people were aware of what I had done, or the torment I was going through, but each comment or remark chipped away at my soul until I felt as though there was nothing left.

In April of 2018 at the age of 27, I discovered I was pregnant. After suffering from severe endometriosis my entire adult life, no one was more surprised than me. I had made my peace long before this that I was unlikely to bear my own children even though I so longed to be a mother.

Upon finding out I was pregnant, I was filled with a mix of emotions and confided in my closest friends. Their support was paramount to my survival and for the very turbulent months to come.

You see, I'm not your typical story. I had always longed to be a mother and didn't think it would ever happen for me, I was progressing in my career and owned my own home. But deep down, I knew this was not the right time. The father of my baby was not someone I was in a relationship with, nor someone I wanted to raise a child with. I couldn't face the idea of being a single mother and I wasn't emotionally ready for the impact having a baby would have on my life. Falling pregnant had been an accident, and one I would carry with me forever.

So, I had a choice to make. A choice I agonised over and making this choice I knew that I could be giving up something I had always wanted that may never happen again. Single-handedly the most difficult decision I have ever had to make and likely ever will make and certainly not one that was taken lightly.

At this point in my life taking time off work to travel to England was not an option, I was working in a very fast paced career, working 12-hour days and my decision window was closing in and a few months prior to this spending all my savings on my new home I didn't have the money to travel.

At this point I had spoken to someone who had pointed me in the direction of a women's rights charity overseas who would mail me the medication to complete my abortion at home. I knew it was illegal and that if I was caught, I was facing prison. Prison, over the agonising decision I made to have the right to decide what to do with my own body.

I was desperate at this stage, so I ordered the medication. It took roughly two weeks to arrive, and once in my possession at 8 weeks pregnant, I had an illegal abortion in my home. Without access to the medical care, support or safety provided to other members of the United Kingdom, purely because I was from Northern Ireland and in Northern Ireland at this time, we did not hold the rights to choose over our own bodies. Forced to be ashamed and alone, putting my health at risk in secret.

I wasn't sure what would come next, or what to expect but I can assure you that the events that followed were nothing like what I had anticipated. Having suffered from endometriosis I have endured significant pain throughout my life, and heavy bleeding, but this was nothing I had ever experienced. The bleeding and clotting were constant, the pain was enough to make me violently vomit for hours on end. After around four hours of excruciating pain, there was a break. A window of relief which led me to naively believe it was over. The break was short lived, and what followed was the worst moment of my life to date. I felt a sudden movement as if my insides were falling out, I stood up, raced to the bathroom and what felt like the entire tissue of my womb fell from my body and I knew that that was it. The torment and anguish I felt in that moment will never leave me, the immediate overwhelming rush of emotions, feelings of guilt and regret that I now know after time with a counsellor is completely normal.

In the days and months that followed I quite rapidly spiralled, my mental health deteriorating. I cried constantly, unable to get out of bed, jeopardising my career and friendships. I was constantly angry, internalising my guilt and acting out completely isolating myself until I decided that I wanted to kill myself. In my eyes I did not deserve to live. I obsessively read the comments on the news articles on the referendum over and over again and convinced myself that I was a monster and a murderer. Letting strangers' comments define me and allowing their words to speak to the inner hatred I already had for myself intensifying the desire I had to end my life. I was worthless, after all I'd killed my baby, they told me. Should've kept my legs closed, there's adoption you know? Slut, using abortion as birth control. These comments cried out to the downward spiral I was on as I was nearing the bottom, the bottom being where my life would end.

I returned to work, almost euphoric knowing that it was all to be over soon. Just another troubled girl who took her own life they would say. When in reality, a young girl who was in dire need of accessible support and healthcare after going through a very traumatic experience.

One morning on the walk to work, I thought about the letters I would leave my family and friends later that night and what I would say, and, in that moment, something changed. A moment of clarity amongst the grief, that I had friends and family, people who loved me who didn't deserve what I was contemplating doing and the effects it would have on them. I wasn't just ending my own grief; I was creating theirs.

So, from this point on my journey of recovery began. The grief, guilt and self-hatred subsided over time paving the way for acceptance that I had made a choice, the right choice for me at that point in my life. I learned that all the emotions and feelings that I had felt after my abortion were normal. Had I had access to the relevant support offered in the Mainland UK, Doctors and Nurses to put me at ease and discuss with me what would happen, I firmly believe that I wouldn't have come so close to ending my life. Instead, I felt like a criminal, ashamed and alone.

Today is 21st October 2019, today is the day that as of midnight tonight abortion is legalised in Northern Ireland. Women will have the accessible, safe and free right to choose. I understand that there are people who have very strong opinions on abortion, but if you take anything from my story, please remember that you may have friends or colleagues who are going through or have been through a story just like mine, and you don't know how your comments may trigger them.

Abortion legalisation is about the right to choose. You have the right to choose not to have one just like I deserved the right to choose mine.

—

#NotACriminal
#NoShame
#AbortionRightsNI
#TheNorthIsTODAY

If you would like to anonymously share your experience, please email ihsnorth@gmail.com or message this page. Your story will be treated with the utmost respect and your personal information will be kept confidential.

A selection of comments:

This was a very very tough read, I'm so sorry you were failed by a flawed system. What makes this worse is that these very people who are pro-life are hypocritically sharing mental health status' in the month of October do not for once consider every aspect of mental health. Whoever you are I thank you for bravely sharing your story. I hope that no girl/woman will ever have to endure the suffering you have. I wish you well on your path to recovery ♡

You're a brave and strong woman. Your story is inspiring yet tells of the horrors you have survived. I salute you and support you. Choice is one of the things that makes people free.

Tremendous personal story, courage, loss, recovery and survival, thank goodness you've come out the other side now. Best wishes to you and all grateful today for prioritising actual women's lives.

From: In Her Shoes NI <ihsnorth@gmail.com>
Sent: 24 October 2019 14:35
To: EE
Subject: Re: Changed my mind

Hi EE,

I hope you don't mind me getting back in touch!
I was just wondering how you feel having shared your story? I hope you have seen how supportive the comments are.
Best wishes,
Ashleigh x

From: EE
Sent: 24 October 2019 21:04
To: In Her Shoes NI <ihsnorth@gmail.com>
Subject: Re: Changed my mind

Hey Ashleigh

Not at all I really appreciate it, thank you so much! I feel like a weight has been lifted off my shoulders, honestly you were completely right it really helped to share my story and not to feel alone.
What you guys do is amazing. You've helped so many people including myself, thank you again for the support xx

From: In Her Shoes NI <ihsnorth@gmail.com>
Sent: 24 October 2019 21:08
To: EE
Subject: Re: Changed my mind

EE,

I am so glad it has helped you, that's why we do what we do. And your lovely message has made my evening.
I'm delighted for you!
Thank you again for sharing, it takes a lot of courage.
Much love,
Ashleigh x

It is not only an honour to be able to be the public voice for these stories, but it is also an added pleasure to have been able to support people who have suffered from the lack of access and lived with their secret shame for many years. In Her Shoes Northern Ireland is one of my proudest achievements and I hope to see it continue to grow in order to support others while eliminating shame and stigma once and for all.

15

What sort of state were we in? Alliance for Choice tackle Westminster

Emma Campbell

This chapter delves into the balancing act that AfC undertook as part of a coalition for Northern Ireland (NI) decriminalization in Westminster and as the representative voice of at least 70,000 abortion seekers who were exiled or criminalized up until 21 October 2019. It will highlight key partners and political touchstones in Parliament, but it will also detail the difficult conversations around lobbying the British political establishment who had intentionally ignored the problem for decades (Thomson this volume).

Along with the Women's sector, Trade Unions and grassroots organizations in NI, AfC facilitated the cooperation of civil society to lobby Westminster, in addition to ongoing work which encompassed protests, art auctions, community education work, global solidarity work, activist recruitment and training, abortion pills destigmatization, social media campaigns, direct provision of pills and one-on-one abortion advice. It's difficult to encompass everything AfC took on board, but few approaches were ignored,

> … taking an active role in legal challenges before the Northern Ireland courts, organising and leading consultation sessions on draft guidelines for medical professionals, engaging with political parties to help inform and educate party members on the restrictive law and its impact, engaging with the public through efforts such as information stalls and media appearances, and engaging with faith organisations.
>
> (Bloomer et al., 2020, p. 3)

The specific nuances of an unstable post-conflict NI grappling with abortion as a human rights issue necessitated the CEDAW abortion inquiry (Cross O'Rourke Simpson, this volume). AfC often commented that 'England's difficulty was our opportunity' (Campbell, 2019), referencing the (post)colonial barriers strewn through the path to abortion decriminalization for NI. We understood quickly that the perfect storm of Brexit, a power-sharing collapse in Stormont and the Repeal the 8th Abortion Campaign in Ireland was the gift we needed. The pivotal role of AfC ensured the lived experiences of abortion seekers were centred and responsibility for traumatic experiences lay with state lawmakers. This chapter offers the perspective of one AfC co-convenor on the momentous change of 21 October 2019.

> It's almost as if certain fundamentalists in Ulster believe that if they keep saying NO they can undo a thing. Undo homosexuality, undo abortions … as if NO is enough of a response, sure say no more.
>
> (Campbell, 2018)

Why Westminster?

The focus on Westminster for change in the abortion law in NI was a significant gearshift for AfC since their devastating disappointment with a Labour Government in 2008 and resulting concentration on the local Assembly (Thomson this volume; O'Dowd Cross Bloomer, this volume). It required careful negotiation within their own membership, with wider communities in NI and with their allies. The Stormont collapse in early 2017 and record-breaking lack of government for three years were a national disgrace and an international embarrassment. This was also during the 2016 UK-wide Brexit Referendum, which despite the Remain vote in NI being the majority with 55.8 per cent, it found itself tethered to an unusually intent England on beguiling NI to the power of the Union (McCann and Hainsworth, 2016). NI continually failed to meet minimum international human rights standards on abortion, and the UN had been highly critical of the refusal of the UK Government to amend abortion law in NI (Allamby and Cross O'Rourke Simpson, this volume). Although intense, the political campaigning was never at the expense of other direct grassroots work, which continued all the while,

> Activists were doing many things at once, often across many different institutional, political, and community environments, and recognising that different dispositions towards law are required and appropriate in different settings. They might be drafting legislative amendments in one environment and distributing 'illegal' (but safe) abortion medication in another.
>
> (Enright, McNeilly and de Londras, 2020, p. 9)

After the May 2016 Northern Ireland Assembly (NIA) elections, AfC undertook private meetings with most of the political parties in the Stormont Assembly to explore the establishment of an all-party group on abortion law reform. AfC reached out to all political parties; all bar the DUP and TUV responded and met with AfC and brokered relationships that are still maintained today. These political discussions were about to bear fruit, with a cross-section of the political spectrum ready to support the all-party group, including members of Sinn Féin and the UUP, just as the NI Executive collapsed. The implosion was a result of the Deputy First Minister Martin McGuinness's resignation precipitated by several scandals (NAMA, RHI Heating scandal, removal of funding for an Irish language group) which had dogged the NIA (Al-Othman, 2018).

Following the May 2016 election, almost a year of talks failed to produce adequate cross-party agreement on several major issues, this resulted in another snap Assembly election being called in March 2017. This left the Unionist parties no longer commanding a majority in the NIA, this DUP loss of MLAs meant they no longer had the power to issue a petition of concern, which had been used repeatedly to stop reform of both abortion and same-sex marriage (Pierson, this volume). Matthews and Pow (2017) outline the parties' positions after the significant 2016 election, where the AfC 'Trust Women' campaign (O'Dowd Cross Bloomer, this volume) made inroads into influencing the language around abortion. The DUP along with the SDLP did establish a working group to review abortion on grounds of fatal foetal abnormalities (FFA) and sexual crimes. No recommendations have, to date, been implemented. 'Sinn Féin and Alliance supported an extension of abortion availability on grounds of rape, incest and FFA. The Ulster Unionists defined both [abortion and same sex marriage] matters as issues of conscience, thus refusing to adopt an official position' (Matthews and Pow, 2017, p.313).

The Westminster election result on 12 June 2017 saw al NI's middle-ground MP's (UUP, SDLP) lose their seats, additionally Teresa May's flimsy majority left the Conservatives in need of support from NI's DUP. This had ramifications not just for UK politics but destabilizing the negotiations for a power-sharing executive in Stormont. As the DUP settled into Westminster and Sinn Féin focused on joining a coalition government in the Republic, the motivation for the NIA to be functional rapidly lost momentum.

The Conservatives/DUP coalition led to much bemoaning of the DUP 'dinosaurs' by commentators in the English press. Few had paid any attention to their political manoeuvring up to 2017, only as the dangerous potential of the DUP's fundamentalist attitudes might impact on English people, did any concern arise: the abuses of DUP power were fine if they only affected NI.

> That the DUP will be calling the shots – even if the Tories win a majority – augurs very badly indeed for power-sharing talks at Stormont (but well for a Brexit deal that incorporates a fudge on the Irish border).
>
> (Maguire, 2017, p. 1)

However, this did galvanize both the Voice for Choice group to include NI more actively in their ongoing lobbying and London Irish Abortion Rights Campaign (LIARC) had a much greater political opportunity to exert pressure on the UK government (Sanquest, volume 2). (Voice for Choice is a national coalition of organizations working alongside the All Party Parliamentary Pro-Choice and Sexual Health Group in Westminster that campaigns on abortion.)

The Stormont collapse in January 2017 happened nine months after the arrest of a young woman found guilty of accessing pills online for a home abortion in April 2016 (McDonald, 2016b; O'Dowd Cross Bloomer, this volume). AfC rallied outside the High Court in Belfast and saw solidarity rallies across Ireland (Brennan, 2016). It was clear that NI did not want women and pregnant people prosecuted for having abortions, and this arrest made the reality of criminalization all too clear. The public outcry was pivotal for AfC (Cahill, 2015). Previously the public discourse had been limited to cases of FFA and Rape only (O'Dowd Cross Bloomer, this volume) in a hierarchy of abortions, yet from the arrest of an unlucky few, the calls for 'free, safe and legal' abortion (Lazare, 2017) were becoming amplified by previously quiet members of the public. One AfC member and Rally for Choice founder Suzanne Lee was interviewed at the protest, Suzanne, 'who took the pills in August 2012 during her third year at university, said: 'Either you arrest me and charge me, or you change this law' (McDonald, 2016a, p. 1). This sentiment was mirrored by over 200 AfC activists who signed a letter stating they had all either bought or helped buy the pills, and if one woman was arrested, each signatory should also be arrested (Campbell, 2016).

The election campaign just prior to the collapse of Stormont was one where members of almost all parties, bar the DUP, were calling for 'mercy' regarding the arrests of those charged under the OAPA regarding use of abortion medication (O'Dowd Cross Bloomer, this volume). AfC members were invited to speak about the arrests at a live television husting. Afterwards, one MLA discussed, off-camera, how the issue needed more thought and cited European examples where decriminalization was until ten/twelve weeks. This and countless more off-the-record conversations with local politicians helped AfC sense the changing tides, especially from previously 'pro-life' people. Despite this, Stormont failed to pass a motion on abortion just prior to their collapse (Thomson this volume); even this small vestige of hope and narrow relaxation of FFA law was vanquished (Bailie, 2018). AfC, including campaigners and directly affected women, were heartbroken, yet everyone continued to push for change, little did they know what the coming three-and-a-half years would bring.

Beyond Stormont

AfC had several meetings with civil society groups in NI between 2014 and 2016 (O'Dowd Cross Bloomer, this volume). We also engaged with a few supportive political parties, or individuals who were personally supportive, such as People Before Profit's Gerry Carroll and Fiona Ferguson, some Alliance Party members, some Sinn Féin members, most notably Carál Ní Chuilín, Megan Fearon and Mary Ellen Campbell, the Green Party of Northern Ireland, most notably Clare Bailey, members of the Ulster Unionist Party including Doug Beattie and Sophie Long of the Progressive Unionist Party. AfC has had to regroup after a crisis before (O'Dowd Cross Bloomer and Thomson this volume), so were mentally and structurally prepared for a pivot in approach. Therefore, they begun useful discussions even before the collapse about what the potential could be for both LGBTQ+ rights and abortion rights if suddenly NI had to look to Westminster. AfC were not acting alone, the advent of exponential engagement in our online abortion activism allowed for expansive, strategic thinking around abortion that moved beyond national borders,

> The potential to engage in solidarity actions globally, the potential for telemedicine to provide direct help to women who need access to abortion while living under restrictive regimes, the ability to connect with those who may not feel comfortable making their activism public, the space to share successful strategies and knowledge, and most importantly, the space to share abortion stories and experiences.
>
> (Bloomer, 2020, p. 89)

AfC had also been periodically sending shadow reports to CEDAW (Cross O'Rourke Simpson, this volume) on the continued denial of abortion rights to women and pregnant people in NI, and laying the responsibility for those rights, directly at the door of British government. Westminster continues to be the state party responsible for upholding human rights in NI, if we remain a part of the UK, even with a devolved government. However, this was and remains a complex argument for public discourse, and hard to navigate considering the sensitivities around national identity and sovereignty in NI. As a contested state with an immature democracy, NI is governed using principles of consociation, with the power-sharing, cross-community, proportional representation system constructed with the aim of greater minority view representation, to protect against discriminations. Instead, the outcome is two opposed ethno-national groups that fiercely protect their opposing Irish and British identities, often to the detriment of social justice issues (Bloomer et al., 2020; Enright, this volume). However, AfC's continued reporting to CEDAW along with NIWEP had built up an awareness amongst the community, the politicians and the media, of the UK's failures to uphold our rights despite the longstanding refusal of movement from the Stormont Assembly.

Right around the brink of the Stormont collapse, AfC, FPA NI and NIWEP's request for a CEDAW inquiry into abortion in NI had been granted. By that September we coordinated the list of who CEDAW should speak to including women directly impacted by the lacuna in provision. Due to ongoing relationships with several women who had linked into previous AfC work, such as the Abortion Diary Podcast, art projects, our court cases and more, AfC facilitated thirteen women, including Ashleigh Topley and Sarah Ewart, to give their personal testimony to the investigators when they came. The Special rapporteurs were incredibly moved by the witness statements and were incredulous at the callous treatment of pregnant people. Fast-forward to February 2018, just as the Supreme Court was to pass judgement on the landmark case including Ashleigh Topley, Sarah Ewart and Denise Phelan, CEDAW published its damning report (UNCEDAW, 2018).

NI has a difficult relationship with Human Rights bodies especially when it comes to women (Galligan, 2013), but the significance of the CEDAW report cannot be overstated, given it would become the fabric of the legislation passed on abortion NI in 2019.

A jurisdictional journey

In 2017, the London Irish Abortion Rights Campaign formed. From their very formation they included a sub-group on NI contacting AfC before they were formed to ensure the name would not be considered exclusive for any NI activists as it did not specify NI. From that inception, the NI situation on abortion was a key tenet. Their main goal was of course the Repeal of the 8th Amendment in Ireland, and as members of the Irish diaspora in London, they were building on huge community support which they passed on to us and the Abortion Rights Campaign (ARC) in Ireland.

Two points of note: firstly, Diana Johnson, MP for Hull, had been working on a decriminalization of abortion Bill for England and Wales for a significant amount of time by 2016. AfC Belfast have been part of Voice for Choice since around 2014. Up until the involvement of LIARC and Stella Creasy in the campaign for NI abortion rights, AfC had many terse meetings with Voice for Choice and the people working on the Diana Johnson Bill, that they could not add NI as it was seen within Parliament as too controversial and 'a devolved issue'. As discussed in the Creasy and Sanquest Chapter, in March 2017, this caution turned out to be misplaced, when it became clear that the widespread disbelief about the particularity of NI's access and the lack of equality across all countries in the UK would create the fervour necessary to engage more MPs positively to support a future bill, rather than wishing to harm its success.

Secondly, AfC had made a concerted decision beginning in 2013 not to ask for an extension of the 1967 Act, but instead to aim for 'free, safe and legal' which in the North meant to repeal the OAPA sections 58/59, the legislation that maintained the latent criminality of abortion, even in England and Wales. There were a number of reasons for this, in a country divided by national identity it was difficult for NI republicans to ask the British government to intervene to extend the '67 Act (a British law) to NI, also the '67 Act would still criminalize the use of abortion pills, still mandated that all abortions needed to be in a medical setting, and it's 'exception to the law' framework which was interpreted liberally by UK providers was thought to allow for a stricter interpretation, likely in a culturally more conservative NI. Finally, AfC always considered itself an integral part of the ARC having been members of the core steering group soon after its inception in 2012 and their call was for 'free safe and legal' abortion – all of which led to AfC's aim to have a piece of bespoke legislation. In the end this was significantly helpful for gaining cross-community support and for navigating the differing circumstances surrounding enacting a new law in a less culturally ready context. Additionally, this was when Human Rights NGOs in NI were beginning to catch up – so we could widen the scope.

LIARC decided that NI abortion access was something a UK MP should do something about, in the absence of any supportive NI MPs (Sinn Féin do not take their seats in the UK parliament). So various members were charged with going to their local MPs to say, 'this issue is something that I, as a constituent of yours, feel very passionately about and so should you'.

Stella Creasy had attended a fundraiser for abortion rights in the United States and this caused LIARC to focus in on her as a sympathetic MP where they had constituents who could approach her, from then Stella became deeply and continually involved. A meeting was set-up with BPAS, MSI, ASN, LIARC Amnesty and FPA, but Clarke of ASN questioned why there was not an AfC member at the table, so from the second meeting, AfC became a key part of the Westminster discussions on abortion. Despite the Supreme Court A and B case losing out to the UK Department of Health just before the results of that 2017 election, the fast-thinking action of Stella Creasy and LIARC around adding the funding of NI abortions to the Queen's Speech, ensured that for the first time ever, women and pregnant people travelling from NI to access abortion care in England and Wales would no longer have to pay.

How do we get to the Repeal of OAPA 58 and 59 in October 2019?

Again, it was a multifaceted strategy, always in partnership, with our organizing colleagues in LIARC and all the members of VfC, our work on the ground in NI with the women's sector, latterly the LGBT sector, political parties and journalists, our relationship with the Repeal Movement most especially ARC in the South and the support of international organizations such as Inroads, Women on Web and Women Help Women.

Abortion campaigners assume that if there is a vacuum of knowledge, dangerous myths and precedents can be set (Pierson and Bloomer, 2017), which is why AfC strove to give activists on the ground as much information as possible and to workshop destigmatizing language for other activists, media, decision-makers and the public to adopt. Early examples of this were evidenced during the 2016 Trust Women campaign when MLAs began to use segments of the AfC briefings verbatim, demonstrating that for some, a lack of sound medical information was the only barrier to it being shared. The difference made by inserting preferential terms were incalculable; this is a common tactic of actualization utilized by social movements globally. When common discourse biases are repeated frequently by those in power, controversial challenges in narrative are often required to encourage the requisite number of the population to unlearn deeply held beliefs. Grassroots movements, such as AfC, can effectively ignite such contentious politics, encouraging non-violent transformation of society's moral compass, and troubling the claims of parties such as the DUP, who try and hold on to an outdated sense of moral authority. (Jaggar, 2014)

Like the assertion that neither lobbying, marching, or creating culture alone will deliver the asks of any campaign, our goals were never met by appealing to one of the jurisdictions without the others. AfC has always been a cross-community group; we aim to not leave anyone behind, right down to our #TheNorthIsNext and #AbortionRightsNI hashtags on social media (Campbell, 2019) which aim to include Nationalists, Loyalists and all in between. However, our concerted action geared towards Westminster was not faring well in all quarters in NI. Some organizations who were steadfastly pro-choice, were not convinced because we might be asking Westminster to 'breach' devolution, other organizations could be said to be using the cover of devolution to obfuscate their anti-choice position.

We had been unremittent in our support and solidarity for the Repeal the Eighth Campaign. We had galvanized support in the North, fundraised to pay for campaign buses across the border counties and more (Roberts, volume 2). We held events, responded to widespread press interest, relentless support on social media, joined several offshoots (Parents for Choice, Strike for Choice, the X-ile project, MERJ, the Coalition to Repeal the Eighth Amendment and finally Together for Yes) (Gallen, this volume; Roberts, volume 2). This was no small effort, made by a tiny core number of AfC organizers and our allies. However, this huge amount of work we put into solidarity for the Repeal Campaign, seemed disregarded by some, who felt that our decision to lobby Westminster was foolish at best and sectarian at worst.

This somewhat justified concern after the actions of Westminster in 2008 (O'Dowd Cross Bloomer, this volume; Thomson this volume) was not confined to allied groups, it was even present within our own Steering Committee; at our May 2019 strategy event, there were still a few members for whom it felt a pointless and even anti-Irish endeavour. Our internal workaround was to assign lobbying roles only to invested people, thus avoiding the Westminster work falling to anyone who had a political aversion to it, luckily, we had a majority who supported it.

The backdrop of the Repeal Referendum

The details of our support for the Repeal the 8th Campaign will be dealt with by Roberts in volume 2, but the impact it had on organizing and galvanizing activists in the north cannot be underestimated. The long history of solidarity between the campaigns for bodily autonomy in the North and South has been conscientiously maintained, most especially in the relationship between the ARC and AfC, as pointed out by Enright et al., 'Activists are conscious that women who live in one jurisdiction may, in future, need to access services in the other' (Enright, McNeilly and de Londras, 2020, p.11); however, the unwillingness for this solidarity to be acknowledged legally by the Dáil, frustrated any equal island-wide access post-Repeal. Similarly, despite the incredible solidarity from ARC, it was not possible to forge real, legal solidarity whilst our invisible borders remain. However, across both jurisdictions ARC and AfC recognized that though the change in law was necessary for harm reduction amongst the most marginalized populations (Enright, McNeilly and de Londras, 2020), legal change would always only be the beginning of universal and equitable access to abortion on the island. Legal change from Westminster was also fraught with the prickly fallouts of political pragmatism; having to work with political actors even on the right, whose positions on other issues were ethically questionable and elicited disgust from activists. It was evident that for the majority of Westminster the NI abortion issue was a question that hinged on a sense of UK equity, promoted by supporters of the Union, balanced against the strength of the powers of devolution, human rights be damned. Emma Gallen, the long-serving volunteer and stall organizer of AfC had this to say the day after the Irish Repeal Referendum result,

> Theresa May is a self-proclaimed feminist, yet she is the one who got into bed with the DUP – which is vocal about its opposition to women accessing abortions – in order to keep hold of her job as prime minister. As a woman living in Northern Ireland, I feel let down by the government and the British public. It is unacceptable that women are forced into life-threatening situations just because our Prime Minister cannot stand up to the reactionary, misogynistic ideology represented by the DUP.
>
> (Gallen, quoted in Arthur, 2018, p. 1)

This reaction to having to ask the Conservative Government for the change needed was echoed more strongly by both Kellie O'Dowd, who was co-chair of AfC at the time, and Kellie Turtle, who was Women's Sector Lobbyist for the Women's Resource and Development Agency (WRDA). Even by the spring of 2019, both long-time feminist activists were wary of asking Westminster for change due to the Irish Nationalist question and were resistant to working with Stella Creasy MP, concerned that it would only serve her interests. Convincing the WRDA that this was the best avenue for change was vital, as they hold a respected position amongst the women's centres of NI. AfC had led education work with the women's centres to establish a supportive base, so it was not anti-choice positioning, but some activists believed they would not be able to convince all the women's centres that we should work with the British state, dependent on their community allegiances. Fortunately, in September 2018, Amnesty International published a cross-party public letter saying that Sinn Féin leader Michelle O'Neill, Colum Eastwood of the SDLP, Alliance leader Naomi Long and Doug Beattie of the UUP, jointly signed the statement declaring the 919 women:

> … who travelled to England in 2017 for this healthcare service and countless others purchased abortion pills online, in doing so risked prosecution. We call on UK Government to decriminalise abortion by repealing sections 58 and 59 of the 1861 Offences Against the Person Act and to ensure a human rights compliant framework governing access to abortion.
>
> (Crockett, 2018)

Within Westminster AfC also had to work hard to win over the SNP, the majority pro-choice Parliament supported the right to choose, but the SNP had difficulties bridging the devolution gap. On 7 October 2018, AfC and the NI Reproductive Health Law and Policy Advisory group alongside Engender Scotland, produced and facilitated a session at the SNP conference in Glasgow, launching a report (Bloomer et al., 2018b) including AfC testimonies on aiding women accessing illegal pills online. On 21 November 2018 they co-hosted a drop-in session at Westminster to encourage SNP to support a motion which troubled their stance on devolution principles with a briefing paper (Pierson et al., 2018). This proved successful when SNP MPs supported the final Executive formation bill in July 2019 citing human rights and a lack of devolved governance (Creasy and Sanquest, this volume). The session also saw several Lib Dem and Conservative MPs and researchers, visiting to find out more about the support for decriminalization from within NI, leading to a greater support from MPs previously on the fence about 'imposing' legislation from Westminster.

AfC's multiple methods of pushing towards decriminalization would not have worked without the community-building, legal demystifying and constant social media pressure on the key players in Parliament. From urging the public to write handwritten letters to ministers, to an unrelenting presence in social and traditional media, to countless protests, to campaigners calling peers on their phones on the days of voting, no stone was left unturned.

AfC, working closely with Cara Sanquest from Creasy's office and Katherine O'Brien from BPAS in July 2019, managed to get the exact wording of the CEDAW recommendations directly into the legislation that was overwhelmingly passed, by proposing it as one of several suggestions for the clerks to approve. It is unique for a UNCEDAW report on Human Rights breaches to end up in primary legislation. There are continuing problems with over-restrictive regulations and the lack of provision even within those regulations as of April 2020, however, to get from 2016 and a vote on abortion only to allow for exceptions of Fatal Foetal Anomaly failing in Stormont, to the passing of decriminalization laws on 21 October 2019, was seismic.

Despite Westminster being the locus of power and being named as the holder of our rights by the CEDAW Inquiry, despite the lack of political traction with asking for access in Ireland for people in the six counties, despite the impossibility of getting change from Stormont without a sitting Assembly and despite there being no other avenue left open to us for change, working with Westminster was difficult for many in the women's sector in NI. Navigating this and the trio of jurisdictions any social justice campaigner must deal with in the North required herculean efforts from the activists and support network of allies in Ireland, England and at home. It would be foolish to assign any one of AfC's actions or methods as the key to decriminalization, suffice to say the broad spectrum of talents and tenacity helped remove the risk of prosecution for even those most marginalized by a strict abortion law. Additionally, AfC is under no illusion that the work is ever done, even now, pressure on local government is ongoing for delivery and funding of services (AfC, 2020). As such AfC continues to nourish and educate our broad spectrum of supporters and the new and exciting task of working alongside our dedicated abortion providers.

16

Alliance for Choice Derry: Delivering decriminalization – activism in the north-west

Maeve O'Brien

Introduction

This chapter documents the rise of pro-choice activism in the north-west of Ireland from the 1980s to the present day. While there has been limited work done on the history of abortion in the north, we know very little about activists' experiences in Northern Ireland (NI). By interviewing activists from throughout this era, this chapter offers an examination of some of the key figures, important moments and the evolution of pro-choice activism in the Derry city area and surrounds. By relying primarily on oral histories, the different strategies and methodologies employed by pro-choice activists in the north-west will be explored as well as the cultural and institutional barriers to abortion access experienced. This chapter will consider the importance of the Derry Women's News Sheet, campaigns in favour of extending the 1967 Act, the impact of pills on the fight for abortion rights, redirection of strategy towards decriminalization as well as the grassroots and political lobbying that took place across the decades. Presenting a picture that transcends the typical sectarian divide of nationalist and unionist, this chapter documents the existence of a feminist and social justice-minded praxis in the north-west of Ireland – one that has more often than not been hidden due to the dominant narrative of The Troubles taking centre stage. This dissenting perspective is detailed strikingly by Anita Villa, one of the founding members of the pro-choice movement in Derry who said, 'I feel I had very much an alternative view of the world – thinking outside of the Troubles. I grew up in the Bogside – two down, one up, no kitchens and fourteen in the house. In the 1970s I was involved with the anti-apartheid movement and anti-nuclear groups' (Interview with Villa, 19th August 2020). For Villa, raised in a predominately Catholic, deprived neighbourhood and educated in a conservative Catholic school, the issue of abortion was one she came to in her twenties, but it intrinsically related to her left-wing activism: 'When I made the decision about abortion, or started thinking about it, I was already politicized as a socialist, so it was part of the package if you like that I accepted and had no problem.'

It was under the weight of The Troubles and an institutionally misogynistic Stormont and local government system that the existing feminist activisms of secret networks (see McCormick, 2015) began to grow into a coherent pro-choice movement in Derry. Villa pinpoints the origins of group activism in 1986, where likeminded women connected with each other when they took part in a university access course exploring women in Irish History, taught by Goretti Horgan – a Cork native who at that time was relatively new to the city. For lecturer Horgan, her pro-choice awakening had occurred years before her arrival to Derry – working in Newcastle upon Tyne, she was introduced to the issue of abortion when told by a colleague of the death of her sister due to a botched abortion in the pre-1967 years. From that moment, Horgan became a committed pro-choice activist, working with the Women's Right to Choose group in the Republic of Ireland and going on to become the national organizer of the anti-amendment campaign in the early 1980s. From there, Horgan embarked on lifelong sustained campaigns to thwart the misinformation of SPUC and other assorted anti-choice groups as well as opposing the censorship of information about contraception in the south. Moving to Derry in 1986, Horgan was surprised to find there was 'very little going on regarding abortion [...] I assumed there would be a more developed pro-choice movement'. In the classes she taught, she ensured that the issue of abortion was platformed and encouraged the women who participated to engage with the issue. Horgan remembers: 'We had a meeting, I think in the Dungloe bar, and asked ourselves "what should we be campaigning about?" I suggested abortion' (Interview with Horgan, 10th August 2020).

For Villa, the access to university course was an opportunity to 'get away from the kids for a few hours', but it ended up becoming much more as the close-knit bond between the women saw them attend community initiatives, socialist meetings and start to put their voices to the fore. Villa remembers: 'Four of us went on to Magee after the course and we saw that the minute women get in a room, the dynamic changes – and we started talking about making changes' (Interview with Villa, 19th August 2020). Villa also recalls, in and around 1986, attending a course on community organizing at Pilot's Row Community Centre on Rossville Street, organized by activist Mary Kay Mullan. Here, Villa and Mullan began to learn the practical dynamics of activism and organizing.

Coming out of this course, they asked themselves – how do we get information out there? 'And', says Villa: 'the idea of the Derry Women's News Sheet came out of that'. Working alongside women such as Geraldine Quigley, Deirdre McCarron, Therese Friel and Ann McClean amongst others, the *Derry Women's News Sheet* was a monthly publication that ran from 1986 to 1989 and is one of the earliest tangible examples of the existence of a pro-choice movement in the north-west.

The *Derry Women's News Sheet* was written only by women and all women on the editorial board were pro-choice. Priced at 10p, women from a variety of different political backgrounds brought relevant information to the news sheet, making it a nucleus for feminist activism in the city. Abortion was not the only topic written about or highlighted – the women went to socialist meetings, anti-toxic waste campaigns, profiled cancer screenings, conducted surveys on the attitudes of local pharmacists to selling condoms and campaigned for child-care assistance. Says Villa: 'Most of the women had children and understood the need to take a holistic view of our activism – women should have choice to have children or not, which meant fighting for childcare, better pay and conditions, healthcare, contraception and of course social justice. Abortion was part of that range of issues' (interview with Villa, 19th August 2020). Here in this news sheet, the work of reproductive justice was being carried out. In terms of distribution, Horgan recalls standing outside of shops such as Wellworths and at public meetings selling the news sheet, with little to no backlash. For Villa, the news sheet was a publication that was largely untouched by the sectarian divide that dominated 1980s life in NI: 'People thought we were a bit rigid in our approach and that we were always angry but also where we became known as the "feminist group". Women in the group came from different political backgrounds – socialists, some republicans and many didn't define themselves along community lines. Women from all backgrounds would come and write for the news sheet' (interview with Villa, 19th August 2020).

'A crazy group of activists'

Not only were the *Derry Women's News Sheet* group gaining a reputation as a 'crazy group of activists' (interview with Villa, 19th August 2020). By writing about abortion and sharing information about how to procure an abortion, Villa recounts that 'women who needed help to travel for abortion often came to the group'. Meeting in a range of venues including the upstairs of the Women's Aid offices on Pump Street, the group regularly supported desperate women from all communities seeking advice and financial assistance. As a result, the news sheet group found their activism increasingly more focussed on helping women in the community travel to England to access abortion healthcare. Due to this increase in abortion activism, the Women's Right to Choose Group was formed in the late 1980s. And the group only continued to grow with Roisin Barton, Margo Harkin, Hilary Morton, Ann Hamilton and Eileen Blake among others becoming active during this time: 'A lot of what was done was supporting women – a lot of time was spent getting money and helping women travel' (interview with Villa, 19th August 2020). Indeed, a key discussion for the Women's Right to Choose Group in the mid-1990s was the debate between assisting women individually or attacking the core institutional and governmental issue of restricted access. This dilemma between public activism and playing a supportive role to women privately was largely answered with the clear emergence of a focus on tackling endemic issues. And while the Women's Right to Choose Group did continue to raise funds to support women in their decision to travel for abortion care, they also tackled the core issue of the illegality and lack of abortion access in NI on a more public stage.

Against the background of an ultra-conservative Stormont, evidence of the growing pro-choice movement is perhaps best exemplified in the 1987 International Tribunal of the Northern Ireland Abortion Law Reform Association (Walker, this volume). Both Horgan and Villa recount a convoy of women from the north-west attending this event. Hearing accounts of the 'enormous emotional and psychological distress and unacceptable financials as a result of the lack of abortion provision in Northern Ireland', the tribunal asserted the 'obligation' of the British government to extend the 1967 Abortion Act to NI (Northern Ireland Abortion Law Reform Association, 1989, pp. 29–30). Such statements galvanized activists in the north-west – Villa remembers that another issue, the 1990 Human Fertilization and Embryology Bill, as a further example of the targeting of a core issue and issuing petitions, marching with placards and raising awareness of the effects of bill. Further, Horgan's 1990 pamphlet publication 'Abortion: Why Irish Women Must Have the Right to Choose' particularly interrogated how the lack of state-funded childcare, health cuts and social class provided the main barrier to abortion. Making the salient observation, 'richer women can sidestep the effects of all these cuts. In the same way as money has always allowed them the choice of having an abortion, so money allows them the choice of having a child on their own terms', Horgan noted 'at every level it is working class women who are the least free to choose;

and with the cuts biting ever deeper they can't even be sure that the few facilities they have will still be there tomorrow' (Horgan, 1990, p. 23). And it is this point that time and time again those involved in the Women's Right to Choose Group returned to – with members continually campaigning for myriad issues that all intersected with abortion; in particular, campaigns around childcare and social security issues occupied much of the group's time.

Undoubtedly, it was the X Case of 1992 that provided a lightning bolt of activity for the Women's Right to Choose Group – inflaming the sense of injustice that long-time and new activists felt. For Horgan, the X Case was 'convulsive' and ensuing protests demonstrated a 'scream of anger' from the women of Ireland (interview with Horgan, 10th August 2020). Derry women travelled to Dublin to take part in X Case rallies, but given the often spontaneous nature of these protests, it was difficult to attend all events. More locally, Horgan recalls a queue of people in Derry City Centre waiting to sign a petition in support of Miss X. In 1992, organizations began to respond to the issue of abortion. The Women's Centre Derry – an educational and social hub for women in the city – declared a pro-choice position and provided a postal address for the Women's Right to Choose Group activists which, to this day, is still used. Around this time, in the mid-to-late 1990s, Sara Greavu and Helen Harris became increasingly involved in individual and group pro-choice efforts in the city. These women brought artistic flair in terms of posters and a penchant for rogue graffiti as well as a sustained injection of queer and feminist theory to the group.

For Greavu – previously a campus organizer for National Abortion Rights Action League in the United States – the dilemma of feminist organizational structures was a recurrent issue in pro-choice activism in the north-west. The Women's Right to Choose Group defined itself as a purposefully leaderless and non-hierarchical group, feeling this inclusive and eglatarian organizational setup reflected their feminist values. This premeditated decision was in keeping with radical feminist and socialist practices, for example, the group prioritized self-fundraising as not to be obligated or restricted by the demands of funding bodies. Additionally, the non-hierarchical structure of the group also allowed activists (the majority of whom were women and had caring and work responsibilities to varying degrees at different stages in their lives) to drop in and drop out of activism depending on availability. For Horgan and Villa, the structureless formation of the Women's Right to Choose Group was integral to the radical formation of the group, 'we didn't think that having a chair or secretary was productive – we wanted to make collective decisions. We wanted to be a group that was action based, not lobbying'. However, for Greavu, this notion of non-hierarchical or structureless organizing can be more nuanced than it may first appear. Says Greavu, 'Structureless is great in many ways, but it also often creates a situation where there are invisible and unspoken structures and hierarchies' (Interview with Greavu, 17th January 2021). Greavu's perspective illustrates the ongoing discussions and reflections within the group, as members continually assessed the best approaches to their activism. It is perhaps because of these differences of opinion, the Women's Right to Choose Group grew from strength to strength in the 1990s with increased engagement between the north-west and activists and reproductive rights figures from outside of the island of Ireland. For example, there were increased interactions between the Women's Right to Choose Group with Marie Stopes International – with Villa and Horgan visiting the MSI headquarters in London in 1994, with a plea that Marie Stopes to return to the north.

The growth of the pro-choice movement

For the rest of the late 1990s and early 2000s, the Women's Right to Choose Group continued their work of supporting women who needed to travel abroad for abortions, as well as campaigning for the extension of the 1967 Act and other systemic anti-women issues. With activists such as Robin Whittaker, Ann Hamilton, Diana King, Cliona Boyle, Dee Sykes and many others joining the fight, there was a need for a more coherent organization to be formed, and so AfC was founded in 1997. At the same time and building on the momentum of the Labour Government victory of 1997, there was some movement on abortion rights for NI at a Westminster level with the formation of the Voice for Choice group where pro-choice voices from the region began to be heard in London. Since its inception, Horgan has maintained strong links with Voice for Choice, but it must be noted that AfC was under no illusion that change was coming as a matter of urgency. For Villa, 'British expedience was the general policy – whatever suited them – women in the north would not be provided for unless it met the needs of Westminster' (interview with Villa, 19th August 2020). Closer to home, the popularity of the centrist Northern Ireland Women's Coalition did little to bolster a pro-choice movement on the political stage, with the party declining to declare a stance on abortion until near the end of their political tenure in 2005. Nevertheless, Horgan believes Voice for Choice was important in inserting the conversation of NI and abortion into Westminster.

For Horgan, up until then, abortion had not been seen as an issue that was on Westminster's radar (interview with Horgan, 10th August 2020).

By the turn of the century, a significant development in reproductive healthcare had made its way to the shores of Ireland. Mifepristone and misoprostol – more commonly known as abortion pills – when taken orally, meant that abortion could now be carried out at in private, at home. For activists this was a revolutionary moment. Procuring these pills meant that abortion healthcare could be taken into the hands of those who needed it and for those under ten weeks gestation, travelling to England was no longer necessary. AfC began working with abortion-pills organizations such as Women on Waves in 2001 to bring an abortion ship to Dublin. In 2005, AfC connected with Women on Web, using the postal service to establish a covert network of pills suppliers and receivers. This meant that activists could receive pills in the post and then deliver the pills to women in need in the north-west and further afield, including the Republic of Ireland. This landmark moment in reproductive healthcare revolutionized how abortion could be procured and for activists, and the pills changed everything. Given that the procurement of abortion pills directly violated the 1861 Offences against the Person Act, AfC engaged in the practice of civil disobedience to supply women with local abortion access. Further, the group generated key strategic relationships locally, nationally and internationally to secure sustained access to abortion pills. Termed by Rawls as 'a public, nonviolent, conscientious, yet political act contrary to law usually done with the aim of bringing about a change in the law or policies of the government', the use of civil disobedience became a standard practice for Derry activists who saw the urgent need for reproductive justice, which continued to be ignored by politicians in this region and at Westminster (Rawls, 1971, p. 364).

With members such as Sharon Meenan, Jim Collins, Julia Black, Denise Meenan, Shá Gillespie, Catherine Pollock, Jacqui Doherty, Christiane McGuffin, Catherine O'Rourke and Tina McLaughlin joining AfC during this time, a great deal of public engagement was done by arts-based protest – a tactic that would become synonymous with pro-choice activism in the north-west. Determined to keep abortion as an issue to the fore, in 2008, AfC held protests where forty masked people stood on the steps of the Guildhall in Derry City Centre to represent the forty women per week travelling to England for abortion care. This protest gave a literal and physical representation of the journeys made by women from their region. This protest also became the subject of a poster created by the group and an indication of just how vitriolic anti-choice opposition was at this time can be seen by AfC struggling to get forty women to share their photographs as part of the poster artwork. In a striking show of solidarity, forty women from England took photographs of themselves and consented to their images being used for the purposes of furthering the pro-choice fight in NI. Highlighting the intimidation experienced by pro-choice activists during this time says, Shá Gillespie,

> I knew a lot of women who had to go to England for an abortion. We were all being treated like second class citizens. I was being spat at on the street because I was a queer woman, and I was also being spat at on the streets for wanting to stand up for a woman's right to choose. It was a no-win situation back then.
>
> (Interview with Gillespie, 27th October 2020)

Despite these threats and acts of aggression, AfC continued their work using interesting and innovative practices to further the pro-choice message on the streets by engaging with and challenging public opinion. The creation of a 'washing line' where each item of clothing on the line contained a story was a particularly memorable idea. The washing line was hung along the streets of Derry alongside AfC information stalls, which were usually held at least one Saturday a month. Each story explained the complex and varied reasons for and experiences of abortion. Other posters created included the text: 'AfC – 40 Years behind – Women Demand Equality – Extend the Abortion Act' and a black and white A3 page featuring a smiling woman reminiscent of a 1950s American-styled housewife holding a sign stating, 'My Body My Choice'. AfC also repeatedly utilized the Derry Walls, carrying out banner-drops with words such as 'Extend the Abortion Act' draped over the seventeenth-century stones.

The move towards decriminalization

By the mid-2000s, with growing activism occurring in Belfast, AfC split into two key groups, with each centre of urban activity having its own organization. For the now-named AfC Derry, campaigning continued along the same lines as it had always done – helping individual women and engaging in activism to target key systemic and institutional issues. The organization held conferences in Derry City and continually engaged with local and national media in order to keep the issue of abortion to the fore. The year 2008 saw an opportunity for meaningful change when Diane Abbott MP's amendment to the Embryology and Human Fertilization bill would have extended abortion rights to NI. Speaking to *The Guardian* (O'Hara, 2008), Horgan predicated the failure of this attempt to grant abortion rights in the north, noting the British government had offered a 'trade-off' with the DUP whereby their votes in favour of a government-led proposal of a forty-two-day detention period would negate Abbott's amendment. Activists note that this period in 2009 was extremely demotivating for AfC Derry, with many feeling that the pro-choice fight lost. Together with recommendations from legal experts, key thinkers from Amnesty International in 2014 and others, post-2008 saw the development of a new strategy for the pro-choice movement in NI that galvanized activism once more. By turning attention away from extending the 1967 Act and instead advocating for the decriminalization of abortion in the north, pro-choice activists gained a fresh perspective and new target to work towards.

By re-centring the key goal as decriminalization, the pro-choice movement in NI was able to generate solidarity with other activist groups such as Sex Workers Association Ireland who had long been campaigning for the decriminalization of sex work as well as marriage equality groups – so much so that Derry's Rainbow Project allowed AfC free use of meeting rooms for monthly meetings. These links helped foster a larger and more connected movement in the fight for decriminalization and this redirection brought fresh energy, providing a wave of enthusiasm that saw members such as Becca Bor, Suzanne McGilloway, Eimear Willis, Colleen O'Neill, Mel Bradley, Maeve O'Neill, Maev McDaid, Nadia Kaczmarczuk, Jacquie and Annie Ward and others becoming involved in activism during this time. Further innovative and artistic forms of protest were utilized by the group, for example the 'Lumiere' art piece in 2013, the year that Derry held the UK City of Culture title.

In literal terms, decriminalization of abortion in NI meant repealing Sections 58 and 59 of the Offences against the Person Act, thereby removing it from criminal law. In order for decriminalization to happen, a seismic shift would have to occur in order to bring abortion once more to the political fore. It was with the death of Savita Halappanavar in Galway in October 2012 that the tremors necessary to put abortion on the mainstream political agenda occurred. Halappanavar's needless death sent a convulsive reaction through the island of Ireland not seen since the X Case and once more activists from Derry and across the island took to the streets, this time utilizing social media in the form of Facebook and Twitter profiles to create a strong grassroots community of networks with the goal of repealing the 8th Amendment in the Republic of Ireland and work towards decriminalization in the north. Kate Mukungu notes the increased acts of civil disobedience in the north post-2012, for example the open letter signed by over 100 activists and published in local newspapers addressed to the PSNI stating they had procured and supplied abortion pills – directly violating the 1861 Offences against the Person Act (Mukungu, 2018). Further tensions rose in the north in April 2016 with the arrest of a young woman in Belfast who had been reported to the PSNI by her housemates and was given a one-year suspended sentence under the 1861 Offences against the Person Act for carrying out an abortion (McDonald, 2016b). As a direct response to these criminal proceedings, in May 2016, AfC Derry activists Collette Devlin, Diana King and Kitty O'Kane handed themselves into the Strand Road Police Station in Derry, requesting that they too be prosecuted for procuring and distributing abortion pills. In a statement, these three activists said: 'We're involved in AfC and had always raised money to help wee girls get to England for legal abortions ... the nine-week pill, as we call it, is cheaper and it's a safe, efficient way of triggering a miscarriage.' Stating that their civil disobedience helped 'girls here in Northern Ireland', the activists also acknowledged the cross-border aspect of their pill distribution: 'but being in Derry, near Donegal, aye we would help some girls from Donegal too. We would help any girl anywhere if they or their family or friends asked us' (Holland, 2016). To date, no charges have been brought against Devlin, King and O'Kane which suggests that the criminalization of women in NI has an added implication of class vulnerability, given that the young woman prosecuted was of a working-class background.

When a referendum in the south was called for May 2018, AfC Derry worked alongside Abortion Rights Campaign Donegal and Abortion Rights Campaign Inishowen to campaign for Repeal. Members canvassed in towns such as Letterkenny, Buncrana, Ballybofey, Stranorlar, Donegal Town, Ballyshannon and Bundoran and worked with Together for Yes nationally to fundraise, promote, engage, lobby and inform the general public and politicians in the south to win the Repeal of the 8th. Following this landmark achievement, AfC Derry continued their fight to decriminalize abortion in the north. Working with Belfast and with the newly formed Mid-Ulster for Choice, significant pro-choice rallies were held in Belfast in September 2018 and 2019, with a cross-border and cross-community population marching in the streets that once held the bellows of misogynistic political forces such as Ian Paisley doggedly opposing any form of social or cultural progress in the north. Both Repeal and the campaign for decriminalization attracted a new cohort of young activists such as Sophia McFeely and Bethany Moore who joined AfC Derry in 2019. Says Bethany, 'I had done some canvassing for Repealing the 8th and I had also been a part of the student movement in Belfast for nearly a year. I wanted to get more involved in my local community, as I knew there were people at home who needed our help too' (interview with Moore, 18th September 2020).

Campaigns spearheaded by AfC Derry during this period between the Repeal of the 8th Amendment in May 2018 and the decriminalization of abortion in NI in October 2019 were many and varied – and often extending beyond the city of Derry. Pro-choice stalls were held in Omagh and Coleraine, AfC Derry donated pro-choice t-shirts to singers performing onstage at the Limavady-based Stendhal Festival and theatre performances were all examples of the artistic protest responses used by the group. Significant battles began to be won. The year 2018 saw the NHS finally pay the fees for abortion healthcare for those women forced to travel to England (Creasy and Sanquest, this volume). On the crest of this wave, activists continued to mobilize and push for systemic change. In 2019, the production of hundreds of black and white t-shirts stating DECRIMINALIZE provided a social act of resistance – mirroring the impact of the REPEAL jumpers used in the run up to the referendum in the south. Creative, colourful and imaginative poster-making sessions were held regularly by artists such as Shannon Patterson – whose 'pro-choice chick' and 'you are not entering Free Derry' badges took on cult status among young activists. Monthly meetings as well as weekly stalls kept the issue of decriminalization to the fore with women such as Aine O'Doherty, Ellie Bergin, Kerry-leigh McCartney, Taryn DeVere, Amy-Louise Merron, Maja McGill and many others working together to organize buses to rallies, fundraising pro-choice film nights and sending countless letters and emails to MLAs as well as MPs in support of Stella Creasy and Conor McGinn's decriminalization and marriage equality amendments (Creasy and Sanquest, this volume). This swathe of activism mirrored repeated statistics coming from organizations like the Amnesty International affirmed that over three-quarters of the population in NI support abortion law change (Amnesty International, 2020). These figures correlate with the recent referendum in the Republic of Ireland, where 66.4 per cent of the population voted to Repeal the 8th Amendment from the Irish constitution, illustrating that the island of Ireland does support liberalization of abortion laws.

On the 21st of October 2019, abortion was decriminalized in NI. AfC Derry held a banner drop in commemoration of the women who suffered untold trauma and tragedy under the criminalization of their healthcare. Celebrating marriage equality, a banner supporting trans rights was dropped and quoting from poet Audre Lorde's 'A Litany for Survival' and in a nod to the internationalism that radical activism in Derry has always embraced, a banner read: 'but when we are silent/we are still afraid/So it is better to speak/remembering/we were never meant to survive' (Lorde, 2002, p. 256). These words carried a deep resonance for activists, who endured endless threats, violence and abuse throughout their campaigning. Later, in the left-wing bar Sandino's, activists from every era and incarnation of the organization took part in a countdown to midnight celebration that featured spoken word poetry, female singer-songwriters and a curated DJ session from artist SOAK.

Undoubtedly, the Repeal of the 8th Amendment in the Republic of Ireland put pressure on the British Government to remove abortion from criminal law in the north. The decriminalization of abortion and latterly marriage equality can be viewed as evidence of the sea-change in public opinion in the north. Polls by Amnesty International and the Northern Ireland Life and Times surveys clearly demonstrate how politicians in this region were out of step with public views (Gray, volume 2). However, the seeds of this change in public opinion were sown by those women in secret networks, those who procured pills and raised monies, those who created the *Derry Women's News Sheet* – culminating in a cross-generational and cross-community grassroots feminist movement that defies traditional definitions of politics and activism in the north. Now in 2021, abortion may have been removed from the criminal law books but the Health Minister of NI and the Department of Health's refusal to commission services means that once more activists are utilizing strategies of the past to ensure a better future for those who can get pregnant and do not want to be. It is with deep gratitude that I thank those who consented to be interviewed for this book chapter. The names of activists cited in this piece are by no means a comprehensive list of everyone involved in AfC Derry. More work on the radical pro-choice feminist activism in the north-west must be done to ensure names and experiences are compreshenively documented.

17

Dismantling the walls of silence surrounding abortion in Northern Ireland

Ruairi Rowan and Audrey Simpson

Introduction

This chapter begins by providing a synopsis of the motivation for a Judicial Review against the failure of the Department of Health, Social Services and Public Safety (DHSSPS) as it was then known, to issue guidance for healthcare professionals on the provision of abortion services in Northern Ireland (NI). The legal challenge was led by the Family Planning Association in Northern Ireland (FPA NI) who at the time argued that the issue of abortion was surrounded by walls of silence. The chapter tracks the outcome and impact of this case: the campaigning carried out by FPA NI, the eventual closure of that organization and the establishment of Informing Choices NI (ICNI). It ends with the establishment of the central access point into early medical abortion (EMA) services in NI and the ongoing challenges in securing reproductive rights for all women and girls.

Ruairi Rowan was Advocacy Manager of FPA NI from 2015 to 2019 and is currently ICNI's Director of Advocacy and Policy.

Audrey Simpson was Director of FPA NI from 1988 to 2015 and is currently Chair of ICNI.

FPA NI

FPA was one of the UK's leading sexual health charities working to enable people to make informed choices about their sexual and reproductive health. In NI the organization provided a non-directive and non-judgemental counselling, support and information service for women and girls faced with an unplanned or crisis pregnancy. This service began in 1988 and following the closure of the

Ulster Pregnancy Advisory Association (UPAA) in 1999, after intimidation and coercion involving aggressive picketing outside the homes of some of their counsellors and the firebombing of their premises, FPA NI was the only organization based in NI that supported and provided information on all pregnancy options, including abortion (Holland, 1999).

FPA NI's offices in Belfast and Derry/Londonderry were targeted for over twenty-five years (McDonald, 2016c). Individuals belonging to anti-choice groups assembled around the entrance to the buildings each day and attempted to start unsolicited conversations with women on their reasons for entering. This included forcing misleading and distressing leaflets on to them which contained inaccurate information and offensive language such as 'Abortion does not unrape the mother – it makes her the mother of a dead baby'. They displayed graphic images, followed clients and their families as they left FPA NI's premises and used emotive and coercive language to dissuade visitors from medical treatment, under the assumption that any woman entering or leaving the building was pregnant and considering an abortion.

Experiencing these behaviours impacted negatively on clients and their families and influenced their decision to access, or not access, FPA NI's counselling service. Below is an extract from a client evaluation:

> Obviously, it's beyond the control of FPA, but I think it's a real shame there are protestors outside the building. It is very intimidating, and I feel it could put a lot of vulnerable girls off going to discuss their options, or to have a counselling session. I was told if I wanted, I could return for a further session, but I definitely wouldn't feel comfortable to do so. I think it is difficult enough without having to face questioning and judgements along with accusations from people who have absolutely no idea what each person is going into the building for. FPA provides an invaluable service and all staff I had dealings with both on the phone and in person were very helpful.

The judicial review

In the 1990s FPA NI, building on the work of the Northern Ireland Abortion Law Reform Association (NIALRA), developed campaigning and advocacy activities to secure abortion rights for women and girls in NI. Apart from AfC, a grassroots organization in NI, unlike many other international countries embroiled in the fight for abortion rights, the women's movement and human rights and equality bodies in NI were notable by their silence.

Furthermore, most women and girls who were considering or who had travelled to England to secure an abortion were rendered invisible due to the social stigma resulting from the illegality of abortion. In effect the issue was surrounded by walls of silence, and for many years FPA NI was a lone voice as a publicly funded organization within NI which was prepared to speak publicly regarding the issue.

The organization's campaign activities were carried out within NI, at Westminster and internationally through its membership of International Planned Parenthood Federation. These took place during sustained periods of direct rule, when the main priority of the UK government was the peace process and restoration of a power-sharing legislature in NI. Many Westminster politicians viewed NI as having a conservative, deeply religious culture which they judged as having no appetite for abortion reform.

Whilst lobbying served to raise awareness of the issues surrounding abortion and garner political support, it was evident that securing reform, through traditional campaigning activities, was not immediately realistic. Given the political apathy at Westminster and the political vacuum, FPA NI decided that the judicial system offered the greatest potential to effect change.

When a public body decides, or acts unlawfully, there are several ways that those affected can challenge that decision, one of which is through a process known as a Judicial Review. Via a court case, a judge or judges decide whether a public body has behaved lawfully. It offers a route to justice for those adversely affected and enables the courts and judiciary to have oversight of government decision-making.

In 2000 funding was secured (a condition of which was anonymity – indicating the stigma attached to abortion) to appoint a London-based legal team with extensive human rights experience. The next nine months were spent building a unique case whereby the greatest potential for change was to argue that DHSSPS was failing in its statutory duty by not issuing official guidance to health professionals on the circumstances in which abortion was lawful in NI; the means by which women could access abortion services; the ways in which general practitioners and other clinicians could refer women for abortion services; and the places in which abortion services could be provided. It was felt this would clarify the law and mainstream and legitimize abortion services in NI.

The confusion surrounding the law was exemplified by the 'K' case in 1993. 'K' became pregnant at fourteen years old. She lived in a children's home, was suspected of substance abuse and had physically and verbally abused staff. The

Northern Health and Social Services Board sought an order for her to avail of an abortion based on statements made that she would take her own life if the pregnancy was not terminated.

'K's' mother had not seen her since she was five years old. She refused social workers' requests to meet with her pregnant daughter but went to court to state her opposition to the abortion. 'K's' father, who had maintained contact with his daughter, indicated that the abortion should proceed. The judge concluded that an abortion would be in the best interests of 'K', but no doctor could be found in NI to carry out the procedure. Although those consulted had no conscientious objection to undertaking the procedure, they were wary of the girl's mother initiating legal proceedings given the uncertainty of the law. Consequently 'K' had to travel to England to obtain a private abortion.

It was FPA NI's experience that legal uncertainties, exacerbated by the lack of guidance from DHSSPS, caused doctors to be extremely cautious and had a chilling effect on their willingness to provide proper or sufficient services to women requiring abortion services. It was also clear from FPA NI's conversations with healthcare professionals that the availability of abortion services varied across and within each Health Trust. This is exemplified by the experiences of the following two women:

1. FPA NI were contacted by a twenty-one-year-old woman living in a community housing and support project. She had been in psychiatric care on a regular basis for several years as her father had sexually abused her from a young age. On a return visit to her home, she was raped by her father and became pregnant. She was twelve weeks pregnant when she attended FPA NI for counselling. During the session she showed the counsellor where she had cut herself in a previous act of self-harm. Her GP confirmed the pregnancy and referred her to a psychiatrist with the aim of obtaining an abortion in NI. The psychiatrist refused, saying that there was no power to refer the woman for this type of treatment. The woman took out a private loan and travelled to England to access an abortion.
2. The experience outlined above contrasts with that of a thirty-two-year-old woman who attended FPA NI for post-abortion counselling. She had also become pregnant as a result of rape, but her father, a retired GP, had arranged an NHS abortion for her in NI.

These and many other inconsistencies in abortion provision in the healthcare system, experienced at first hand by FPA NI in its day-to-day work with girls and women accessing its counselling service and contacting its helpline, underlined the need for clarity in the law. Therefore, FPA NI had a legitimate and direct concern in challenging the Health Minister's failure to provide guidance for healthcare professionals.

Despite FPA NI's clear interest in resolving the issues arising from a lack of clinical guidance, there were risks involved in proceeding with the case, not least that the organization was proposing to take their main funding source, DHSSPS, to court.

However, it was felt that the publication of guidance would have an important educative and normative effect on attitudes to the provision of abortion services in NI, helping to challenge myths and remove the culture of secrecy and blame that surrounded the issue.

On 13th June 2001 FPA NI's application for a Judicial Review was heard in Belfast High Court and leave was granted (BBC News, 2001). The full hearing took place on 21st and 22nd March 2002 (BBC News 2002). Inside the courtroom FPA NI were opposed by five legal teams representing three anti-choice organizations, the Northern Bishops (representing the Catholic Church) as well as the Government. Outside the court anti-choice protests intensified in their numbers as did the levels of harassment against FPA NI.

Judgement was finally given on 7th July 2003. The presiding Judge, Mr. Justice Kerr, ruled that DHSSPS was not failing in its statutory duty to issue guidelines but thought it would be prudent if they did so (BBC News, 2003). (Justice Kerr was latterly appointed to the UK Supreme Court and fifteen years later would rule that NI's abortion law constituted a breach of women's human rights.)

Following this decision papers were lodged by FPA NI on 28th July 2003 appealing the outcome and a hearing was eventually heard by a panel of three judges from the 24th to 26th of May 2004 (BBC News, 2004a). On 8th October of that year the Court of Appeal ruled in favour of FPA NI and ordered DHSSPS to consider what steps it should take to fulfil its duties by carrying out an investigation and issuing appropriate guidance (BBC News, 2004b).

Twelve years to secure legal compliance

In 2005 DHSSPS set up a working group to take the process forward which included a workshop for healthcare professionals and circulating a questionnaire to the Chief Executives of the Health and Social Care (HSC) Trusts, GPs, gynaecological nurses, midwives and obstetricians.

After numerous letters from FPA NI expressing grave concern at the lack of progress, draft guidance was finally issued for consultation in February 2007, three years after the Court of Appeal decision.

In October 2007 the Northern Ireland Assembly (NIA) debated the following motion tabled by then DUP MLAs Iris Robinson and Jeffrey Donaldson:

> That this Assembly opposes the introduction of the proposed guidelines on the termination of pregnancy in Northern Ireland; believes the guidelines are flawed; and calls on the Minister of Health, Social Services and Public Safety to abandon any attempt to make abortion more widely available in Northern Ireland.
>
> (Hansard, 2007)

In response to this attempt by Stormont to abandon the creation of clinical guidelines the Health Minister of Health, Social Services and Public Safety explained that he was proposing to establish another working group 'to consider the way forward' taking account of responses received in the consultation of the draft guidance (BBC News, 2007).

After yet more legal letters from FPA NI to the Minister another version of the guidance was eventually issued for consultation in July 2008. In November 2008, frustrated by the delays, FPA NI's solicitor informed the Minister that the intention was to return to court if guidelines were not issued by the end of 2008. The Minister responded by stating that he was anxious to avoid further legal challenge and that the guidance had been put to the Executive on 11th December. The document was finally published on 13th March 2009 (BBC News, 2009).

This prompted several legal challenges by anti-choice groups, in particular the Society for the Protection of the Unborn Child (SPUC), and on 30th November 2009, the Court ordered DHSSPS to withdraw the guidance and re-write the sections on conscientious objection and non-directive counselling. In February 2010 DHSSP released an interim document minus the two contested sections.

Another version of the guidance which included the re-drafted contentious sections was issued for consultation in July 2010 but in November 2011, frustrated by the numerous delays, FPA NI formally wrote to the Minister requesting that the guidance be issued without delay. A reply indicated that revised guidance had been prepared but in January 2012 FPA NI was advised that the Minister had asked for the guidance to be redrafted. FPA NI responded by advising the Minister that unless the revised guidance was submitted for Executive approval within twenty-one days legal action would be initiated.

No response was received; so in March 2012 FPA NI issued DHSSPS a Judicial Review Pre-Action Protocol letter. Application for leave was granted in September 2012 with hearing dates set for 21st and 22nd of January 2013 (BBC News, 2012). However, DHSSPS backed down on the morning of the Judicial Review and agreed to issue guidance to the Executive within weeks.

Over twenty weeks later yet another version of the guidance, with a revised title of 'The Limited Circumstances for a Lawful Termination of Pregnancy in Northern Ireland', was issued for consultation in April 2013 with a closing date of 29th July 2013 (BBC News, 2013). The opening paragraph of the document stated:

> The aim of the health and social care system must be protection of both the life of the mother and her unborn child. The objective of interventions administered to a pregnant woman must be to save the mother's life or protect against real and serious long-term or permanent injury to her health. Intervention cannot have as its direct purpose the ending of the life of the unborn child.
>
> (Department of Health NI, 2013a)

The document continued by specifying that:

> the circumstances where a termination of pregnancy is lawful in Northern Ireland are highly exceptional. This document is intended to guide clinicians on the application of the very strict and narrow criteria that are consistent with the law. It details the very limited circumstances under which a termination of pregnancy may be lawful in Northern Ireland.
>
> (Department of Health NI, 2013a)

Remarking that this version was significantly different from the previous guidance issued, the Royal College of Midwives in Northern Ireland said:

> The tone and language used throughout the document is intimidatory and threatening – both for women and for health care professionals. The document would appear to have been written in such a way as to create uncertainty and fear of possible criminal or legal repercussions amongst those working in this area of healthcare and thereby exert a 'chilling' effect' on the provision of abortion services for women in Northern Ireland.
>
> (RCM, 2013)

Commenting on the potential criminal consequences, the Royal College of Psychiatrists in Northern Ireland highlighted the danger this could have on a woman's health:

It is well recognised that over 1000 women from Northern Ireland each year travel to England to terminate a pregnancy, however it is increasingly possible for women to procure medication over the internet to terminate an unwanted pregnancy. This is potentially dangerous. The College is extremely concerned that if women taking these medications were aware that health professionals had an obligation to report to the police then they might delay or be deterred from seeking medical assistance with potentially very serious, even life-threatening consequences to their health.

(RCPSYCH, 2013)

Reflecting on the document the Royal College of Nursing in Northern Ireland said:

Nurses and other health care professionals in Northern Ireland have now been waiting for the best part of a decade to receive definitive guidance from the DHSSPS on the termination of pregnancy in Northern Ireland. They deserve better than to be subjected to the inadequacies of the current draft, or to have to wait another nine years for helpful and useful guidance.

(RCN, 2013)

At the conclusion of the consultation process on 22nd October 2013, DHSSPS officials gave evidence to the Committee for Health, Social Services and Public Safety and commented:

We are accepting, based on the comments that we have received, that we probably have not got the language or the tone quite right. There is scope to reflect the law accurately in a way that does not make someone feel that they are being intimidated by what the guidance is saying.

(DHSSPS, 2013b)

Fourteen months later the guidance had not been issued; so on the 19th December 2014 FPA NI's lawyer wrote to DHSSPS reminding them that they are in breach of the court order by not issuing the guidance and failure to do so could result in further court action.

In response, on the 12th of January 2015, the Departmental solicitor replied that the guidance is subject to a new Judicial Review and the applicant had been granted anonymity. It later emerged that a woman from County Antrim initiated legal action claiming that the ongoing delays by DHSSPS to provide revised guidance compounded the trauma of losing her babies. She travelled to England in 2013 to terminate twins with fatal foetal abnormalities as doctors said they could not carry out the abortion in NI due to uncertainty around the law. Shortly after initiating legal proceedings the woman found out that she was carrying another unviable pregnancy. On this occasion she was able to have an abortion in a different hospital in NI than the one she first attended after consultants assessed that continuing the pregnancy would have serious consequences to her mental health.

Finally, on 25th March 2016 the NI Executive approved 'Guidance for Health and Social Care Professionals on Termination of Pregnancy in Northern Ireland' (BBC News, 2016c).

This document stated that 'this guidance recognises that women must be made aware of the options and choices available to them under the law in Northern Ireland. Support and advice must respect the personal views of the woman and enable her to make her own informed choices'. It also stated that 'regardless of where a termination of pregnancy has been carried out, were necessary, support must be provided for individuals through aftercare services including counselling and other psychological support services. It is the responsibility of Health and Social Care Trusts to provide access to aftercare support for all women where it has been assessed to be required' (Department of Health, 2016).

Fifteen years of campaigning

Although it took fifteen years from the beginning of the Judicial Review process and twelve years from the Court of Appeal ruling to secure publication of the guidance, FPA NI successfully achieved its aim of gaining legal and clinical clarity as regards abortion in NI, and the case laid the foundation for further legal challenges that followed. It also stimulated a dialogue around reproductive rights in NI which placed women's experiences at its centre, gradually started to break down the walls of silence surrounding abortion and achieved other positive outcomes, directly and indirectly.

Firstly, the legal challenge attracted significant media attention during the three years in which the case was being heard. This was not only focused on NI, but throughout Great Britain and internationally which raised awareness of the stigmatization, discrimination and emotional and financial hardship experienced by girls and women with a crisis pregnancy. This generated an enhanced understanding of the realities of a crisis pregnancy, among the general public, politicians, clinicians and health professionals and increased empathy for girls and women faced with an unplanned or crisis pregnancy.

Secondly, it gradually 'gave permission' for clinicians and health professionals to begin to speak publicly about the impact of the absence of any official guidance for their clinical practice. The hostile environment, which surrounded the abortion debate in NI, had fostered a culture of fear and silence. Doctors were aware of colleagues in the United States being physically threatened, with some even being shot, and the ongoing presence of protestors outside FPA NI's premises in Belfast and Derry/Londonderry heightened concerns about personal safety.

It is noteworthy that prior to the publication of the guidance, unlike the Republic of Ireland, it was rare for any clinician or health professional to comment on abortion except to condemn it as murder. However, the Court of Appeal order to DHSSPS to publish guidance on the provision of abortion services meant that in effect, abortion became a mainstream healthcare service in NI. This empowered clinicians and health professionals to make public comments just as they would about any other aspect of the health service.

Thirdly, during this time period more NI politicians, despite official opposition from their parties to any abortion reform including the publication of guidance, were off the record, offering support to FPA NI in their campaigning for change. This support was confirmed by confidential surveys of MLA attitudes to abortion carried out by FPA NI which revealed higher levels of support for abortion reform than was publicly stated.

Fourthly, whereas human rights and equality bodies had been silent when FPA NI began the judicial review process, gradually over the years their voices began to be heard in support of the girls and women of NI. For example, in 2014 Amnesty International (AIUK) began campaigning to reform NI's abortion law and the following year launched their global 'My Body, My Rights' campaign. AIUK went on to play a leading role in the campaign to reform abortion law in NI and formed a strong partnership with FPA NI, both of which had a significant presence at Westminster in the lead up to the law finally being changed.

The Northern Ireland Human Rights Commission (NIHRC) began their own legal proceedings in 2015 challenging the compatibility of the law on abortion in NI with Article 3 (the prohibition of torture and of inhuman or degrading treatment), Article 8 (the right of everyone to respect for their private and family life) and Article 14 (the prohibition of discrimination) of the European Convention on Human Rights insofar as the law prohibits abortion in cases of serious malformation of the foetus, pregnancy as a result of rape and/or pregnancy as a result of incest.

Campaigning by women's groups also became increasingly more visible. This enabled FPA NI to form an important partnership with the Northern Ireland Women's European Platform (NIWEP) who provided a platform for women in NI to influence and shape social, economic and political policies at a local, national,

European and international level; and with AfC who had grown over the years to become an important voice for women in the community who travelled to England for an abortion or taken pills illegally. The three organizations worked together to prepare a submission to the CEDAW Committee requesting an inquiry into access to abortion in NI (Cross, O'Rourke Simpson this volume). Ultimately the findings of this inquiry provided the basis of the legislation to reform abortion law in NI in July 2019.

Lastly, throughout the years of campaigning by FPA NI very few girls or women, who had experienced a crisis pregnancy, were prepared to participate in the public debate. This was understandable given the vitriolic language often used by some NI politicians and the harassment they may have experienced, by anti-choice protestors, when trying to access FPA NI's counselling service. But throughout the elongated guidance publication process girls and women became more frustrated by the lack of progress and consequently began to join in the public debate by, for example, relating their experiences in the print and broadcast media and eventually officially through legal proceedings.

The judgement by the Court of Appeal, for the first time, clarified the law and indicated that abortion was legal in NI, albeit in limited circumstances. The eventual approval by the NI Executive and publication of the 2016 guidance document endorsed FPA NI's long-standing argument that abortion was indeed legal in NI.

The walls of silence were now being dismantled, but FPA NI continued to campaign for further reform, including the decriminalization of abortion which was eventually achieved in October 2019.

Establishment of Informing Choices NI

Regretfully, FPA NI was not around to witness the momentous change that was decriminalization. In May 2019 the London-based Trustees of FPA UK took the decision to place the organization into voluntary administration. However, a new organization, Informing Choices NI (ICNI), was quickly formed. A Board of Trustees was recruited, and their first meeting took place on 8 May 2019, a week before FPA UK was placed into administration. The organization registered with Companies House on 20 May 2019 and was subsequently granted charitable status. Through the Board of Trustees and staff team ICNI holds much of the history associated with FPA NI and the role it played in contributing to the improvement and change in societal attitudes towards sexual and reproductive health in NI. This work now continues, and is evolving, through ICNI.

Launch of the Central Access Point (CAP) Service

ICNI maintained all contracts previously held by FPA NI and following the introduction of the Abortion (Northern Ireland) Regulations 2020 worked alongside healthcare professionals to establish an interim early medical abortion (EMA) service which was integrated into existing sexual and reproductive health services in all HSC Trusts in NI (The Irish News, 2020; Morgan McLaughlin Kavanaugh Kirk, volume 2).

A vital part of the EMA service is the ease of the referral pathway through the CAP service provided by ICNI which enables people from across NI to contact a single telephone number where they can also access non-directive information, pregnancy choices counselling if requested, and referral into an EMA service within their HSC Trusts.[1] Seamless access to follow-up support is also available via ICNI's post-pregnancy counselling service.

In addition, ICNI undertakes all safeguarding assessments with girls aged between thirteen and fifteen years old, including their ability to consent to medical treatment using the Fraser guidelines, and also with clients who disclose domestic or sexual abuse. ICNI refers daily to the HSC Trusts, a medical consultation is offered within a few working days and a time is then agreed to attend an HSC clinic for treatment.

2,182 women and girls contacted the CAP service between 15 April 2020 and 14 April 2021. The average age of those who sought support was twenty-nine years old and the parliamentary constituency with the highest number of women self-referring was North Belfast (ICNI, 2021).

The EMA clinical leads in each HSC Trust have said that the CAP service provides an invaluable safety net for them as clinicians providing abortion care and have stated that from an NHS and HSC Trust perspective, currently there is nothing in place that remotely replicates what ICNI has to offer, including from a counselling aspect.

Access to support and counselling is one of the recommendations in the NICE Abortion Care Guideline published in September 2019, which states, 'These recommendations should make it easier for women to get support after an abortion and reduce the variation in what support is offered.'

Due to COVID-19 ICNI's counselling service has adapted by delivering uninterrupted telephone counselling sessions. Telephone counselling ensures the service remains accessible for those who are shielding, have dependents or cannot travel. It also expands the reach of the service and is a convenient avenue of support.

One in five women will experience a mental health issue during pregnancy. This is exacerbated by the pandemic which can limit access to their normal support pathways. Having trialled telephone counselling, we know it to be effective and has shown to significantly improve attendance rates. Clients value the services we provide and feedback from patient evaluations has been consistently excellent as one service user highlights:

> I just wanted to say a big thank you. You helped me out when I had nowhere else to turn and I honestly don't know what I would off done if I hadn't found Informing Choices. Thank you so much. Everyone I was on the phone to was amazing also. You are doing an amazing job keep it up. Thank you again!

It must be noted, however, since the introduction of the new abortion Regulations in March 2020, it has been left up to individual HSC Trusts and ICNI to absorb the needs of women and girls, and without additional resources we have seen the services struggle to cope. For example, on Monday, 5th October 2020, the Northern HSC Trust ceased providing their EMA service. They stated that they were unable to continue to deliver the unfunded EMA service, and as other HSC Trusts did not have the capacity to accommodate women who fell within this area an EMA pathway to care was no longer available to all women in NI (ITV News, 2020).

As a result, people living within this area once again had their options limited to travelling to England through the UK government-funded central booking system; travelling to the south of Ireland and paying privately to access abortion care at a cost of around €450; or accessing medication outside of NHS/HSE provision through an independent online telemedicine provider such as Women Help Women.

The service in the Northern HSC Trust was subsequently reinstated on 4 January 2021. The following day the South Eastern HSC Trust suspended their EMA service stating unforeseen circumstances resulting in no senior medical cover. (The consultant leading the service had begun her maternity leave.) As a result of the suspension women and girls living within this area faced the same limited options as outlined above. This service was subsequently reinstated on 1 February 2021. On 23 April 2021 the Western HSC Trust suspended their EMA service which had been maintained over the previous year by a single doctor working without any support. At the time of writing the service maintains suspended, and ICNI continues to monitor the situation closely and work with the Western HSC Trust to resume the service.

As many as 167 people living in the Northern, South-eastern and Western HSC Trust areas self-referred into the CAP service between October 2020 and June 2021 and requested access to abortion, but there was no local EMA service in which they could receive the care they needed and are legally entitled. This number will continue to increase unless services are commissioned, as all are susceptible to collapse without adequate funding in place.

Conclusion

FPA NI, and latterly ICNI, played a leading role in breaking down the walls of silence which surrounded the issue of abortion in NI for many years, and subsequently helped construct the building blocks which led to decriminalization.

A significant challenge for ICNI was to step in to provide an interim CAP service as an emergency response to COVID-19 and ensured that there was no delay in EMA services being established in NI. By doing so the organization demonstrated how a service can operate and the willingness of healthcare professionals in NI to provide such a service. Most importantly a vital local service was provided to women and girls during a global health pandemic. Such a ground-breaking service would not have been possible without ICNI.

Despite resistance from the health minister and the NI Executive to commission full abortion services, the dedication of local healthcare professionals and ICNI has meant that as of January 2022 2,794 women and girls accessed abortion services in NI since the new regulations took effect from 31 March 2020. ICNI will continue to work to advance sexual and reproductive rights and to ensure that no woman or girl is forced to leave NI to access abortion care that should be available locally.

Note

1   Despite the Secretary of State for Northern Ireland issuing a Direction in July 2021 which included an immediate requirement for the Department of Health to continue to support the Central Access Point provided by ICNI, no additional funding was provided and their service ceased on 1 October 2021. Since then there has been no local service; the British Pregnancy Advisory Service (BPAS) has provided an interim referral point, based in England, which is also unfunded.

18

Alliance for Choice volunteers

Emma Gallen

Abortion in NI has become my hobby since 2016. I began wanting to write about the people involved and instead became one of the people involved. There've been many volunteers for AfC over the years, even long before my time with the organization and there will be more still to come. I can't clearly remember the date of my first stall as they had been ad hoc when I started. I can't remember my first AfC meeting either, but I know it was on a Tuesday evening in Realta (or was it Queens?).

Getting involved in the AfC stall was about being there for advice, a call to action and as a barometer for public feelings and a place for people to ask questions about what was happening. It was usually on a Saturday 2 pm–4 pm and somewhere near Corn Market or Church Lane in Belfast City centre and at events and conferences and once or twice in other counties.

The driver for me to become more involved was the conviction, in April 2016, of a young woman who was reported by her housemates to the police for having taken abortion pills at home. I had been to a few AfC events before this, but the injustice of the prosecution spurred me to get further involved. Regularly organizing the stall was a tangible thing I could do that I felt would be of use. At the time, the Belfast Feminist Network reach was bigger than AfC's, I was organizing the monthly book club and monthly meetings for them, as well as being an admin for their Facebook group and page. There was, and still is, a huge overlap amongst the core organizers of both organizations. This is where the core group of the stall volunteers came from. People who I knew were feminist, some friends from the book club and friends of friends who could be vouched for.

Ceardha Morgan was one of the first women to volunteer to become a stall regular, she detailed why she got involved:

> I was offered the chance to join the stall. When you have the chance to do the right thing, you need a lot of good reasons not to do so. And somehow fear

of abuse, attack, embarrassment and censure just weren't enough to turn that chance down. No matter how often those fears rattled through my head.

The constant rage at living my entire life in jurisdictions that essentially persecuted women was festering in me. And so, the rage overcame the fears. Any reasons I had to refuse weren't reason enough for me anymore. Here was a chance; join in, make change.

I suppose I was tired of living in a state of passive fear and rage. I have always been pro-choice; this was my chance to be pro-active.

The 'Trust Women' postcards to Stormont calling for abortion in NI and a free vote to all MLAs had started before my involvement and was our main action on the stall until summer 2017. It had been successful in changing the discourse within party politics and moving the public conversation beyond the debate around 'good and bad abortions'. The slogan was subsequently adopted by Sinn Féin during the Irish Repeal Campaign in 2018; a little after we had decided to move on to a more inclusive call to action. The Assembly collapsed in January 2017, and we eventually abandoned the appeals to Stormont, even though we continued for a little while, not knowing there would be no Assembly for three years.

During this time, the Repeal the Eighth campaign led by the Abortion Rights Campaign in Ireland had been getting bigger, and members of the public in Belfast began asking us more about what they could do to effect change in NI (Roberts, volume 2). At this point, we had moved beyond friends of friends and now had an 'Activist 101' training for people to do before they would be representing AfC on the stall. We became aware of the need to ensure people understood the laws about abortion as well as the strict Belfast City Council rules around leafleting, what our main conversation goals and campaigning goals were and to vet potential new activists.

Karen Carson shared when and why she got involved with AfC:

> I got involved volunteering for AfC after the police raids on International Women's Day 2017. I had tried to get involved before that, but it clashed with work commitments. That International Women's Day though I was absolutely furious at how low the powers that be would stoop in their endeavours to silence the women of NI and stop us from having access to abortion healthcare. I emailed Dawn Purvis who directed me to AfC. I wasn't working at that point, so I was able to throw myself into doing the stall and I loved it. The support was overwhelming. Yes, there were some people who voiced their views against access to abortion healthcare but the majority of ordinary people who approached the stall absolutely supported a woman's right to choose. That's what I remember most, people's support for change.

On 29th June 2017, many AfC activists messaged each other in sadness and in anger that the A and B case narrowly lost in the Supreme Court in June 2017, challenging lack of NHS funding for abortion services for women from NI. However, within hours we were messaging with happiness as Stella Creasy had secured an amendment to the Queen's Speech forcing the UK government to make a U-Turn and placate the backbenchers furious with the DUP coalition post-election (Creasy and Sanquest, this volume). The new proposals allowed for the Government Equalities Office to ensure those in need of abortion in NI were able to get their abortions in England paid for.

Our next job on the stall was to explain what this meant, who this helped, who this left behind. For many people, that abortion was only now free in England was news to them! They had always assumed it was free, presumably because they hadn't needed to get one. Then came the news that it was going to be available in Scotland too; so many people who visited the stall had thought you could get the boat to Scotland, and it would be free there. Our job on the stall was often to fill the vacuum on up-to-date and accurate public information about abortion access in NI and Ireland. In a land with little to no non-religious sex education, it was often a huge gap in knowledge.

As the group of volunteers got bigger and the information was getting more complex, we started putting together cheat-sheets and 101s to try to explain what we wanted and how we thought we could achieve it. We also further developed the training and now it was 'So you want to talk about abortion?' and I often co-facilitated the sessions with Kellie O'Dowd and Emma Campbell to let the new recruits know about what to expect if they did volunteer.

Kathleen Girvan, who lives and works in Belfast, explains why she wanted to volunteer:

> As a teenager whose favourite film was Dirty Dancing, I'd always been interested in the issue of illegal abortion and was aware of (and angered by) the restrictions faced by women in Ireland. When I was a student in Dublin, I had supported the Abortion Rights Campaign and attended the Marches for Choice. I moved to Belfast and came across AfC on social media and began following them with the intention of somehow getting involved. Meeting stall organiser Emma Gallen at a feminist book club in 2017 gave me the opportunity to take part in activist training and volunteer with the stall.

This is also when the only abortion clinic on the island of Ireland, the Marie Stopes clinic, closed after opening controversially in 2012 (Biernat and Johnston, volume 2). One of our volunteers, who didn't want to be named, said:

I was motivated to volunteer for AfC following the closure of the Marie Stopes clinic in Belfast in late 2017. Prior to this, I volunteered as a client escort at the clinic. This involved escorting clients out of the clinic, past the protestors assembled outside, and walking with them to a location where they felt they could safely continue alone. Over the two years I spent at Marie Stopes, I witnessed the intimidation of women who were seeking to access necessary healthcare, and the volunteers who were trying to protect them. In addition, given the location of the clinic in a large, centrally located office building in Belfast, this experience made me aware of how any woman entering that building for any reason might be subject to harassment upon leaving the building. As someone who has always been strongly pro-choice, witnessing these efforts to control women's bodies only strengthened my resolve to continue with pro-choice activism. Volunteering with AfC provided me with a way to continue my activism in a way that felt meaningful. I learned from the reactions of passers-by to the protesters at Marie Stopes that there were some who agreed with – or would readily turn a blind eye to – their stance (if not perhaps their behaviour). Volunteering on the stall in Belfast city centre on Saturday afternoons provided a way to directly engage with the general public to discuss access to abortion and also show solidarity with anyone passing by who might need it. Being involved with AfC provided me with a way to involve myself in activism in the ways that I feel comfortable with, and to be part of the broader network of pro-choice and feminist activists in Belfast.

In the run up to the Repeal Referendum in Ireland (Roberts, volume 2), we still had stalls where people would ask us what was happening with the vote, ask us what we thought would happen and ask us what was going on in NI. Our cheat-sheets now had explanations as to the law in the North and how it differed to Ireland's position. There was a slight surge in volunteers post-Repeal from people who had been canvassing, but much like with ARC it slowly waned.

Úna McNulty, an artist and activist who lives in Belfast but is from the south of Ireland, explained why she got involved:

> It was the Repeal the 8th that reawakened my attention. It coincided with me giving up teaching work that I had been doing on Saturdays which freed me up to volunteer on the stall. I wanted to do my bit for the Repeal Campaign and also do my bit to support the extension of Abortions Rights to Northern Ireland. I came into the Repeal Campaign late but had been active in campaigning for Abortions Rights in the South in the late 80's and early 90's. I joined the campaign bus from Belfast to Monaghan and that reminded me how much I enjoyed interacting with people to hear what they have to say and share what I felt about Abortion Rights. So, when it came to doing my bit for the North's Abortion rights, I knew

the stall was the best place for me to be. I enjoyed my time at the stall and felt empowered by it, as I was doing something, however small an action it was, to support the campaign for Abortion Rights in Northern Ireland. I like the phrase 'doing my bit'. It really speaks to me and not just because of its historical connotations. What I had learnt from my past involvement in campaigning was that it's everyone doing 'their bit', no matter how insignificant it feels at the time, that brings about tides of change. I am now 52 years old and what I have learnt is that positive change can happen, and a society can be transformed by that tidal wave of everyone doing their bit.

The first stall after Repeal was one of the worst for abuse of the volunteers. People had largely ignored us before when they disagreed or shouted their disapproval as they walked past. After Repeal, people who opposed us felt entitled to a debate, felt entitled to call you names and felt you owed them a watertight debate as to why abortion should be allowed in NI. A special shout-out to our volunteer Elaine Crory for how well she handled that first post-Repeal stall. On that day she demonstrated how to shut down unhelpful conversations, especially those where greater empathy and understanding are not on the table.

Post-Repeal, Britain once again realized that actually NI didn't have abortion that was free, safe and legal on their doorstep the way most British people did. There was now a little isolated corner of Britain and Ireland that still insisted women had to travel for abortions. Yes, it was free but that wasn't good enough. We have always maintained that the abortion laws overly hurt working-class people, those in precarious employment and those on benefits. Even when travel and treatment is funded, it is the most marginalized or least able to access childcare, time off work, freedom from abusive financial, physical or emotional control and the right to travel who get left behind. The work we do is always about the people who continue to fall through the net, but also to recognize we deserve to be treated at home.

Sometime later the Conservative Minister Women's and Equalities for Penny Mordaunt publicly said that abortion in NI should be investigated; so, began 'Penny Post' a handwritten letter writing campaign to get the abortion law changed in NI. We knew from previous lobbying that emails were often dismissed, particularly if they followed a template. We'd been advised that a template email would count as one response from a group rather than looked at as all the individuals who were responding. These letters then became part of an impetus for the Women and Equalities Committee inquiry into abortion in NI, chaired by Maria Miller MP; the letters were even mentioned in a tweet from Penny Mordaunt. So, we continued to ask people to write to engage with the inquiry on the stall. Letter writing is not easily done with an audience, especially if there is a hostile street environment. Yet, people were interested, and again a special mention to Elaine Crory for managing the first stall with Penny Post. One of my favourite moments of solidarity came from Penny Post when a man came up and gave us two books of stamps to post the letters. It was a small gesture of a man amplifying women's voices.

Once the inquiry closed, we had to think of a new campaign, what we needed people to engage with, what might be legitimately interesting to them and something we might be able to achieve. We had free travel, but we didn't want to travel. We would soon be able to access abortions across the border in the twenty-six counties of Ireland, but it would cost a small fortune plus two doctor's visits and a three-day wait in between, no thanks. After a small meeting in a Belfast Cafe, we settled on 'Pen to Pengelly', asking Richard Pengelly, the Permanent Secretary for Health to make clear what abortion services are available in NI and that travel to England is an option. There were other, more controversial titles we considered for the campaign which we decided against. His response was to write back one volunteer and tell her that what we were asking him to do is the job of such organizations as AfC, an activist group, not a public health organization.

We had email campaigns running alongside the Saturday stall campaigns. Both Lives Matter, an anti-abortion group closely tied to the Evangelical Alliance, called for local councils across NI to take an anti-abortion stand when they realized they needed to counter our claims of NI being a largely pro-choice country, in much the same proportions as Ireland.

On 5th July 2019, Stella Creasy, alongside several abortion rights organizations, including AfC, drafted an amendment, for a second Executive Formation Bill, which said that if the Northern Ireland Assembly (NIA) was not up and running by 21st October 2019, Westminster would pass the primary legislation and decriminalize abortion in NI writing the CEDAW recommendations into law (Campbell; Creasy and Sanquest, this volume). This was the game changer. This also brought out the complications of being an activist within the context of NI into sharper focus.

'We're having abortion imposed on us from Westminster' was the new complaint. My personal thoughts were 'who cares! I'm going to have so much free time' but more on having to be careful what you wish for later.

The stall's role now was to explain what decriminalization meant to the confused public, who had been fed a lot of unsubstantiated nonsense from anti-choice organizations through the vehicle of local media and social media, scare mongering really. We had to explain carefully what would be allowed and what wouldn't. Although we have always strived for 'Free, Safe, Legal, Local' since 2016, we also had to explain that this did not mean abortion 'on demand' beyond twelve weeks. We encouraged people to contact their MLAs and say why they were glad this was about to be enacted. On 21st October, the NIA was recalled but no Executive was formed, despite some pantomime antics by the DUP. On 22nd October abortion was decriminalized in NI, many photos of celebratory drinks were shared on WhatsApp that night and many of our faces ended up on the walls of the streets of Belfast as part of an art project, as one of our members paid tribute to all of us who gave our time and passion to the fight. We had a low-key get together with volunteers past and present that evening. And we took that next Saturday off.

I emailed all the stall volunteers post-decriminalization and we met to discuss what they wanted to do. We agreed to meet on 30th November for Reclaim the Night with the idea being we'll take at least December and January off the stall. The last stall was 16th November 2019.

We heard that the NIO was about to announce the consultation process for the regulations on abortion. It was not a process we wanted to happen, but we had to engage with it all the same. We held the first Consultation Café on the 23rd November 2019 just over a month since decriminalization had happened and no woman or pregnant person could be arrested for accessing pills online and the woman and her daughter facing criminal charges were now safe from prosecution. However, the process wasn't over; we had been urged by the NIO to facilitate first-hand responses for their consultation as to what abortion services should look like. The Cafés were groups of pro-choice women meeting in a café with laptops and hard copies of the consultation to discuss what each question meant and how to best answer it. We reached out to people in the greater Belfast area to hold several of these until the consultation ended on 16th December.

I also organized a 'Stitch and Bitch' for choice, which was a session on learning how to crochet in a pro-choice environment and discussing the sort of standstill we had reached with campaigning, i.e. we didn't have abortion in NI, but we also knew that it was due to come.

Tina Campbell lives and works in Belfast and ran the Stitch and Bitch.

After moving home from Canada last year, I was so grateful to be invited to a wonderful feminist book club in a city I was reacquainting myself with. I immediately felt such warmth and acceptance from the group and when I discovered that most of the members also belonged to AfC, I was keen to get involved. At this time, we were marching and protesting for abortion rights in Northern Ireland and when, on October 21st, the law changed, I was lucky enough to witness the celebrations of these women and people that worked so hard for change. Having taken part in the Happy Activist training, I knew I wanted to get more involved in the group and when some of the women who had now become friends asked in passing if I would ever teach them how to crochet, our fearless leader, Emma, saw an opportunity. Crocheting is something I've enjoyed as a hobby for many years, and it was a privilege to get to teach others my skill in a safe space with important conversations regarding abortion rights. I'm looking forward to starting the classes outside of zoom chats when lockdown is lifted, and I feel so proud to work with such an amazing group.

We had decided that we would meet in March 2020, once we got the abortion guidelines to strategize what to do next, but COVID-19 and social distancing have meant that our next stages are not clear yet. Some of us had to help in much more practical ways with pills access, reminiscent of the pre-decriminalization and repeal days since COVID, and the network of volunteers being willing to help has been so important for people who would have otherwise had no access. We have also been able to participate in online webinars about self-managing abortion with pills, Happy Activist training and emailing MPs and MLAs to try and get them either to commission services or stop delaying commissioning. As ever, the dedicated team of volunteers engage online magnifying the voice of AfC, as well as signposting to pills when needed and help explain the ever-changing availability of abortion in NI. Our volunteering may change shape but while there's still work to be done, there will be people willing to give their time and energy until we have free, safe, legal, local abortion.

19

Conclusion

Emma Campbell and Fiona Bloomer

This book set out to establish how decriminalization of abortion was achieved in NI focusing on the themes of law, campaigning and activism. We began with a chapter foregrounding the universality of the need for abortion access; we travel through social, cultural and political strategies across the years, via powerful personal testimonies and determined actors. When we envisioned this book, it was intended to guard against the potential retellings of our journey that we had witnessed happening in Ireland, where often the real protagonists were omitted, or their contributions minimized. It is precisely because of this that we invited authors from a wide range of backgrounds to tell their own stories, to present their analysis of how decriminalization was achieved. Our aim in providing the vehicle for this is a feminist intersectional one, where we tried to imagine the voices that are not usually uplifted in retelling of how history was made.

AfC appears frequently in the book; yet still this volume does little justice to the range, depth and imagination of their work. They have been the warp and weft of the movement in the North, and their growth, adaptability and strength growing from a few people in a café to thousands on the streets have really been phenomenal for feminism in NI. Yet even such a tremendous force could not have done this work alone, which is why we pay tribute also to the outliers like MLA Anna Lo, who understood other people's oppression as if it were her own, to the unlikely hero of an English MP, Stella Creasy, who demonstrated how to take advantage of her backbench position with relentless parliamentary questions and amendments. It's why we establish the complexities and seeming immutabilities of the NI abortion legislation and the political system(s) that it resides within, in order to establish just how insurmountable the task seemed to many. Pierson's analysis is embedded within the understanding of her attendance at rallies and activist meetings as well as observation of anachronistic Stormont debates with precise critical analysis.

Les Allamby came to the NIHRC amid a controversial abortion Judicial Review and proved himself and the Commission worthy of the status of Human Rights defenders, even if it had not come soon enough for frontline activists who couldn't wait for CEDAW declarations to prove what they already knew daily – anti-abortion laws save no one and harm women and pregnant people every single day. Thomson succinctly captures the neglect of the British State, unwilling to right the wrong they enacted in 1861, and dashing the hopes of NI activists in 2008, causing a reluctance amongst some to work with Westminster, as outlined by O'Dowd, Cross and Bloomer. Whilst acknowledging the pain of the 2008 debacle, the authors moved to illustrate some of the other tactics employed to build a solid community base, address cultural stigma and bring more allies on board in the years that followed Westminster's chaos.

O'Brien demonstrates the vivacity of grassroots work in Derry and brings to life the urgency and dedication of a network of volunteers utterly committed to free, safe, legal and local access. Walker, a stalwart in her own right and a legend to many, brings in many voices from across the decades to help us understand what foundations had been laid to allow for groups like AfC, Rally for Choice and In Her Shoes NI to become what they were. Some of her account intersects with Simpson and Rowan's illumination of the role of the FPA NI/ICNI in changing the legislation, whose pregnancy counselling helpline provided the only safe access to abortions in England for many. Their continued passion and defence of the rights of women and pregnant people in the face of ongoing harassment from anti-choice protestors are hugely admirable. As the official voice of abortion in the public sector, for many years they had a foot in the table where AfC couldn't, equally AfC were able to provide information and access in a way FPA NI couldn't as AfC had no public funding and no charitable status at risk if they crossed the law. Enright's incisive analysis captures the breath of AfC's efforts to actively produce legal change and reshape the established boundaries of formal law-making authority. The radicalism of their actions extends now into an organized abortion doula network, working in the space that decriminalization has provided to assist abortion seekers.

Though it was sometimes a struggle, finally getting larger organizations on board with the pro-choice message was worth the effort. As Teggart and Rowan's chapter demonstrates, Amnesty in partnership with FPA NI utilized their reputational weight in legal and political arenas and recount the frantic days between court and Parliament. The battle fought by Sarah Ewart with her mum Jane Christie by her side and later joined by Amnesty provides insight into the huge personal effort made to bring about change (McKay's chapter).

The full impact of a lack of services is also felt so keenly in the chapter by Ashleigh Topley. Topley sacrificed five years to the legal process of the Judicial Review, gave evidence to CEDAW, spoke to countless journalists and politicians, came on dozens of marches and protests and hosted In Her Shoes NI from the position of someone who was denied the care she needed but wanted to help others. Her, Sarah Ewart and Denise Phelan all gave so much of themselves and their personal tribulations towards making the possibilities they never had, a reality for other women and pregnant people in NI. We knew we could never tell any of this story without including them.

In Lourenco's chapter, she describes the experience of intersecting marginalization, which could have seen her bereft, but instead her urge to organize and her disbelief at the north's lack of access to abortion, helped her find her community of likeminded souls. Equally Gallen's chapter describes a sliver of the vital work that volunteers attended to on behalf of abortion seekers everywhere and the delight and frustration that comes with that kind of direct engagement. Almost everyone in this volume will have either had an abortion or assisted others with their abortions, all of us will additionally hold countless people's private accounts of their own abortion journeys or those of partners, friends, parents, children because as Enright notes in her chapter about what constitutes legal work, we are all part of a critical community of care which encourages a greater tolerance of necessary disobedience. Her chapter elevates the service work and community building of AfC to legal world-building and frames the many legal transgressions for what they were, an attempt to provide survivability to abortion seekers.

This volume touches on some of the messiness of organizing in a contested state, around a topic deemed controversial to most and through any and all available channels. Importantly we hope it has demonstrated that no one single action can ever deliver social change, not even one group or one politician regardless of who writes the bill or lays down the gavel in the end. If we have any lessons at all to impart, it is that this work only ever reaches its goals via partnership and solidarity even when there isn't full consensus across all the detail. Contained in these pages are people who disagree vehemently on some finer points, who vary across the social divides and political spectrum, but none of whom could countenance the ongoing devastation caused to women and pregnant people who had until recently been effectively banished to England.

Abortion is simple and abortion is complicated. Yes, all we want is free, safe, legal and local abortion for everyone who needs it, but as we have seen, the law and medicine also require consideration. Social change has rarely been delivered benignly by those in power. First, we state the need, we gather evidence, we are often forced to demonstrate our denigration, then show the strength of opinion, when our rights should never spring from popular vote but from a recognition of our autonomy and freedom. This volume lifts the lid on some of that work, much of which can remain invisible outside of the circle of campaigners. Some of the complications can emerge from medical developments, technology, movements in feminism, legal change and language; this is why we have included an extensive appendix, containing contextualizing timelines both internationally and in NI, a glossary to explain key organizations, terms, changes or abbreviations, a bibliography for reference and further reading and an index for ease in searching around themes.

If readers look at this volume as way of capturing a series of parallel and occasionally overlapping modes of political and cultural change, hopefully the vastly different narrative styles, perspectives and roles of the authors can illustrate the required complexities at hand. When we discuss abortion in almost any global context, not just NI, we are addressing one of the totems of the culture wars, we are challenging the tangled knots of sexuality, gender, power, control, health, class, race and more. It is ever present, it is common, for most it is merely five tablets, and yet it generates political heat in a depressingly consistent way worldwide. Perhaps access to abortion and the transgressive ways in which much of the world must access it is a reminder that even when so much power has been taken away from us, we can survive like wildflowers with flecks of dirt and light. Pragmatic adaptability means people with unsupportable pregnancies have always done whatever it takes to get their abortions. These skills translate easily into civil transgression; furthermore, if abortion is deemed so wrong, what else do people need to re-evaluate, in what other transgressive ways can community serve us better than the laws and the institutions supposedly designed to help? Revolutionary ideas can begin at home and for many in this volume, they began in the vacuum left by being abandoned by the state which was filled by the pro-choice community.

We acknowledge that there will always be abortion work to be done, either in defence of the rights we have won or in a push for greater access, wider cultural awareness, less stigma and a deeper understanding. If your interest remains whetted by this volume and you wish to know more, we are publishing a second volume by Bloomsbury. This will cover themes such as pragmatic activism, cultural work, civic society solidarity, international solidarity, the work of local medical providers, as well as research highlighting the importance of the medical abortion pills and their ease of use, and the socio-cultural discourse surrounding abortion in contemporary NI. The two volumes offer different themes and allow for books that still relatively easy to carry.

What this book offers

Both volumes of this book weave the complex, multi-layered story of how decriminalization of abortion was achieved in NI, across a lengthy time period, across three jurisdictions and drawing on the extensive experience of the authors. They demonstrate that abortion activism has successfully changed the law and created history in doing so.

The sustained attention that this book provides presents a series of lessons for the global activist audience, eager to understand how this monumental success was achieved. The book offers a compelling primary resource for scholars, across many disciplines, who will seek to understand further how decriminalization was achieved and how we challenged dominant narratives to focus on the needs of those needing abortion.

Finally, we are grateful to our readers for supporting the work of abortion in NI and hope that each one of you can learn something new, as we did whilst collating all the chapters. Overall, this book hopes to ensure that the views of people directly affected remain a core part of the story of change in NI. Thanks for reading.

Timeline of key events: Global, Ireland, UK, NI

Global timeline of when jurisdictions introduced abortion on request

1950	North Korea
1953	Hungary
1955	Armenia, Azerbaijan, Belarus, Estonia, Georgia, Kazakhstan, Kyrgyzstan, Latvia, Lithuania, Moldova, Russia, Tajikistan, Turkmenistan, Ukraine and Uzbekistan as part of the Soviet Union
1965	Cuba
1973	Denmark, Tunisia, the United States
1974	Singapore, Sweden
1975	Austria, France, Vietnam
1977	Bosnia and Herzegovina, Croatia, Montenegro, North Macedonia, Serbia, Slovenia as part of Yugoslavia
1978	Italy, Luxembourg
1979	China, Norway
1983	Turkey
1984	The Netherlands
1986	Cape Verde (Czech Republic, Slovakia as part of Czechoslovakia), Greece
1988	Canada
1989	Mongolia
1990	Belgium, Bulgaria, Romania
1992	Germany
1995	Albania, Guyana
1997	Cambodia, South Africa
2002	Nepal, Switzerland
2007	Portugal
2010	Spain
2012	São Tomé and Príncipe, Uruguay
2015	Mozambique
2018	Cyprus, Ireland
2019	Iceland, Northern Ireland
2020	New Zealand
2021	Argentina, Australia, South Korea, Thailand

Ireland timeline (source: IFPA 2018)

1861   The Offences Against the Person Act is introduced in the British Empire (Ireland remained as a part of since 1801, though British occupation of various forms dated back to 1169), Sections 58 and 59 criminalized those who sought an abortion at any stage in a pregnancy, and those who helped/performed an abortion.

1921   Twenty-six counties, majority Catholic, in Ireland become independent from the British state, forming the Republic of Ireland, six with most Protestants remain, forming Northern Ireland.

1983   Referendum on Eighth Amendment of the Constitution (Article 40.3.3) is passed after a bitter campaign; 53.67 per cent of the electorate voted, with 841,233 votes in favour and 416,136 against. Article 40.3.3 of the Constitution reads: 'The State acknowledges the right to life of the unborn and, with due regard to the equal right to life of the mother, guarantees in its laws to respect, and, as far as practicable, by its laws to defend and vindicate that right'.

2011   Irish government establishes expert group to advise on implementation of ECHR judgement in *A, B and C v Ireland*, which ruled that state failure to implement existing constitutional rights to a lawful abortion when a woman's life is at risk violates Applicants C's rights under Article 8 of the European Convention on Human Rights.

2012   Savita Halappanavar dies in Galway University Hospital in circumstances where she was refused a termination during inevitable miscarriage because a foetal heartbeat was detectable.

2013   President Michael D. Higgins signs the Protection of Life During Pregnancy Act into law. The Act is intended to implement the 1992 judgement of the Supreme Court in the X case and the 2010 ECtHR in the case of *A, B and C v Ireland* and provide for lawful access to abortion where a pregnant woman's life is at risk.

2014   The UN Human Rights Committee (HRC) criticizes Ireland's abortion laws and urges legislative and constitutional change to bring these laws in line with human rights standards.
Concerns are raised about the adequacy of the Protection of Life During Pregnancy Act after a young migrant woman, known as Ms Y, who was pregnant as a result of rape, sought an abortion on grounds of suicide under the 2013 Act but was subsequently delivered of her baby by caesarean section.

2015   The UN Committee on Economic, Social and Cultural Rights (CESCR) criticizes Ireland's 'highly restrictive' abortion laws and urges the Government to amend the legislation and Constitution.

2016   The UN Committee on the Rights of the Child (CRC) expresses several concerns regarding the impact of Ireland's abortion laws on girls' human rights.

Government commits to establishing a Citizens' Assembly which will be asked to make recommendations on the Eighth Amendment.

2017   The UN Committee on the Elimination of Discrimination against Women (CEDAW) criticizes Ireland's abortion laws.

The Citizens' Assembly recommends by an overwhelming majority (87 per cent) that Article 40.3.3 (Eighth Amendment) of the Irish Constitution should not be retained in full. The Assembly shows very strong support for progressive regulation of abortion with 64 per cent voting in favour of access to abortion with no restriction as to reason.

The Joint Committee on the Eighth Amendment of the Constitution, tasked with considering the report and recommendations of the Citizens' Assembly on the Eighth Amendment of the Constitution, meets for the first time. The Committee is comprised of fifteen members of Dáil Éireann and six members of Seanad Éireann.

The United Nations Committee against Torture expresses concern at the 'severe physical and mental anguish and distress experienced by women and girls regarding termination of pregnancy due to the State policies'.

2018   Referendum to change the Constitution passed with 66 per cent votes in favour to repeal the Eighth Amendment.

2019   The Health (Regulation of Termination of Pregnancy) Act 2018 was enacted. Abortion access available without reason up to twelve weeks, conditions applied thereafter.

UK timeline (source BPAS https://www.bpas.org/get-involved/campaigns/briefings/abortion-law/)

1861   Offences against the Person Act introduced in England Scotland Wales, extended to countries in British Empire, Sections 58 and 59 criminalized those who sought an abortion at any stage in a pregnancy, and also those who helped/performed an abortion.

1929   Infant Life (Preservation) Act 1929 was passed. The Act criminalized the deliberate destruction of a child 'capable of being born alive'.

1938   *R v Bourne:* Abortion in case of risk to physical and mental health included in risk to life. Decision also implemented by some British territories and their successors.

1968   The Abortion Act 1967 is introduced in England Scotland Wales, providing grounds for exemption from the 1861 Offences against the Person Act.

1990   Human Fertilization and Embryology Act 1990 amends the Abortion Act 1967; time limits were lowered from twenty-eight to twenty-four weeks for most cases on the grounds that medical technology had advanced sufficiently to justify the change. Restrictions were removed for late abortions in cases of risk to life, foetal abnormality, or grave physical and mental injury to the woman.

2008   Human Fertilization and Embryology Act 2008, MPs voted to retain the
         current legal limit of twenty-four weeks. Amendments proposing reductions
         to twenty-two weeks and twenty weeks were defeated.

2016   Abortion was devolved to the Scottish Parliament via the Scotland Act 2016.

A note on convictions

Throughout the UK there have been several prosecutions in recent years relating to
the unlawful procuring or administration of abortion (primarily under the Offences
Against the Person Act) (BMA, 2017). These include cases of:

- Individuals illegally supplying abortifacients
- Women self-administering abortifacients
- Individuals covertly procuring or administering abortifacients.

**Timeline of events towards legal reform of abortion law in Northern Ireland
2010–20**

9 December 2010	Submission from Family Planning Association, NI Women's European Platform and AfC to CEDAW committee that abortion laws in NI amounted to grave and systematic violations of human rights.
30 July 2013	CEDAW committee publishes its concluding observations on periodic review of the UK.
2013 and 2014	Correspondence between NIHRC and Department of Health and Department of Justice raising concerns of compatibility of abortion law with human rights.
20 January 2014	The UK government submitted observations to the CEDAW committees request for an inquiry rejecting allegations of breaches of human rights law.
8 October 2014	Department of Justice issues consultation document on abortion law reform in cases of fatal foetal abnormality and for victims of sexual crimes. The NIHRC seeks a legal opinion on whether the law on abortion is compatible with human rights.
11 December 2014	The NIHRC lodges papers for judicial review.
March 2015	CEDAW committee decides to hold an inquiry into abortion law in NI.
16 April 2015	Department of Justice publishes responses to consultation on abortion law reform.

August 2015	ICCPR committee publishes concluding observations of its periodic review of the UK government's implementation of treaty obligations.
30 November 2015	High Court rules that the law on abortion is incompatible with human rights in cases of fatal foetal abnormality and victims of sexual crimes.
January 2016	The UK government agrees to visit of CEDAW members to Belfast and London.
12 February 2016	NI Assembly debates amendments to Justice (No2) Bill to allow for abortion in limited specific circumstances. All amendments were rejected.
11 July 2016	Ministers of Health and Justice agree to establish an inter-departmental working group on fatal foetal abnormality.
12 and 14 July 2016	CRC and ICESCR committees issue concluding observations on their periodic review of the UK government's implementation of treaty obligations.
10–19 September 2016	Visit of CEDAW committee designated inquiry members to Belfast and London.
11 October 2016	Report of the interdepartmental committee submitted to ministers.
12 January 2017	NI Executive collapses.
29 June 2017	NI Court of Appeal unanimously upholds the appeal of the Department of Justice and Attorney General against High Court ruling.
14 August 2017	UNCRPD treaty committee issues its concluding observations on periodic review of the UK government's implementation of its treaty obligations.
26 September 2017	Irish government announces decision to hold a referendum on abortion.
24–26 October 2017	Supreme Court holds a hearing on the NIHRCs appeal against NI Court of Appeal decision.
23 February 2018	CEDAW inquiry into abortion law published hold the law in NI constitutes grave and systemic violations of human rights. Observations of the UK government published rejecting the conclusions of grave and systematic violations found by the CEDAW inquiry.
25 April 2018	The interdepartmental report on fatal foetal abnormality is published.

26 May 2018	Ireland votes by 66.4 per cent to repeal the Eighth Amendment to the Constitution.
7 June 2018	The Supreme Court rules that the NIHRC does not have standing to bring a case without a victim, but indicates that abortion law in not compatible with human rights in cases of fatal foetal abnormalities and for victims of sexual crimes.
September 2018	The House of Commons Women and Equalities Select Committee launches an inquiry into abortion law in NI.
25 April 2019	The Women and Equalities Select Committee publishes its report.
9 July 2019	The House of Commons passes an amendment by Stella Creasy to the Northern Ireland Executive Formation Act to implement the CEDAW abortion inquiry recommendations in full.
24 July 2019	The Executive Formation Bill passes into law.
21 October 2019	Abortion is decriminalized in NI.
31 March 2020	The law to allow abortion where a woman's health is at risk comes into effect.

UN Treaty monitoring bodies' observations and recommendations on abortion law in Northern Ireland

UN Convention of Elimination of Discrimination Committee (CEDAW)	'The United Kingdom should expedite the amendment of anti-abortion law in Northern Ireland with a view to decriminalising abortion' (30 July 2013)
International Covenant on Civil and Political Rights Committee (ICCPR)	'The State party should as a matter of priority amend its legislation on abortion in Northern Ireland with a view to providing for additional exceptions to the legal ban on abortion including in cases of rape, incest and fatal foetal abnormality. The State party should also ensure access to information on abortion, contraception and sexual and reproductive health' (August 2015)
The Children's Rights Convention Committee (CRC)	'The State should decriminalise abortion in Northern Ireland in all circumstances and review its legislation with a view to ensuring girls access to safe abortion and post-abortion care services. The views of the child should always be heard and respected in abortion decisions' (12 July 2016)

International Covenant of Economic, Social and Cultural Rights Committee (ICESCR)	'The Committee is concerned that termination of pregnancy is still criminalised in all circumstances except where the life of a woman is in danger, which could lead to unsafe abortions and disproportionality affect women from low-income families who cannot travel to other parts of the United Kingdom' (14 July 2016)
Convention on the Rights of Persons with Disabilities Committee (CRPD)	'The Committee is concerned with perception in society stigmatising persons with disabilities living a life of less value and the termination of pregnancy at any stage of foetal impairment. The Committee recommends that the State party changes abortion law accordingly. Women's rights to reproductive and sexual autonomy should be respected without legalising selective abortions on grounds of foetus deficiency' (29 August 2017)

Intervenors to NIHRC Judicial Review 2015

1.	Humanists
2.	UNHCR
3.	JR76 (mother prosecuted for providing abortion pills to pregnant fifteen-year-old daughter)
4.	Sarah Ewart (written submission)
5.	Amnesty International (written submission)
6.	Christian Action and Research in Education (written submission)
7.	ADF International (UK) (written submission)
8.	Professor Patricia Carey (written submission)
9.	Centre for Reproductive Rights (written submission)
10.	Family Planning Association (written submission)
11.	British Advisory Service (written submission)
12.	Abortion Support Network (written submission)
13.	Birthrights (written submission)
14.	Royal College of Midwives (written submission)
15.	Bishops of the Roman Catholic Dioceses in NI (written submission)
16.	The Society for the Protection of the Unborn Child (written submission)
17.	Equality and Human Rights Commission (written submission)
18.	AfC (Written submission)

Glossary

Campaigning/lobbying groups/advisory groups

Abortion Rights UK	Abortion Rights was formed in 2003 by the merger of the two long-standing and influential campaigns – the National Abortion Campaign (NAC) and the Abortion Law Reform Association (ALRA).
AfC	Alliance for Choice, Belfast and Derry-based largest abortion activist group in NI.
Amnesty International	An international non-governmental organization with its headquarters in the UK focused on human rights.
ARC	Abortion Rights Campaign, sister grassroots organization to AfC, campaigns for free, safe, legal in the RoI. Was one of three organizational members of Together for Yes in Repeal 8th Campaign.
DFCNI	Doctors for Choice NI, a group of NI clinicians advocating and campaigning for reproductive rights in NI and across the UK.
FPA NI	Family Planning Association NI, non-governmental organization with responsibility for non-directive pregnancy counselling, contraception advice and sex education projects for special education needs schools in NI.
ICNI	Informing Choices NI, borne out of UK-wide closure of FPA took on portfolio of FPA NI.
NIACT	The NI Abortion and Contraception Taskgroup, group of medical doctors, midwives and nurses who provide abortion care in NI and lead on research and training.
NIHRC	NI Human Rights Commission, funded by the UK government, but is an independent public body that operates in full accordance with the UN Paris Principles. Established on the basis of the Belfast (Good Friday) Agreement, following conflict, rebuilds, respects and upholds human rights standards and responsibilities.
NIWEP	NI Women's European Platform, an NGO that instrumentalizes the UNCHR bodies to assert rights and submit to optional protocols and shadow reports.
Precious Life	Anti-abortion lobby group

RfC	Rally for Choice, Belfast-based activist group organizing counter-demos to pro-life marches
RHLPAG	Reproductive Health Law and Policy Advisory Group is a joint initiative between academics interested in reproductive health and rights. Its founding members are Dr Fiona Bloomer (Ulster University), Dr Kathryn McNeilly (QUB) and Dr Claire Pierson (the University of Liverpool).
VfC	Voice for Choice – UK-based organization campaigns for liberal access across England, Wales, Scotland and NI.

Abortion terms

EMA   Early Medical Abortion, abortion method, using medication, safely self-administered, up to twelve weeks six days gestation according to WHO
Surgical   Abortion using suction methods such as Manual Vacuum Aspiration
FFA   Fatal Foetal Anomaly/Abnormality
SFA   Severe Foetal Anomaly/Abnormality

Government departments

DHSC   The Department of Health and Social Care (England and Wales)
DOH   The Department of Health (Northern Ireland)
DOJ   The Department of Justice (Northern Ireland)
PPS   Public Prosecution Service
PSNI   Police Service of Northern Ireland
NIA   The Northern Ireland Assembly, aka Stormont, and the Assembly
NIO   Northern Ireland Office, UK government department with Parliament oversight of NI

Health and Social Care Trusts – responsible for health and social care service delivery in NI, divided into five geographic areas Belfast, Northern, South, South-eastern, Western.

Abortion providers

BPAS   provided abortion to NI women in English clinics; managed central booking line from 2017 to 2020
MSI   provided abortion to NI women in English clinics; managed central booking line from 2021 onwards. Belfast clinic offering EMA March 2013–17.
NUPAS provided abortion to NI women in English clinics.

Women on Web WOW – internet-based providers of EMA
Women Help Women WHW – internet-based providers of EMA

Political parties, Northern Ireland

Alliance Party NI – allows a free vote on abortion, most are supportive of decriminalization, party leader and high-profile MPs and MLAs support decriminalization.

Democratic Unionist Party (DUP) – seeks to maintain the union with rest of the UK, has morally conservative policies on all social issues, is opposed to any reform of abortion legislation, and does not allow party members a free vote on abortion.

Green Party NI (Greens) – supportive of decriminalization and working towards introduction of buffer zones for clinics.

People before Profit (PBP) – is an all-Ireland socialist party widely supportive of decriminalization and Buffer Zones.

Progressive Unionist Party (PUP) is linked to paramilitaries but for a time it described itself as the only left of centre unionist party, which is largely supportive of decriminalization and allows its members a free vote.

Sinn Féin – sees to break the union with rest of the UK and become part of all Ireland, supports abortion legislation in line with law in twenty-six counties of Ireland, does not allow party members a free vote on abortion.

Social Democratic and Unionist Party (SDLP) – seeks to break the union with rest of the UK and become part of all Ireland, allows a free vote on abortion; some members are opposed to any reform of abortion legislation, others are supportive of some reform.

The Good Friday Agreement (sometimes referred to as the Belfast Agreement) was a peace agreement negotiated by the majority of NI's political parties, and an agreement between the UK and the Republic of Ireland. It was signed in 1998 and ratified by public referenda in NI and the Republic of Ireland later that year.

Ulster Unionist Party (UUP) – seeks to maintain the union with rest of the UK, has morally conservative policies on many social issues, allows a free vote on abortion. Some members are opposed to any reform of abortion legislation, others are supportive of some reform.

Political parties, UK

Conservative Party UK – allows free vote on abortion, some hostile to change, majority supportive of decriminalization.

Labour Party UK – allows free vote on abortion, is supportive of decriminalization, although has been supportive of legal change but reluctant to take steps whilst in power.

Scottish National Party SNP – allows free vote on abortion, is supportive of decriminalization, though initially did not want to intervene as it would conflict with their devolved stance.

United Nations organizations

CEDAW UN Convention of Elimination of Discrimination Committee, requires signatories to report every four years on progress to eliminate discrimination, identified the UK as failing to do so NI; conducted inquiry, published in 2018, since written in part, verbatim as NI legislation.

CRC   The Children's Rights Convention Committee (CRC)

CRPDC   Convention on the Rights of Persons with Disabilities Committee

ICCPR   International Covenant on Civil and Political Rights Committee

IESCR   International Covenant of Economic, Social and Cultural Rights Committee

Bibliography

Alliance for Choice (2018) *Decriminalisation Motion in Belfast - Letter to Councillors*. Alliance for Choice. Available at: https://www.alliance4choice.com/news/2019/4/ decriminalisation-motion-in-belfast-letter-to-councillors [Accessed 22 April 2021].

Alliance for Choice (2019a) *Dear People Facing Abortion Pushback, We Know How You Feel*. Alliance for Choice. Available at: https://www.alliance4choice.com/ repeal-58/59/2019/5/dear-people-facing-abortion-pushback-we-know-how-you-feel [Accessed 22 April 2021].

Alliance for Choice (2019b) *Abortion Consultation Guide*. Alliance for Choice. Available at: https://www.alliance4choice.com/abortion-consultation-guide [Accessed 8 July 2021].

Alliance for Choice (2020) *Open Letter to Robin Swann, Health Minister for Northern Ireland*. Alliance for Choice. Available at: https://www.alliance4choice.com/ news/2020/10/open-letter-to-robin-swann-health-minister-for-northern-ireland [Accessed 8 July 2021].

Al-Othman, H. (2018) 'These MPs Say They'll Force the Government to Reform Northern Irish Abortion Law'. *BuzzFeed*. Available at: https://www.buzzfeed.com/ hannahalothman/these-mps-say-theyll-force-the-government-to-reform [Accessed 22 April 2021].

Amnesty UK (2014) Press release, Available at: https://www.amnesty.org.uk/press-releases/amnesty-launches-new-campaign-abortion-northern-ireland [Accessed 29 August 2021].

Amnesty UK (2015) 'Amnesty International and Sarah Ewart Join Court Challenge on Northern Ireland Abortion Law'. Available at: https://www.amnesty.org.uk/press-releases/amnesty-international-and-sarah-ewart-join-court-challenge-northern-ireland%E2%80%99s [Accessed 29 August 2021].

Amnesty UK (2016) 'Northern Ireland: Nearly 3/4 of Public Support Abortion Law Change - New Poll'. Available at: https://www.amnesty.org.uk/press-releases/ northern-ireland-nearly-34-public-support-abortion-law-change-new-poll-0 [Accessed 15 November 2020].

Amnesty UK (2017) 'Northern Ireland: Barriers to Accessing Abortion Services'. Available at: https://www.amnesty.org.uk/files/eur_45_0157_2015_northern_ ireland_-_barriers_to_accessing_abortion_services_pdf.pdf [Accessed 28 August 2021].

Amnesty UK (2018a) 'Northern Ireland: Conservative MPs Reject That Westminster Cannot Act on Abortion, Press Release'. Available at: https://www.amnesty.org.uk/

press-releases/northern-ireland-conservative-mps-reject-westminster-cannot-act-abortion [Accessed 28 August 2021].

Amnesty UK (2018b) 'Kate Beckinsale, Claire Foy, Jodie Whittaker and Olivia Colman Call on Theresa May to Change "Cruel" Northern Ireland Abortion Law Press Release'. Available at: https://www.amnesty.org.uk/press-releases/kate-beckinsale-claire-foy-jodie-whittaker-and-olivia-colman-call-theresa-may-change [Accessed 28 August 2021].

Amnesty UK (2018c) 'Northern Ireland Abortion: 75% of UK Public Want Government to Change Law - New Polls'. Available at: https://www.amnesty.org.uk/press-releases/northern-ireland-abortion-75-uk-public-want-government-change-law-new-polls [Accessed 28 August 2021].

Amnesty UK (2021) 'Abortion Rights Northern Ireland Timeline'. Available at: https://www.amnesty.org.uk/abortion-rights-northern-ireland-timeline [Accessed 29 August 2021].

Anker, K. (2016) *Declarations of Interdependence: A Legal Pluralist Approach to Indigenous Rights*. London: Routledge.

Arthur, J. (2018) *Finally the Injustice of Northern Ireland's Abortion Laws Is Being Recognised – Theresa May Must End This Gross Violation of Women's Rights*. Abortion News Info. Available at: https://abortion-news.info/finally-the-injustice-of-northern-irelands-abortion-laws-is-being-recognised-theresa-may-must-end-this-gross-violation-of-womens-rights/ [Accessed 8 July 2021].

Bailie, C. (2018) 'Abortion in Northern Ireland'. *International Journal of Gynecology & Obstetrics*, 143(2), pp. 131–3.

Bair, D. (1991) *Simone de Beauvoir: A biography*. London: Vintage.

BBC News (2001) 'Abortion Law to Be Reviewed'. 13 June. Available at: http://news.bbc.co.uk/1/hi/northern_ireland/1385897.stm [Accessed 29 July 2021].

BBC News (2002) 'Court Action over Abortion Guidelines'. 21 March. Available at: http://news.bbc.co.uk/1/hi/northern_ireland/1884321.stm [Accessed 29 July 2021].

BBC News (2003) 'Abortion Clarity Request Denied'. 7 July. Available at: http://news.bbc.co.uk/1/hi/northern_ireland/3049652.stm [Accessed 29 July 2021].

BBC News (2004a) 'Appeal over Abortion Guidelines'. 24 May. Available at: http://news.bbc.co.uk/1/hi/northern_ireland/3740729.stm [Accessed 29 July 2021].

BBC News (2004b) 'Landmark Ruling on Abortion'. 8 October. Available at: http://news.bbc.co.uk/1/hi/northern_ireland/3726494.stm [Accessed 29 July 2021].

BBC News (2007) 'Assembly Call over Abortion Guide'. 22 October. Available at: http://news.bbc.co.uk/1/hi/northern_ireland/7057128.stm [Accessed 29 July 2021].

BBC News (2008a) 'Labour MPs May Rebel over Embryos'. 21 March. Available at: http://news.bbc.co.uk/1/hi/uk/7308997.stm [Accessed 29 July 2021].

BBC News (2008b) 'MPs Reject Cut in Abortion Limit'. 21 May. Available at: http://news.bbc.co.uk/1/hi/uk_politics/7412118.stm [Accessed 29 July 2021].

BBC News (2009) 'NI Abortion Guidelines Published'. 20 March. Available at: http://news.bbc.co.uk/1/hi/northern_ireland/7954077.stm [Accessed 29 July 2021].

BBC News (2012) 'Northern Ireland Abortion Guidelines Judicial Review Granted'. 24 September. Available at: https://www.bbc.co.uk/news/uk-northern-ireland-19703370 [Accessed 29 July 2021].

BBC News (2013) 'Draft NI Abortion Guidelines Published by Minister'. 8 March. Available at: https://www.bbc.co.uk/news/health-21712388 [Accessed 29 July 2021].

BBC News (2016a) 'Abortion: MLAs Vote against Legalisation in Fatal Foetal Abnormality Cases'. 11 February. Available at: https://www.bbc.co.uk/news/uk-northern-ireland-35546399 [Accessed 28 August 2021].

BBC News (2016b) 'Woman Who Bought Drugs Online to Terminate Pregnancy Given Suspended Sentence'. 4 April. Available at: https://www.bbc.co.uk/news/uk-northern-ireland-35962134 [Accessed 28 August 2021].

BBC News (2016c) 'New Northern Ireland Abortion Guidelines Published'. 26 March. Available at: https://www.bbc.co.uk/news/uk-northern-ireland-19703370 [Accessed 5 June 2020].

BBC News (2017a) 'Man and Woman Cautioned over Abortion Pills'. 18 January. Available at: https://www.bbc.co.uk/news/world-europe-38669974 [Accessed 28 August 2021].

BBC News (2018) 'NI Abortion Reform: More than 170 Politicians Sign Letter'. 22nd July. Available at: bbc.co.uk/news/uk-politics-44914252 [Accessed 5 June 2020].

BBC News (2019a) 'Arlene Foster: *"Serious Negotiations" to Restore NI Devolution'*. 21 July. Available at: https://www.bbc.co.uk/news/uk-northern-ireland-49063374 [Accessed 5 June 2020].

BBC News (2019b) 'Abortion: Who is NI Law Challenger Sarah Ewart?' 3 October. Available at: https://www.bbc.co.uk/news/uk-northern-ireland-49921229 [Accessed 5 June 2020].

BBC News (2019c) 'Northern Ireland Abortion Protests Held at Westminster'. 26 February. Available at: https://www.bbc.co.uk/news/uk-northern-ireland-47373175 [Accessed 28 August 2021].

BBC Newsbeat (2017) 'I was Forced to Carry My Baby, Knowing She Would Die'. 11 April. Available at: http://www.bbc.co.uk/newsbeat/article/39437961/i-was-forced-to-carry-my-baby-knowing-she-would-die [Accessed 5 June 2020].

BBC Radio Ulster (2013) 'The Nolan Show'. 9 October.

Belfast City Council (2018) 'Agenda and Minutes, Council – Monday'. 9 April, 2018 6.00 pm. Available at: https://minutes.belfastcity.gov.uk/ieListDocuments.aspx?CId=164&MId=8740&Ver=4 [Accessed 28 August 2021].

Belfast Telegraph (2012) 'Fury at Larkin: Anger over Abortion Like "Bullet in Head" Comments'. *Belfast Telegraph*. 22 October. Available at: https://www.belfasttelegraph.co.uk/news/northern-ireland/fury-at-larkin-anger-over-abortion-like-bullet-in-head-comments-28876770.html [Accessed 11 July 2020].

Birrell, D. (2012) 'Intergovernmental Relations and Political Parties in Northern Ireland'. *British Journal of Politics and International Relations*, 14 (2), 270–84.

Blackford, I. @Ianblackford_MP (2019) 'For Those Asking, I Strongly Support Equal Marriage, and Women's Right to Choose on Abortion'. *Twitter.* 9 July, 11:07. Available at: https://twitter.com/Ianblackford_MP/status/1148534042192744448 [Accessed 29 July 2021].

Bloomer, F. (2020) 'Abortion in Northern Ireland-We Have Decriminalisation, What Comes Next?' *(OxHRH Blog).* Available at: https://ohrh.law.ox.ac.uk/abortion-in-northern-ireland-we-have-decriminilisation-what-comes-next/ [Accessed 8 July 2021].

Bloomer, F. and Fegan, E. (2014) 'Critiquing Recent Abortion Law and Policy in Northern Ireland'. *Critical Social Policy,* 34 (1), 109–20.

Bloomer, F. and O'Dowd, K. (2014) 'Restricted Access to Abortion in the Republic of Ireland and Northern Ireland: Exploring Abortion Tourism and Barriers to Legal Reform'. *Culture, Health and Sexuality,* 16 (4), 66–380.

Bloomer, F.K., O'Dowd, K. and Macleod, C. (2017) 'Breaking the Silence on Abortion: The Role of Adult Community Abortion Education in Fostering Resistance to Norms'. *Culture, Health and Sexuality,* 19 (7), 709–22.

Bloomer F., Pierson C. and Estrada, S.C. (2018a) *Reimagining Global Abortion Politics.* Bristol: Policy Press.

Bloomer, F., McNeilly, K. and Pierson, C. (2018b) 'Northern Ireland and Abortion Law Reform, Briefing Paper'. September 2018. Available at: https://pure.ulster.ac.uk/en/ publications/northern-ireland-and-abortion-law-reform-westminster [Accessed 8 July 2021].

Bogdanor, V. (2001) *Devolution in the United Kingdom,* Oxford: Oxford University Press.

Bogdanor, V. (2010) 'The West Lothian Question'. *Parliamentary Affairs,* 62 (1), 156–72.

Brennan, C. (2016) 'Demonstrations Taking Place around Ireland in Solidarity with Woman Charged with Taking Abortion Pills'. *The Journal.ie.* Available at: https:// www.thejournal.ie/pro-choice-abortion-pills-2550754-Jan2016/ [Accessed 22 April 2021].

British Medical Association (BMA) (2017) *Decriminalisation of Abortion: A Discussion Paper from the BMA.* Available at: https://www.bma.org.uk/media/1142/bma-paper-on-the-decriminalisation-of-abortion-february-2017.pdf [Accessed 30 July 2021].

British Pregnancy Advisory Service (BPAS) (1997) *Abortion Law Reformers: Pioneers of Change, Interviews with People Who Made the 1967 Abortion Act possible.* BPAS. Available at: https://www.bpas.org/js/filemanager/files/abortion_pioneers.pdf [Accessed 27 April 2015].

British-Irish Parliamentary Assembly (2019) *Report from Committee D (Environment and Social) on the Cross-jurisdictional Implications of Abortion Policy in the BIPA Jurisdictions.* Available at: http://www.britishirish.org/committee-d-reports/ [Accessed 22 July 2021].

Butler, D. (2018) *Prime Minister Must Stop Turning Blind Eye to Northern Ireland Abortion Rights, Labour Press Release, 24th October.* Available at: https://labour.org. uk/press/prime-minister-must-stop-turning-blind-eye-northern-ireland-abortion-rights/ [Accessed 25 July 2021].

Byrnes, A. (2013) 'The Committee on the Elimination of Discrimination against Women'. In Hellum, A. and Aasen, H.S. (eds.), *Women's Human Rights: CEDAW in International, Regional and National Law*. Cambridge: Cambridge University Press, 27–61.

Cafolla, A. (2019) 'Northern Ireland's Abortion Law Shaped My Identity'. *The Refinery*. 23 October. Available at: https://www.refinery29.com/en-gb/2019/10/8573152/growing-up-northern-ireland-abortion-law [Accessed 25 July 2021].

Cafolla, A. (2020) 'Abortion Has Come Grudgingly to Northern Ireland in the Wake of Coronavirus'. *The Guardian*. 13 April. Available at: https://www.theguardian.com/commentisfree/2020/apr/13/abortion-northern-ireland-coronavirus-women-stormont-rights [Accessed 25 July 2021].

Cahill, M. (2015) 'Pro-choice Woman Dares Police to Arrest Her for Having Abortion Pills'. *Belfast Telegraph*. 6 July. Available at: https://www.belfasttelegraph.co.uk/news/northern-ireland/pro-choice-woman-dares-police-to-arrest-her-for-having-abortion-pills-31356634.html [Accessed 25 July 2021].

Calkin, S. (2020) 'Transnational Abortion Pill Flows and the Political Geography of Abortion in Ireland'. *Territory, Politics, Governance*. https://doi.org/10.1080/21622671.2019.1704854.

Campbell, E. (2016) 'Think Women Seeking Abortion in Northern Ireland Have Other Options? Here's the Reality'. *The Guardian*. 5 April. Available at: https://www.theguardian.com/commentisfree/2016/apr/05/abortion-northern-ireland-sentencing. [Accessed 23 April 2021].

Campbell, E. (2018) 'It's Only the North's Leaders Who Say "No" to Abortion Rights'. *The Times*. 28 May. Available at: https://www.thetimes.co.uk/article/it-s-only-the-north-s-leaders-who-say-no-to-abortion-rights-m7p0966h9 [Accessed 22 April 2021].

Campbell, E. (2019) 'Now for NI: Fighting for Abortion Rights in the North'. *Irish Broad Left*. Available at: https://irishbroadleft.com/2019/02/21/now-for-ni-fighting-for-abortion-rights-in-the-north/ [Accessed 8 December 2018].

Campbell, E., Connor, N., Heaney, S. and Bloomer, F. (2021) 'Training Abortion Doulas in Northern Ireland: Lessons from a COVID-19 Context'. *BMJ Sexual and Reproductive Health*. http://dx.doi.org/10.1136/bmjsrh-2021-201098.

Cannold, L. (2002) 'Understanding and Responding to Anti-choice Women-Centred', *Reproductive Health Matters*, 10 (19), 171–9.

Centre for Reproductive Rights (2021) *World Map of Abortion Laws*. Available at: https://maps.reproductiverights.org/worldabortionlaws [Accessed 8 July 2021].

Children by Choice (2021) *Australian Abortion Law and Practice*. Available at: https://www.childrenbychoice.org.au/factsandfigures/australianabortionlawandpractice [Accessed 8 July 2021].

Connor, N. (2019) 'The North Is Today: Two Weeks on'. *Brook Blog* (blog). 4 November. Available at: https://brookblog.health.blog/2019/11/04/the-north-is-today-two-weeks-on/ [Accessed 8 July 2021].

Cooper, D. (2019) 'Conceptual Prefiguration and Municipal Radicalism: Reimagining What It Could Mean to Be a State'. In Cooper, D. Dhawan, N. and Newman, J. (eds.), *Reimagining the State*. London: Routledge, 171–90.

Crockett, M. (2018) 'The Campaign to Change Northern Ireland's Abortion Laws Explained'. Stylist. Available at: https://www.stylist.co.uk/long-reads/northern-ireland-abortion-law-explained-case-legislation-policy-human-rights-supreme-court/210864 [Accessed 8 July 2021].

Crockett, M. (2019) 'Alabama Ban Is Disturbing. Northern Ireland's Is Even Worse'. *Stylist.* Available at: https://www.stylist.co.uk/life/alabama-abortion-law-northern-ireland-countries-states-abortion-banned-without-exception/267150 [Accessed 8 July 2021].

Davies, M. (2016) 'Law's Truths and the Truth about Law: Interdisciplinary Refractions'. In Munro, V.E. (ed.), *The Ashgate Research Companion to Feminist Legal Theory.* London: Routledge, 77–94.

Davies, M. (2017) *Law Unlimited.* London: Routledge.

Delaney, D. (2010) *The Spatial, the Legal and the Pragmatics of World-Making: Nomospheric Investigations.* London: Routledge.

Department of Health Northern Ireland (2016) 'Guidance for Health and Social Care Professionals on Termination of Pregnancy in Northern Ireland'. March.

Department of Health and Social Care (2018) 'Central Booking System for NI Women Seeking an Abortion in England'. Available at: https://www.gov.uk/government/news/central-booking-system-for-ni-women-seeking-an-abortion-in-england [Accessed 28 August 2021].

Department of Health, Social Services and Public Safety (DHSSPS) (Northern Ireland) (2013a) 'The Limited Circumstances for a Lawful Termination of Pregnancy in Northern Ireland: A Guidance Document for Health and Social Care Professionals on Law and Clinical Practice'. In *Draft.* Belfast: DHSSPS.

DHSSPS (2013b) 'Northern Ireland Assembly, Guidance on Termination of Pregnancy in Northern Ireland: DHSSPS Briefing'. Available at: http://www.niassembly. gov.uk/assembly-business/official-report/committee-minutes-of-evidence/session-2013-2014/october-2013/guidance-on-termination-of-pregnancy-in-northern-ireland-dhssps-briefing/ [Accessed 29 July 2021].

Dickson B. and Davison, M. (1990) 'Family Matters'. In Dickson, B. (ed.), *Civil Liberties in Northern Ireland.* Belfast: Committee for the Administration of Justice, 186–204.

Dorsett, S. and McVeigh, S. (2012) *Jurisdiction.* London: Routledge.

Drapeau-Bisson, M.L. (2020) 'Beyond Green and Orange: Alliance for Choice – Derry's Mobilisation for the Decriminalisation of Abortion'. *Irish Political Studies,* 35 (1), 90–114.

Duffy, D.N. (2020) 'From Feminist Anarchy to Decolonisation: Understanding Abortion Health Activism before and after the Repeal of the 8th Amendment'. *Feminist Review,* 124 (1), 69–85.

Edgerton (Walker) L. (1974) *Women's Rights in Ulster Morning Star.* 22nd March, page 4.

Elgot, J. (2017) 'Rudd Enters Row on NHS Charging Women from Northern Ireland for Abortions'. *The Guardian.* 28 June. Available at: https://www.theguardian.com/world/2017/jun/28/rudd-row-nhs-charging-woman-from-northern-ireland-for-abortions-in-england [Accessed 28 August 2021].

Elgot, J. and McDonald, H. (2017) 'Northern Irish Women Win Access to Free
Abortions as May Averts Rebellion'. *The Guardian*. 29 June. Available at: https://
www.theguardian.com/world/2017/jun/29/rebel-tories-could-back-northern-
ireland-abortion-amendment [Accessed 21 July 2021].

Enright, M., McNeilly, K. and de Londras, F. (2020) 'Abortion Activism, Legal Change,
and Taking Feminist Law Work Seriously', *Northern Ireland Legal Quarterly*,
71 (3(OA) OA7–OA33.

Eric-Odorie, J. (2015) 'How Long Can Northern Ireland's Draconian Abortion Laws
Survive?' *New Statesman*. 30 June. Available at: https://www.newstatesman.com/
politics/2015/06/how-long-can-northern-ireland-s-draconian-abortion-laws-survive
[Accessed 21 July 2021].

Fearon K. (1999) *Women's Work: The Story of the NI Women's Coalition*. Belfast:
Blackstaff Press.

Fegan, E. (2010) 'Abortion Law in Northern Ireland: Behind the Iron Curtain'. *Address
to the Pro-choice Society at Queens University Belfast*. 9 February.

Fegan, E.V. and Rebouche, R. (2003) 'Northern Ireland's Abortion Law: The Morality of
Silence and the Censure of Agency'. *Feminist Legal Studies*, 11 (3), 221–54.

Ferguson, A. (2019) 'Unionists to Return to Stormont in Last-Ditch Attempt to Block
Abortion Law'. *The Irish Times*. 21 October. Available at: https://www.irishtimes.
com/news/ireland/irish-news/unionists-to-return-to-stormont-in-last-ditch-
attempt-to-block-abortion-law-1.4057009 [Accessed 21 July 2021].

Fletcher, R. (2005) 'Abortion Needs or Abortion Rights? Claiming State Accountability
for Women's Reproductive Welfare'. *Feminist Legal Studies*, 13 (1), 123–34.

Fletcher, R. (2018) 'RepealedThe8th: Translating Travesty, Global Conversation, and the
Irish Abortion Referendum'. *Feminist Legal Studies*, 26 (3), 233–59.

Flynn, A. (2016) 'Regulating Critical Mass: Performativity and City Streets'. *Windsor
Rev. Legal and Soc. Issues*, 37, 98–112.

Fox, M. (2009) 'The Human Fertilisation and Embryology Act 2008: Tinkering at the
Margins'. *Feminist Legal Studies*, 17 (3), 333–44.

FPA (2015) 'Abortion Practice and Provision in Northern Ireland – Factsheet'.

FPA (2017) 'FPA Affidavit, in the Matter of an Application for Judicial Review by JR76'.
April 2017.

FPA NI (no date) Internal Document, Pregnancy Choices Counselling Service,
Evaluation Form.

FPA NI Re an Application for Judicial Review [2003] *NIQB* 48; [2004] NICA 39

Francome, C. (1994) 'Gynaecologists and Abortion in Northern Ireland'. *Journal of
Biosocial Science*, 26, 389–94.

Francome, C. (2004) *Abortion in the USA and the UK*. Ashgate: London.

Francome, C. (2011) 'Attitudes and Practices of Gynaecologists towards Abortion in
Northern Ireland'. *Journal of Obstetricians and Gynaecologists*, 31 (1), 50–3.

Freeman, M.A., Chinkin, C. and Rudolf, B. (2012) *CEDAW Commentary*. Oxford and
New York: Oxford University Press.

Gallagher, C. (2019) 'Women and Equalities Committee 27th February 2019'. *Oral evidence: Abortion Law in Northern Ireland (HC 1584).*

Gallen, E. (2018) 'The Women Joining Forces across the Border to Fight Ireland's Abortion Laws'. *Dazed.* 21 May. Available at: https://www.dazeddigital.com/politics/article/40101/1/northern-ireland-women-joining-forces-border-to-fight-irelands-abortion-laws [Accessed 21 July 2021].

Galligan, Y. (2013) 'Gender and Politics in Northern Ireland: The Representation Gap Revisited'. *Irish Political Studies*, 28(3), pp. 413–433.

Ganiel, G. (2006) 'Ulster Says Maybe: The Restructuring of Evangelical Politics in Northern Ireland'. *Irish Political Studies*, 21 (2), 137–55.

Gentleman, A. (2016) 'I Needed an Abortion but My Consultant Told Me: "I'm Not Going to Prison"'. *The Guardian.* 7 January. Available at: https://www.theguardian.com/world/2016/jan/07/northern-ireland-abortion-ban-sarah-ewart-interview [Accessed 29 August 2021].

Gillen, A. (1999) 'The Other Troubles'. *The Guardian.* 17 August.

Glass Clark, M. (1995) '*Introduction*'. In Furedi, A. (ed.), *The Abortion Law in Northern Ireland.* Belfast: Family Planning Association Northern Ireland, 1–9.

Gorman, T. (2020) 'Stormont Assembly Votes against Abortion Regulations'. *RTE.* 2 June. Available at: https://www.rte.ie/news/ulster/2020/0602/1145056-stormont-assembly-abortion/ [Accessed 21 July 2021].

Graham, N., Davies, M. and Godden, L. (2017) 'Broadening Law's Context: Materiality in Socio-Legal Research'. *Griffith Law Review*, 26 (4), 480–510.

Gray, A.M. and Birrell, D. (2012) 'Coalition Government in Northern Ireland: Social Policy and the Lowest Common Denominator Thesis'. *Social Policy and Society*, 11 (1), 15–25.

Greening, J. (2017) 'Letter from Justine Greening of abortion in England'. Available at: https://assets.publishing.service.gov.uk/government/uploads/system/uploads/attachment_data/file/623669/Letter_from_Justine_Greening_on_Abortion_in_England.pdf [Accessed 09 April 2020].

Halfmann, D. (2011) *Doctors and Demonstrators: How Political Institutions Shape Abortion Law in the United States, Britain and Canada.* Chicago: University of Chicago Press.

Hansard (1990) 'House of Commons Debate'. 21 June. *HMG.*

Hansard (2007) 'Northern Ireland Assembly'. *Official Report.* October.

Hansard (2008a) 'Human Fertilisation and Embryology Bill [Lords]'. *Consideration of Bill: 22nd October 2008.* New Clause 30.

Hansard (2008b) 'House of Commons Debate'. *House of Commons.* 22 October.

Hansard (2013) 'Official report of the NI Assembly 12th March 2013'.

Hansard (2017a) 'House of Commons Debate'. *House of Commons.* 26 June.

Hansard (2017b) 'House of Commons Debate'. *House of Commons.* 28 June.

Hansard (2017c) 'House of Commons Debate'. *House of Commons.* 29 June.

Hansard (2018a) 'House of Commons Debate'. *House of Commons.* 4 June.

Hansard (2018b) 'House of Commons Debate'. *House of Commons.* 5 March.

Hansard (2018c) 'Northern Ireland (Executive Formation and Exercise of Functions) Act 2018, S.4.

Hansard (2018d) 'House of Commons Debate'. *House of Commons*. 24 October.

Hansard (2019a) 'House of Commons Debate'. *House of Commons*. 30 January.

Hansard (2019b) 'Domestic Abuse Bill'. *HC Bill*, 422.

Hansard (2019c) 'House of Commons Debate'. *House of Commons*. 9 July.

Hansard (2019d) 'Report under Section 4 of the Executive Formation and Exercise of Functions Act 2018'. *House of commons debate, House of Commons*. 30 January.

Hansard (2019e) 'Report under Section 4 of the Executive Formation and Exercise of Functions Act 2018'. *House of commons debate, House of Commons*. 1 May.

Hansard (2019f) 'Northern Ireland Budget (Anticipation and Adjustments) (No. 2)'. *Bill*. 5 March.

Hansard (2019g) 'House of Commons Debate'. *House of Commons*. 5 March.

Hansard (2019h) 'House of Commons Debate'. *House of Commons*. 2 October.

Hansard (2020) 'Official Report of the NI Assembly'. 2 June.

Harding, R. and Peel, E. (2019) 'Polyphonic Legality: Power of Attorney through Dialogic Interaction'. *Social and Legal Studies*, 28 (5), 675–97.

Hellen, N. and Wheeler, C. (2019) 'Abortion reform "blocked to protect DUP deal"'. *The Sunday Times*. 27 January. Available at: https://www.thetimes.co.uk/article/abortion-reform-blocked-to-protect-dup-deal-kpbw8vltt [Accessed 21 July 2021].

Hendry, J. (2019) 'A Legally Pluralist Approach to the Bakassi Peninsula Case'. In Gonzalez-Salzberg D. and Hodson L. (eds.), *Research Methods for International Human Rights Law: Beyond the Traditional Paradigm*. London: Routledge, 123–45.

Hennessy, T. (2008) 'Gordon Brown and Harriet Harman Is Abortion Bust-up'. *The Telegraph*. 12 July. Available at: https://www.telegraph.co.uk/news/politics/labour/2403614/Gordon-Brown-and-Harriet-Harman-in-abortion-bust-up.html [Accessed 21 July 2021].

Hennessey, T., Braniff, M., McAuley, J.W., Tonge, J. and Whiting, S.A. (2018) *The Ulster Unionist Party: Country before Party?* Oxford: Oxford University Press.

Higgins, K. (2020) 'Abortion Rules in Chaos as Northern Ireland Struggles to Cope with New Rules Imposed by Travel Restrictions'. *South West Londoner* (blog). 5 May. Available at: https://www.swlondoner.co.uk/uncategorised/06052020-abortion-rules-in-chaos-as-northern-ireland-struggles-to-cope-with-new-rules-imposed-by-travel-restrictions/ [Accessed 21 July 2021].

Hill, M., Walker, L. and Ward, M. (2019) *A Century of Women*. Available at: https://www.acenturyofwomen.com/ [Accessed 21 July 2021].

Holland, K. (1999) 'Pickets Close NI Pregnancy Advisory Association'. *The Irish Times*. 5 August. Available at: https://www.irishtimes.com/news/pickets-close-ni-pregnancy-advisory-association-1.213559 [Accessed 21 July 2021].

Holland, K. (2016) 'Abortion Pills Trio: Law Making Women Criminals "Absolutely Bad"'. *The Irish Times*. 25 May. Available at: https://www.irishtimes.com/news/social-affairs/abortion-pills-trio-law-making-women-criminals-absolutely-bad-1.2659395 [Accessed 14 January 2021].

Horgan, G. (1982) *Abortion: Why Irish Women Must Have the Right to Choose*. Dublin: Socialist Workers Party.

Horgan, G. (1990) 'Abortion: Why Irish Women Must Have the Right to Choose'. Pamphlet. Dublin, Bookmarks.

Horgan, G. (2017) 'If Northern Irish Women Can Now Have an Abortion in England, Why Not Here?' *The Guardian*. 22 August. Available at: https://www.theguardian.com/commentisfree/2017/aug/22/women-northern-ireland-abortion-reproductive-rights-westminster-change-law [Accessed 21 July 2021].

ICNI (2021) 'Beyond Decriminalisation: Pregnancy Choices and Abortion Care in Northern Ireland'. Available at: https://informingchoicesni.org/wp-content/uploads/2021/06/Beyond-Decriminalisation-Report.pdf [Accessed 21 July 2021].

The Irish News (2020) '"Central Access Point" launched for Abortion Services in Northern Ireland'. 16 April. Available at: https://www.irishnews.com/news/northernirelandnews/2020/04/16/news/-central-access-point-launched-for-abortion-services-in-northern-ireland-1903701/ [Accessed 21 July 2021].

ITV News (2020) 'Postcode Lottery for Abortion Services' One Year Since Law Change in NI – Amnesty'. 21 October. Available at: https://www.itv.com/news/utv/2020-10-21/postcode-lottery-for-abortion-services-one-year-since-law-change-in-ni-amnesty [Accessed 21 July 2021].

Jaggar, A.M. (2014) *Gender and Global Justice*. Cambridge: Cambridge Polity.

The Journal IE (2019) 'London Irish Campaigners Taking British Government to Court over Northern Ireland Abortion Laws'. *The journal.ie*, 9 July. Available at: https://www.thejournal.ie/abortion-rights-campaigner-take-uk-govt-to-court-4716741-Jul2019/ [Accessed 21 July 2021].

Kennedy, R., Pierson, C. and Thomson, J. (2016) 'Challenging Identity Hierarchies: Gender and Consociational Power-Sharing'. *The British Journal of Politics and International Relations*, 18 (3), 618–33.

King, D. (2016) 'I Handed Myself in to Police for Helping Women in the UK to Get an Abortion'. *The Independent*, 30 May. Available at: https://www.independent.co.uk/voices/northern-ireland-abortion-protesters-handed-myself-police-helping-women-a7055191.html [Accessed 21 July 2021].

Kinglsey, P. (2017) 'Northern Ireland Is Sinking into a Profound Crisis'. *The New York Times*. 20 November. Available at: https://www.nytimes.com/2017/11/20/world/europe/northern-ireland-stormont-adams.html [Accessed 21 July 2021].

Kleinhans, M.M. and Macdonald, R.A. (1997) 'What Is a Critical Legal Pluralism'. *Journal of Law and Society*, 12 (02), 25–46.

Lazare, S. (2017) 'Free, Safe, Legal: Thousands Demand Ireland Bring Abortion "Out of the Shadows"'. *Common Dreams*. Available at: https://www.commondreams.org/news/2015/09/27/free-safe-legal-thousands-demand-ireland-bring-abortion-out-shadows [Accessed 22 April 2021].

Lorde, A. (2002) '*A Litany for Survival*' the Collected Poems of Audre Lorde. New York: WW Norton & Co.

Mackay, F. and McAllister, L. (2012) 'Feminising British Politics: Six Lessons from Devolution in Scotland and Wales'. *The Political Quarterly*, 83 (4), 730–4.

Maguire, P. (2017) 'The DUP Are the Real Winners of the 2017 General Election'. *The New Statesman*. 6 June. Available at: https://www.newstatesman.com/politics/june2017/2017/06/dup-are-real-winners-2017-general-election [Accessed 2 November 2020].

Matthews, N. and Pow, J. (2017) 'A Fresh Start? The Northern Ireland Assembly Election 2016'. *Irish Political Studies*, 32 (2), 311–26.

McCann, G. and Hainsworth, P. (2016) 'Brexit and Northern Ireland: The 2016 Referendum on the United Kingdom's Membership of the European Union'. *Irish Political Studies*, 32 (2), 327–42.

McCormick, L. (2015). "No Sense of Wrongdoing": Abortion in Belfast 1917–1967. *Journal of Social History*, 49(1), 125–148.

McDonald, H. (2013) 'Northern Irish Women Risk Jail by Admitting Use of Abortion Drugs'. *The Guardian*. 10 March. Available at: https://www.theguardian.com/world/2013/mar/10/northern-irish-women-risk-jail-over-abortion-drug-use [Accessed 21 July 2021].

McDonald, H. (2015) 'Pro-choice Activists Picket Derry Police Station over Mother's Abortion Trial'. *The Guardian*. 15 July. Available at: https://www.theguardian.com/uk-news/2015/jul/15/pro-abortion-campaigners-picket-derry-police-station-mother-prosecution [Accessed 21 July 2021].

McDonald, H. (2016a) 'Pro-choice Activists Plan Belfast Protest over Woman's Abortion Trial'. *The Guardian*. 13 January. Available at: https://www.theguardian.com/uk-news/2016/jan/13/pro-choice-activists-plan-belfast-protest-abortion-trial-northern-ireland [Accessed 22 April 2021].

McDonald, H. (2016b) 'Northern Irish Woman Given Suspended Sentence over Self-induced Abortion'. *The Guardian*. 4 April. Available at: https://www.theguardian.com/uk-news/2016/apr/04/northern-irish-woman-suspended-sentence-self-induced-abortion [Accessed 3 November 2020].

McDonald, H. (2016c) 'Hounded and Picketed: The Targeting of Belfast's Family Planning Advisers'. *The Guardian*. 6 January. Available at: https://www.theguardian.com/world/2016/jan/06/belfast-family-planning-advisers-hounded-and-followed-by-anti-abortion-activists [Accessed 21 July 2021].

McDonald, H. (2017) 'Northern Ireland Police Raided Premises in Search for Abortion Pills'. *The Guardian*. 13 March. Available at: https://www.theguardian.com/uk-news/2017/mar/13/northern-ireland-police-raided-premises-searching-for-abortion-pills [Accessed 21 July 2021].

McHugh, M. (2020) 'Campaigner – Urgent Action Needed for Abortions during Coronavirus Outbreak'. *The Belfast Telegraph*. 30 March. Available at: https://www.belfasttelegraph.co.uk/news/northern-ireland/campaigner-urgent-action-needed-for-abortions-during-coronavirus-outbreak-39087822.html [Accessed 21 July 2021].

McLaughlin, E. (2007) 'From Negative to Positive Equality Duties: The Development and Constitutionalism of Equality Provisions in the UK'. *Social Policy and Society*, 6 (1), 111–21.

Moon, D., Thomson, J. and Whiting, S. (2019) 'Lost in the Process? The Impact of Devolution on Abortion Law in the United Kingdom'. *British Journal of Politics and International Relations*, 21 (4), 728–45.

Moriarty, G. (2020) 'SF Proposes Tightening NI Abortion Legislation over Non-fatal Disability'. *The Irish Times*. 31 May. Available at: https://www.irishtimes.com/news/ireland/irish-news/sf-proposes-tightening-ni-abortion-legislation-over-non-fatal-disability-1.4267082 [Accessed 21 July 2021].

Mukungu, K. (2018) 'But What Do You Do When You Believe That the Law is Wrong? Civil Disobedience in Pro-choice Activism in Northern Ireland.' In *North East Crime Research Conference*. 25 April. York, England: York St John University.

Murphy, J. (2017) 'Theresa May Suffers Abortion Vote Chaos in First Test of DUP deal'. *The Evening Standard*. 29 June. Availableat:https://www.standard.co.uk/news/politics/theresa-may-suffers-abortion-vote-chaos-in-first-test-of-dup-deal-a3575861.html [Accessed 21 July 2021].

NIACT (2021) 'Report on Sexual and Reproductive Health in Northern Ireland'. *NIACT*. Available at: https://pure.ulster.ac.uk/en/publications/report-on-sexual-and-reproductive-health-in-northern-ireland [Accessed 21 July 2021].

Northern Ireland Abortion Campaign (1982) *Abortion in Northern Ireland-Results of a Survey Carried out by NIAC amongst General Practitioners in NI*. NIAC.

Northern Ireland Abortion Law Reform Association (1985) *Why We Need the 1967 Abortion Act*. NIALRA.

Northern Ireland Human Rights Commission (2001) *Making a Bill of Rights for Northern Ireland*.

O'Dowd, K. (2018) 'Britain Is Denying Abortion Rights to Northern Ireland'. *Green Left. Northern Ireland*. 21 June. Available at: https://www.greenleft.org.au/content/britain-denying-abortion-rights-northern-ireland [Accessed 21 July 2021].

O'Hara, M. (2009) 'We're Talking about Women's Lives'. *The Guardian*. 17 October.

O'Rourke, C. (2016) 'Advocating Abortion Rights in Northern Ireland: Local and Global Tensions'. *Social and Legal Studies*, 25 (6), 716–40.

O'Rourke, C. (2019) 'Bridging the Enforcement Gap? Evaluating the Inquiry Procedure of the CEDAW Optional Protocol'. *American University Journal of Gender, Social Policy and the Law*, 27 (1), 1–31.

Palmer, J. (2009) 'Seeing and Knowing: Ultrasound Images in the Contemporary Abortion Debate'. *Feminist Theory*, 10 (2), 173–89.

Pierson, C. (2018) 'Rights versus Rites? Catholic Women and Abortion Access in Northern Ireland'. In Burgess, T.P. (ed.), *The Contested Identities of Ulster Catholics*. London: Palgrave Macmillan, 39–55.

Pierson, C. (2019) 'Gendering Peace in Northern Ireland: The Role of United Nations Security Council Resolution 1325 on Women, Peace and Security'. *Capital and Class*, 43 (1), 57–71.

Pierson, C. and Bloomer, F. (2017) 'Macro-and Micro-Political Vernaculizations of Rights: Human Rights and Abortion Discourses in Northern Ireland'. *Health and Human Rights*, 19 (1), 173–85.

Pierson, C. and Bloomer, F.K. (2018) 'Anti-abortion Myths in Political Discourse'. In McQuarrie C., Pierson C., Bloomer F. and Shettner, S. (eds.), *Crossing Troubled Waters: Abortion in Ireland, Northern Ireland, and Prince Edward Island*, Prince Edward Island: Prince Edward University Press, 184–311.

Pierson, C., McNeilly, K. and Bloomer, F. (2018) 'Devolution and Abortion Law Reform in Northern Ireland. Briefing Note October 2018'. Available at: https://pure.ulster. ac.uk/en/publications/devolution-and-abortion-law-reform-in-northern-ireland-briefing.

Press Association (2016) 'Drone Delivers Abortion Pills to Northern Irish Women'. *The Guardian*. 21 June. Available at: https://www.theguardian.com/uk-news/2016/jun/21/drone-delivers-abortion-pills-to-northern-irish-women [Accessed 21 July 2021].

Proctor, K. and Steward, H. (2019) 'Abortion Rights Used to Get DUP to Back Brexit Deal, says Stella Creasy'. *The Guardian*. 16 October. Available at: https://www.theguardian.com/politics/2019/oct/16/abortion-rights-used-to-get-dup-to-back-brexit-deal-says-stella-creasy [Accessed 21 July 2021].

Rawls, J. (1971) *A Theory of Justice*. Cambridge: Harvard University Press.

Rossiter, A. (2009) *Ireland's Hidden Diaspora: The Abortion Trail and the Making of a London-Irish Underground, 1980–2000*. London: IASC.

Royal College of Nursing (2013) RCN Consultation Response to 'The Limited Circumstances for a Lawful Termination of Pregnancy in Northern Ireland'.

Royal College of Psychiatrists (2013) RCPSYCH Consultation Response to 'The Limited Circumstances for a Lawful Termination of Pregnancy in Northern Ireland'.

Sanghani, R. (2015) '"Arrest Us": Northern Irish Women Want to Be Prosecuted for Breaking Abortion Laws'. *The Telegraph*. 26 June. Available at: http://www.telegraph.co.uk/women/womens-life/11700651/Abortion-Northern-Irish-women-want-arrest-over-illegal-abortion-pills.htm [Accessed 21 July 2021].

Sharp, K. and Earle, S. (2002) 'Feminism, Abortion and Disability: Irreconcilable Differences?'. *Disability and Society*, 17 (2), 137–45.

Shaw, S. (2013) 'Gender and Politics in the Devolved Assemblies'. *Soundings*, 55, 82–94.

Sheldon, S. (1997) *Beyond Control: Medical Power and Abortion Law*. London: Pluto.

Sheldon, S., O'Neill, J., Parker, C. and Davis, G. (2020) '"Too Much, Too Indigestible, Too Fast"? The Decades of Struggle for Abortion Law Reform in Northern Ireland'. *The Modern Law Review*, 83, 761–96.

Side, K. (2006) 'Contract, Charity, and Honorable Entitlement: Social Citizenship and the 1967 Abortion Act in Northern Ireland after the Good Friday Agreement'. *Social Politics: International Studies in Gender, State and Society*, 13 (1), 89–116.

Socialist Worker (2008) 'The Dates of Ann Widdecombe's anti-Abortion Speaking Tour'. https://socialistworker.co.uk/art/13774/The%20dates%20of%20Ann%20 Widdecombe%27s%20anti-abortion%20speaking%20tour [Accessed 21 July 2021].

Society for the Protection of Unborn Children, Re an Application for Judicial Review [2009] *NIQB* 92.

Sturgeon, N. @NicolaSturgeon (2019) I'm Not in the House of Commons but If I Was, I'd Vote for Amendments on NI Equal Marriage and Women's Right to Choose Twitter, 9 July, 11:16. Available at: https://twitter.com/NicolaSturgeon/ status/1148536432602112000l

Sweeney, J. (2013) 'Mother's Tragic Abortion Story Could Spark Reappraisal of Rules for Northern Ireland Medics'. *Belfast Telegraph*. 10 October. Available at: https://www. belfasttelegraph.co.uk/news/northern-ireland/mothers-tragic-abortion-story-could-spark-reappraisal-of-rules-for-northern-ireland-medics-29648562.html [Accessed 29 August 2021].

Thomson, J. (2016a) 'Explaining Gender Equality Difference in a Devolved System: The Case of Abortion Law in Northern Ireland'. *British Politics*, 11 (3), 371–88.

Thomson, J. (2016b) 'Thinking Globally, acting Locally?: The Women's Sector, International Human Rights Mechanisms and Politics in Northern Ireland'. *Politics*, 37 (1), 82–96.

Thomson, J. (2019a) 'Feminising Politics, Politicising Feminism? Women in Post-conflict Northern Irish Politics'. *British Politics*, 14 (2), 181–97.

Thomson, J. (2019b) *Political Institutions and Abortion Law: Explaining Policy Resistance*. London: Palgrave Macmillan.

Tonge, J. (2020) 'Beyond Unionism versus Nationalism: The Rise of the Alliance Party of Northern Ireland'. *The Political Quarterly*, 91 (2), 461–6.

Tonge, J., Braniff, M., Hennessey, T., McAuley, J.W. and Whiting, S. (2014) *The Democratic Unionist Party: From Protest to Power*. Oxford: Oxford University Press.

Uberoi, E., Watson, C. and Kirk-Wade, E. (2020) 'Women in Parliament and Government'. House of Commons Briefing Paper, No. 01250, 25 February 2020. Available at: https://commonslibrary.parliament.uk/research-briefings/sn01250/ [Accessed 21 July 2021].

UK Government (1861) Offences against the Person Act 1861.

UK Government (1967) The Abortion Act 1967.

UK Parliament (1966) *Medical Termination of Pregnancy Bill* (HC).

UK Parliament (1972) *Abortion* (HC).

UK Parliament (1984) *Abortions* (HC).

UK Parliament (1985) *Abortion* (HC).

UK Parliament (1986) *Abortions* (HC).

UK Parliament (1987) *Abortion* (HC).

UK Parliament (1989) *Abortion (Carlisle Baby Case)* (HC).

UK Parliament (1993) *Abortion* (HC).

UK Parliament (1994) *Birth Control and Abortion* (HC).

UK Parliament (1995) *Abortion* (HC).

UK Parliament (1995) *Birth Control* (HC).

UK Parliament (1998) *Abortion* (HC).

UK Parliament (1998) *Reserved Matters* (HC).

UK Parliament (2000) *Abortion and Contraceptive Services* (HC).

UK Parliament (2008) *Human Fertilisation and Embryology Bill, No. 2* (HC).

UK Parliament (2009) *Abortion Law (Northern Ireland)* (WH).

UK Supreme Court (2017) UKSC 41.

UK Supreme Court (2018) UKSC 27.

Ulster Pregnancy Advisory Association LTD (Undated) Abortions for Women in Northern Ireland (Leaflet) UPPA.

UN CEDAW (1993) Concluding Observations of CEDAW Regarding: The United Kingdom of Great Britain and Northern Ireland, June 1999, 21ˢᵗ session.

UN CEDAW (1999) General Recommendations No.24 (20ᵗʰ session, 1999), *Article 12: Women and Health.*

UN CEDAW (2008) Concluding Observations of CEDAW Regarding: The United Kingdom of Great Britain and Northern Ireland, 18 July, C/GBR/CO/6.

UN CEDAW (2013) Concluding Observations on the Seventh Periodic Report of the United Kingdom of Great Britain and Northern Ireland, 30 July, *CEDAW/C/GBR/CO/7.*

UN CEDAW (2018) Inquiry Concerning the United Kingdom of Great Britain and Northern Ireland under Article 8 of the Optional Protocol to the Convention on the Elimination of All Forms of Discrimination against Women. Available at: https://tbinternet.ohchr.org/_layouts/15/treatybodyexternal/TBSearch.aspx?Lang=en&TreatyID=3&DocTypeCategoryID=7 [Accessed 28th January 2021].

UN CESCR (2009) Concluding Observations of CESCR Regarding the United Kingdom and Northern Ireland, 22 May, E/C. 12/GBR/CO/5.

United Kingdom Government (2018) Observations of the Government of the United Kingdom of Great Britain and Northern Ireland on the Report of the Inquiry Concerning United Kingdom of Great Britain and Northern Ireland of the Committee on the Elimination of Discrimination against Women under Article 8 of the Optional Protocol to the Convention on the Elimination of All Forms of Discrimination against Women, 23 February 2018.

Walker L. (2017) *Living in an Armed Patriarchy-Public Protest Domestic Acquiescence.* Belfast: Communist Party of Ireland.

Ward, M. (2009) *Involving Women: A Key Issue in Security and Peace Reconstruction.* Organisation for Security and Co-operation in Europe. Available at: http://www.osce.org/gender/36863 [Accessed 13 November 2014].

Weaver, M. and McDonald, H. (2019) 'Mordaunt Targets "Appalling" Northern Ireland abortion Laws'. *The Guardian.* 3 July. Available at: https://www.theguardian.com/world/2019/jul/03/penny-mordaunt-targets-appalling-northern-ireland-abortion-laws [Accessed 31 August 2021].

Wilford, R. (1996) 'Women and Politics in Northern Ireland'. *Parliamentary Affairs*, 49 (1), 41–55.

Women and Equalities Committee (WEC) - House of Commons (2019). Abortion law in Northern Ireland. Available at: https://publications.parliament.uk/pa/cm201719/cmselect/cmwomeq/1584/158402.htm [Accessed 18 April 2022].

Women and Media Group (1980) *A Woman's Choice Arguing the Case for a Free Legal Abortion*. Women and Media.

Wright, S. (2015) 'Why I Asked to Be Arrested for Breaking Northern Ireland's Abortion Laws'. *Rights NI*. Available at: http://rightsni.org/2015/07/why-i-asked-to-be-arrested-for-breaking-northern-irelands-abortion-laws/ [Accessed 21 July 2021].

Yeginsu, C. (2020) 'Legal Abortion Begins in Northern Ireland'. *The New York Times*. 10 April. Available at: https://www.nytimes.com/2020/04/10/world/europe/northern-ireland-abortion-uk.html [Accessed 21 July 2021].

Index

9 780755 642571